THE PADMA-PURĀNA

Translated and Annotated by

Dr. N.A. Deshpande

PART X

MOTILAL BANARSIDASS PUBLISHERS
PRIVATE LIMITED • DELHI

Reprint: Delhi, **2010**
First Edition: Delhi, 1992

ISBN: 978-81-208-0897-3

MOTILAL BANARSIDASS

41 U.A. Bungalow Road, Jawahar Nagar, Delhi 110 007
8 Mahalaxmi Chamber, 22 Bhulabhai Desai Road, Mumbai 400 026
203 Royapettah High Road, Mylapore, Chennai 600 004
236, 9th Main III Block, Jayanagar, Bangalore 560 011
Sanas Plaza, 1302 Baji Rao Road, Pune 411 002
8 Camac Street, Kolkata 700 017
Ashok Rajpath, Patna 800 004
Chowk, Varanasi 221 001

UNESCO COLLECTION OF REPRESENTATIVE WORKS—*Indian Series*
This book has been accepted in the Indian Translation Series of the UNESCO Collection of Representative Works, jointly sponsored by the United Nations Educational, Scientific and Cultural Organization (UNESCO) and the Government of India

Printed in India
By Jainendra Prakash Jain at Shri Jainendra Press,
A-45 Naraina, Phase-I, New Delhi 110 028
and Published by Narendra Prakash Jain for
Motilal Banarsidass Publishers Private Limited,
Bungalow Road, Delhi 110 007

ANCIENT INDIAN TRADITION & MYTHOLOGY

TRANSLATED BY

A BOARD OF SCHOLARS

AND EDITED BY

Dr. G.P. BHATT

VOLUME 48

ANCIENT INDIAN TRADITION AND MYTHOLOGY SERIES

[PURĀṆAS IN TRANSLATION]

Volumes Released

ŚIVA 1-4
LIṄGA 5-6
BHĀGAVATA 7-11
GARUḌA 12-14
NĀRADA 15-19
KŪRMA 20-21
BRAHMĀṆḌA 22-26
AGNI 27-30
VARĀHA 31-32
BRAHMA 33-36
VĀYU 37-38
PADMA 39-48
SKANDA, PARTS I-XXI, 49-69

Volumes Under Preparation

SKANDA, PARTS XXII-XXIII, 70-71
VĀMANA 72-73
BHAVIṢYA
BRAHMAVAIVARTA
DEVĪBHĀGAVATA
KĀLIKĀ
MĀRKAṆḌEYA
MATSYA
VIṢṆU
VIṢṆUDHARMOTTARA

PUBLISHER'S NOTE

The purest gems lie hidden in the bottom of the ocean or in the depth of rocks. One has to dive into the ocean or delve into the rocks to find them out. Similarly, truth lies concealed in the language which with the passage of time has become obsolete. Man has to learn that language before he discovers that truth.

But he has neither the means nor the leisure to embark on that course. We have, therefore, planned to help him acquire knowledge by an easier course. We have started the series of Ancient Indian Tradition and Mythology in English Translation. Our goal is to universalize knowledge through the most popular international medium of expression. The publication of the Purāṇas in English Translation is a step towards that goal.

Acknowledgements

It is our pleasant duty to put on record our sincere thanks to Dr. R.N. Dandekar and the UNESCO authorities for their kind encouragement and valuable help in the publication of the volumes in this series.

EDITORIAL

With the publication of this volume the translation of the *Padma-Purāṇa* is now complete. This Part of the Purāṇa comprises the concluding chapters 246-255 of Section VI: *Uttarakhaṇḍa* and chapters 1-26 of the last, Section VII: *Kriyāyogasārakhaṇḍa* plus Index to the whole of the Purāṇa.

The chapters of Section VI included here describe some important events of the life of Śrīkṛṣṇa from Jarāsandha's invasion of Mathurā to the wholesale destruction of the descendants of Yadu in a terrible in-fighting and the sad end of the golden era of Kṛṣṇa. The last Section deals mainly with the details of and the rites and rituals connected with the worship of god Viṣṇu as well as the formalities of the Vaiṣṇava sect. Some interesting features and events we note here in passing.

The founding of the city of Dvārakā by Śrīkṛṣṇa in the sea and its final submergence are allegorically described in chapter 246 of Section VI. Archaeologists have recently unearthed important evidence in this regard which supports the real existence of this city in the remote past. It was to save the population of Mathurā threatened by Kālayavana, a powerful and cruel ally of Jarāsandha, the father-in-law of Kaṁsa, that the city of Dvārakā was built by Śrīkṛṣṇa, where the citizens of Mathurā were shifted in a hurry. Kālayavana is described as a Mleccha king with a huge army of ferocious barbarians approached by Jarāsandha to come to his help when his own army was routed and destroyed by Śrīkṛṣṇa and Balarāma. The word *Kālayavana* means a "black Greek or foreigner". He might have been a cruel invader from the Middle East or Africa. We could as well venture a guess that he might have been one from a Muslim country during the time when the Purāṇas were composed as the total shift of a population implies a fear of general massacre and looting for which the Muslim invaders were notorious.

In Section VI, chapter 249 Kṛṣṇa's eight wives are listed as

Rukmiṇī, Satyabhāmā, Kālindī, Mitravindā, Jāmbavatī, Nāgnajiti, Sulakṣmaṇā and Suśīlā. In addition he had to accommodate in his harem sixteen thousand maidens who were held in captivity by the demon Naraka who had terrorized the world and was killed by Kṛṣṇa. This huge number of females in Śrīkṛṣṇa's harem resulted in an abnormal proliferation of Yādava population in the city of Dvārakā, in which in course of time evil practices, such as drinking, set in and ultimately the whole of which was destroyed in a drunken feud. This series of sad events is described in chapter 252, Section VI. One noteworthy thing here is that the wives of Yādavas committed *Sati* after the destruction, showing a prevalance of this practice, if not in those remote times, at least at the time when the Purāṇas and the Epics were composed.

The Purāṇa condemns those who worship demons, vampires, spirits, ghosts, Bhairavas, Yakṣas and even deities enjoying liquor and flesh. Worship of these was current in pre-Aryan societies and later also under the influence of Tantric ideas.

Recent ecological concern and mobilization of public opinion against pollution are fore-hadowed in this Purāṇa when it declares that "there is no expiation for one who urinates or excretes on the bank of Gaṅgā and he would go to hell who drops phlegm, spittle, rheum, tears or dirt on the bank of Gaṅgā".

Speaking in highly exaggerated terms which is a characteristic feature of the Purāṇic style is very frequently seen here also. Ethically so insignificant an act as bathing the image of Viṣṇu with water from a conch is said to result in freedom from such heinous sins as murder of a brāhmaṇa, a cow, a woman, or causing abortion* or drinking liquor. And, "for as many thousands of Kalpas a man rejoices with Viṣṇu as the steps he would devoutly walk while going round Viṣṇu."

Since the ancient Vedic times the Brāhmaṇa in India enjoys the highest position, for he is said to be born from the mouth of the Cosmic Puruṣa, and the Purāṇas have carried this pro-brāhmaṇism to its extreme limit. This Purāṇa also is no exception as is evident from its declaration that "all the holy places that exist in crores of worlds exist in the right foot of a brāhmaṇa" and

*Control of population was no problem at the time.

also from the fact that it enjoins gifts of garments, food, cow, land, horse, elephant etc. always to a brāhmaṇa. However, this is not unconditional, as the Purāṇa says that all the brāhmaṇas are superior and always respectable, but those who are spoilt by such blemishes as theft, bad conduct etc. are not respectable and gifts should not be given to them. As compared to such brāhmaṇas śūdras with their senses curbed were deemed respectable. Further, "a brāhmaṇa who is not a devotee of Viṣṇu should be known to be inferior to a cāṇḍāla, while a cāṇḍāla who is devoted to Viṣṇu should be known to be superior to a brāhmaṇa." The Purāṇa has even gone to the other extreme by declaring that Viṣṇu is a cāṇḍāla in the city of Puruṣottama (i.e. Jagannātha Purī) and so food offered by cāṇḍālas should be accepted by brāhmaṇas at that holy place. Incidentally, this city is said to be situated on the shore of the "Lavaṇa Sea in the west", which may be taken as showing that the author of this Purāṇa or of this Section (VII) at least was probably a native of Bengal or Assam. As regards śūdras, this much is certain that the social problems connected with this lowest stratum of the Hindu society were not as acute at the time of this Purāṇa as they became in the later and modern period, as is evident from the remark: "The wise ones should honour like Viṣṇu brāhmaṇas, kṣatriyas, vaiśyas and śūdras who have come to their house."

—G.P. Bhatt

CONTENTS

ABBREVIATIONS

Common and self-evident abbreviations such as Ch(s)—Chapter(s), p—page, pp—pages, v—verse, vv—verses, Ftn—Footnote, Hist. Ind. Philo.—History of Indian Philosophy are not included in this list.

ABORI	*Annals of the Bhandarkar Oriental Research Institute*, Poona
AGP	S.M. Ali's *The Geography of Purāṇas*, PPH, New Delhi, 1973
AIHT	*Ancient Indian Historical Tradition*, F.E. Pargiter, Motilal Banarsidass (MLBD), Delhi
AITM	*Ancient Indian Tradition and Mythology* Series, MLBD, Delhi
AP	*Agni Purāṇa*, Guru Mandal Edition (GM), Calcutta, 1957
Arch. S.Rep.	Archaeological Survey Report
AV	*Atharva Veda*, Svādhyāya Maṇḍal, Aundh
Bd. P.	*Brahmāṇḍa Purāṇa*, MLBD, Delhi 1973
BG	*Bhagavadgītā*
Bh. P.	*Bhāgavata Purāṇa*, Bhagavat Vidyapeeth, Ahmedabad
Br.	*Brāhmaṇa* (preceded by name such as Śatapatha)
BS. P.	*Bhaviṣya Purāṇa*, Vishnu Shastri Bapat, Wai
BV. P.	*Brahma Vaivarta Purāṇa*, GM, 1955-57
CC	*Caturvarga Cintāmaṇi* by Hemādri
CVS	*Caraṇa Vyūha Sūtra* by Śaunaka, Com. by Mahīdāsa
DB	*Devī Bhāgavata*, GM, 1960-61
De or GDAMI	*The Geographical Dictionary of Ancient and Mediaeval India*, N.L. De, Oriental Reprint, Delhi, 1971
Dh. S.	*Dharma Sūtra* (preceded by the author's name such as Gautama)
ERE	*Encyclopaedia of Religion and Ethics* by Hastings
GP	*Garuḍa Purāṇa*, ed. R.S. Bhattacharya, Chowkhamba, Varanasi, 1964

GS	*Gṛhya Sūtra* (preceded by the name of the author such as Āpastamba)
HD	*History of Dharma Śāstra*, P.V. Kane, G. O. S.
IA	*The Indian Antiquary*
IHQ	*The Indian Historical Quarterly*
JP	*Purāṇa* (Journal of the Kashiraj Trust), Varanasi
KA	*Kauṭilya Arthaśāstra*
KP	*Kūrma Purāṇa*, Veṅkaṭeśvara Press Edn., Bombay; also Kashiraj Trust Edn., Varanasi, 1971
LP	*Liṅga Purāṇa*, GM, 1960; also MLBD, Delhi, 1981
Manu.	*Manusmṛti*
Mbh.	*Mahābhārata*, Gītā Press, Gorakhpur, VS 2014
MkP	*Mārkaṇḍeya Purāṇa*
MN	*Mahābhārata Nāmānukramaṇī*, Gītā Press, Gorakhpur, VS 2016
MtP	*Matsya Purāṇa*, GM, 1954
MW	Monier Williams' *Sanskrit-English Dictionary*, MLBD, Delhi, 1976
NP	*Nāradīya* or *Nārada Purāṇa*, Veṅkaṭeśvara Press, Bombay
PCK	*Bhāratavarṣīya Prācīna Caritrakośa*, Siddheshwar Shastri, Poona, 1968
Pd. P.	*Padma Purāṇa*, GM, 1957-59
PE	*Purāṇic Encyclopaedia*, V. Mani, English version, MLBD, Delhi, 1975
PR or PRHRC	*Puranic Records on Hindu Rites and Customs*, R.C. Hazra, Calcutta, 1948
ṚV	*Ṛg-Veda*, Svādhyāya Maṇḍal, Auṅdh
Śat. Br.	*Śatapatha Brāhmaṇa*
SC or SMC	*Smṛti Candrikā* by Devanna Bhaṭṭa
SEP	*Studies in Epics and Purāṇas*, A.D. Pusalkar, Bharatiya Vidya Bhavan (BVB), Bombay

CHAPTER TWO HUNDRED FORTYSIX

Jarāsandha Defeated

Śrī Maheśvara said:

1-7. Then Vasudeva performed the thread ceremony of Rāma and Kṛṣṇa according to the Vedic rite. The preceptor Garga performed the ritual for Rāma and Kṛṣṇa. The very strong Rāma and Kṛṣṇa whose purificatory rites were performed by the learned devotees of Viṣṇu, with clean, auspicious baths, went to the house of Sāndīpani. Having saluted him, and having learnt the Vedic texts and the scriptures from that noble best brāhmaṇa, they brought (back to life) his dead son, and gave that as the fee. Having received words of blessing from that noble preceptor, the two best Yadus saluted him and went (back) to Mathurā. Then the very mighty Jarāsandha, the father-in-law of that king (i.e. Kaṁsa), having heard that the invincible Kaṁsa was killed by Kṛṣṇa, came with a very great army having a strength of thousands of akṣauhiṇīs[1] to kill Kṛṣṇa and besieged the city of Mathurā.

8-16. The very powerful Rāma and Kṛṣṇa went out of that excellent city, and saw the flood of his army abounding in elephants and horses. Kṛṣṇa recollected his former, eternal form. Just by means of its recollection, Dāruka, Viṣṇu's charioteer brought the great chariot named Sugrīvapuṣpaka which was ancient and was drawn by ancient horses like Divyapuṣpa, which was equipped with divine weapons like the conch, the disc, the mace etc., was decorated with the flag (having on it the figure) of Garuḍa and was unconquerable (even) for gods. Viṣṇu's charioteer, on reaching the earth, saluted Kṛṣṇa and presented to him the bright chariot, possessed of weapons and horses. Kṛṣṇa too, seeing the great chariot with joy, took himself round it, and being praised by the hosts of gods, got into it along with his elder brother. He, being one with a body having four hands, holding the conch, the disc, the mace, wearing a crown, ear-rings, garlands, proceeded to fight. The strong Balarāma also, taking a pestle and a plough, started killing that army like an-

1. One akaṣuhiṇī=21870 chariots+21870 elephants+65610 horses+109350 foot-soldiers.

other Maheśvara. Dāruka too quickly drove the chariot to the battlefield, as wind (drives) fire in a forest covered with clusters of grass and creepers.

17-24. Then Jarāsandha's soldiers covered that chariot with maces, iron bars, (missiles called) śakti, and hammers. Viṣṇu quickly and easily destroyed them with his disc only, as a great fire destroys many (blades of) grass and (pieces of) wood with its flame. Then taking the Śārṅga (bow) (Kṛṣṇa) destroyed those troops with sharp arrows. Nothing was known about (the massacre). Some very strong ones had their lotus-like faces cut off with the disc. In the great battle some were crushed with the mace; some with (some) other (weapon). Some were cut off with the sword; others were struck with arrows. The necks of some were struck with the tip of the plough; the heads of some were struck with the pestle. Having, in a moment, killed that entire army, the best of the Yadus, Kṛṣṇa, blew his conch, sounding like the sound of the destructive fire. The great warriors, with their hearts rent by the sound of the conch, fell dead along with horses and elephants. Kṛṣṇa alone killed that army consisting of a thousand akṣauhiṇīs along with horses, chariots and elephants. The army had none left in it.

25-32. In half a watch Kṛṣṇa, the holder of the Śārṅga (bow) killed the army. Then all the hosts of gods with their hearts full of joy, dropped showers of flowers, and shouted, "Well (done), Well done!" The supporter of the earth having shed (i.e. removed) the entire burden of the earth, and being praised by gods, shone on the battlefield. The very mighty, wicked Jarāsandha, seeing his army killed, came to fight with Balarāma. The fight between the two not retreating from fights was very fierce. The brave Rāma, taking his plough, knocked down his chariot along with the charioteer on the battlefield, and seizing the very strong one, raised the pestle and set out to kill him. Lord Kṛṣṇa seeing that the powerful Rāma had made Jarāsandha, the best king, face the peril to his life as a lion would do to a great elephant, said to his elder brother: "(Please) let him not be killed." The righteous, very intelligent one got Jarāsandha freed. The immutable Saṁkarṣaṇa freed his enemy at the words of Kṛṣṇa.

33-37. He, along with his younger brother (Sunāman) got into a chariot and entered Mathurā (? Magadha). Having approached Kālayavana, the powerful one, endowed with might, he told him about the valour of Vasudeva's sons. He narrated to him the destruction of the akaṣauhiṇīs, so also his own defeat and the great deeds of Kṛṣṇa. Hearing that the very powerful, angry (Kāla)Yavana, surrounded by thousands of crores of arrogant, very strong and brave mlecchas, went quickly to Mathurā for the help of the king of Magadha.

38-39. Having covered the earth with many countries with his troops, and having placed a large army (outside the city), he besieged the city of Mathurā. Kṛṣṇa too, thinking of the welfare of his citizens then asked the Ocean for (some) land for the people to reside (on).

40-46a. The Ocean gave Kṛṣṇa (a piece of land) having an expanse of thirty yojanas. In the water he created the Dvāravatī city. It had many palaces; its ramparts and arched doorways were golden. It was covered with rows of divine houses having (i.e. decked with) various jewels. It also had many charming gardens and lakes. The lotus-eyed (Kṛṣṇa) fashioned it like Indra's (city) Amarāvatī. Janārdana (i.e. Kṛṣṇa) suddenly, at night, lifted the people that were asleep there, and put them in Dvāravatī. When the people along with their sons and wives got up, they (found themselves) placed in golden mansions and (so) were much amazed. Surrounded by principal houses full of such objects of enjoyments as much wealth, corn, divine garments and ornaments, they stayed there as the hosts of gods (live) in heaven.

46b-52. Then the very powerful Rāma and Kṛṣṇa, the lords of themselves came out of Mathurā to fight with (Kāla)Yavana. Rāma, the great warrior, taking a plough and a pestle, being angry, killed the great army of the Yavanas in the battle. Kṛṣṇa, the son of Devakī, strung the Śārṅga (bow) with arrows resembling flames of fire, and burnt the entire army of the mlecchas. Seeing his army killed, that mighty Kālayavana, the lord of Yavanas, fought with Kṛṣṇa, with a mace. Seeing that great havoc (done) by him for a long time, the lotus-eyed Kṛṣṇa too, turning away from the battle, retreated. (Kālayavana) very speedily followed him, saying, 'Wait, wait'. The very intelligent Kṛṣṇa speedily entered a cave. There the great sage, the king Mucukunda, was asleep.

53-55. Lord Kṛṣṇa remained invisible to the king. The great hero, Yavana also, raising his mace with his hand, and set out to kill Kṛṣṇa, entered that cave. Seeing the king that was asleep, and taking him to be Kṛṣṇa, Yavana struck the great sage Mucukunda with his foot. Then the revered great sage, Mucukunda, woke up.

56-60. He, with his eyes red through anger, made a *hum* sound. Due to his *hum* sound, so also due to looking at (Kālayavana) angrily, the Yavana was completely burnt, was reduced to ash and (thus) gave up his life. Then in front of the royal sage was seen Kṛṣṇa, who was dark like the petals of a blue lotus, whose eyes were like lotuses, who had the conch, the disc, the mace in his hands, and who had put on yellow garments. Seeing him of an unlimited lustre, the great sage suddenly got up and said, "Oh, great luck, great luck (to me)!" With his entire body horripilated, and (his eyes) full of tears of joy, he praising him with shouts of victory repeatedly saluted him (i.e. Kṛṣṇa).

Mucukunda said:

61-66. O highest lord, seeing (you) I am today fortunate; I am blessed. Today my existence is fruitful; my life is fruitful. Salutation to Vāsudeva, Jagannātha (the lord of the world), Śārṅgin (holder of the Śārṅga bow), to Dāmodara, to the god, the treasure of lustres. Salutation to Adhokṣaja, to Hari, who had taken up the form of Man-Lion. Salutation to you, to Rāghava, the lotus-eyed one. Salutation to Acyuta (unfallen), to (A-)Vikāra (changeless) and Ananta (unlimited). Salutation to you, to Govinda, Viṣṇu, Jiṣṇu (conqueror). Salutation to Nārāyaṇa, to the lord of Śrī, to Śrī Kṛṣṇa, to the highest soul. Salutation to you, to Mukunda, to you having four forms. Salutation to you, the highest well-being, to the highest soul. Salutation to Vāsudeva, to Śānta (the peaceful one), to the lord of the Yadus.

Maheśvara said:

67. Having thus praised Govinda, he repeatedly saluted him. The lord, who was pleased, said to Mucukunda, the great sage:

The lord said:

68-70. O royal sage, ask for the boon which is in your mind.

Maheśvara said:

He too asked for liberation free from rebirth. Then Kṛṣṇa gave him the divine ancient world. The very intelligent king also having given up the human form, obtained the same form as of the god, the highest soul. Having mounted upon Garuḍa, he reached the eternal position.

CHAPTER TWO HUNDRED FORTYSEVEN

Rukmiṇī's Abduction

Rudra said:

1-3. After the intelligent Mucukunda had killed Yavana, the descendant of Yadu gave him a boon, and went out (of the cave). Having heard that Yavana was killed, the very wicked Jarāsandha, surrounded by his army, fought with Rāma and Kṛṣṇa. Kṛṣṇa killed the entire army of that wicked one. The lord of Magadha, having fainted, fell on the ground.

4-7a. The lord of Magadha, having regained consciousness after a long time, and being distressed by fear and his body afflicted by fear, could not fight with Rāma in the battle. With his remaining army and followers killed, he, turning away (from the battle) ran away. Taking the (two) Rāma and Kṛṣṇa as unconquerable, he gave up hostility against them and entered his own city. Then the two sons of Vasudeva, along with their army left the city of Mathurā and entered the city of Dvārikā.

7b-10a. Vāyu, sent by Indra, affectionately gave Kṛṣṇa the assembly(-hall) of gods, which was fashioned by Viśvakarman, was decorated with diamonds and lapis lazuli, graced with many seats, which shone with divine golden umbrellas, full of (i.e. decked with) various gems. The kings like Ugrasena along with the traders, on arriving at the charming assembly(-hall), were delighted as hosts of gods (are delighted) in heaven.

10b-12. The king named Raivata, born in the Ikṣvāku family, affectionately gave Rāma his daughter named Revatī who was endowed with all (auspicious) marks. That Rāma duly married that Revatī and amused himself with her as Indra with Śacī.

13-19. Bhīṣmaka, the king of Vidarbha, was pious and virtuous. He had good sons like Rukma. (Bhīṣmaka's) daughter, their youngest sister was Rukmiṇī, of an excellent complexion. She was born with a portion of Lakṣmī and had all auspicious marks. She was Sītā in (the lord's) existence as Rāma, and was Rukmiṇī in his birth as Kṛṣṇa. She accompanied Viṣṇu in his other incarnations also. In the Dvāpara (age) Hiraṇyaka and Hiraṇyākṣa were again born with the names Śiśupāla and Dantavaktra. The two very mighty and brave ones were born in the family of the Cedi (king). His son desired to give Rukmiṇī (in marriage) to Śiśupāla. The beautiful-faced (Rukmiṇī) did not want Śiśupala as her husband. She, of a firm vow, was attached to Viṣṇu from her childhood. That virgin Rukmiṇī, dedicated to Viṣṇu, always worshipped the deities and gave various presents (to brāhmaṇas).

20-21. Highly devoted to practising vows, and thinking of Viṣṇu, the lord of the soul, as her husband, she lived in her father's house. Through his intelligent son Rukmin, the best king tried to get her married to Śiśupāla.

22-23. Intending to have Kṛṣṇa as her husband, she sent a brāhmaṇa, the son of her family-priest (to Kṛṣṇa). He quickly went to Dvārakā. Having approached Kṛṣṇa and Rāma and being duly honoured by them, he told them in private what Rukmiṇī had said.

24-26. Having heard it, the two best among men, Rāma and Kṛṣṇa, along with that intelligent brāhmaṇa, got into the chariot full of all weapons and missiles and moving (even) in the sky along with the noble Dāruka, quickly went to the (capital) city of Vidarbha. All kings, led by Jarāsandha, from all countries had come to witness the marriage(-ceremony) of the intelligent Śiśupāla.

27-30. At the time of the marriage, Rukmiṇī, having put on golden ornaments, went out of the city with her friends to worship Durgā. At that time only Devakī's son (Kṛṣṇa) reached (there). The strong Kṛṣṇa seized her who was in her chariot. Suddenly putting her into his chariot he quickly came home. Then kings like Jarāsandha, full of anger, went along with prince Rukmin, to fight (with Kṛṣṇa). With their army having the four-fold division, the angry ones pursued Kṛṣṇa.

31-35. The powerful Balabhadra, having got down from his excellent chariot, took the plough and the pestle and in a moment struck the enemies. With force he struck the chariots, horses, great elephants and foot-soldiers also with his plough and pestle in the battle. Due to the fall of his plough the rows of chariots were pounded. The elephants also fell on the ground as mountains due to (the fall of) the thunderbolt (on them). The heads of all were broken; all vomitted blood profusely. At that time, in a moment, Balarāma struck down the army along with the horses, the elephants and the chariots in the great battle. On the battlefield there rivers of blood flowed on all sides.

36-42. All the kings that were routed, being tormented by fear, fled away. The powerful Rukmin, through anger, fought with Kṛṣṇa. Raising his bow, he struck Kṛṣṇa with volleys of arrows. Then Kṛṣṇa laughed and taking his Śārṅga (bow) struck with one arrow the horses of his chariot and the charioteer. The supporter of the earth rent his chariot, flag and banner. He, deprived of his chariot, stood on the ground. The powerful Kṛṣṇa cut off his sword with one arrow. Then raising his fist, he struck Kṛṣṇa on his chest. Kṛṣṇa binding him, seized him on the battlefield. Kṛṣṇa (i.e. Viṣṇu), the killer of (the demon) Madhu, smiled, and taking an arrow with a sharp horse-shoe-shaped head, shaved his head and left him. He, full of grief, and hissing like a serpent, entered his own city and stayed there only.

CHAPTER TWO HUNDRED FORTYEIGHT

Rukmiṇī Formally Married to Kṛṣṇa

Rudra said:

1-6. Then getting into the divine chariot along with Rāma, Rukmiṇī and Dāruka, Kṛṣṇa speedily went home. Then having entered the city of Dvārakā, (Śrī Kṛṣṇa) the son of Devakī, married princess Rukmiṇī decorated with (ornaments of) gold according to the Vedic rite on an auspicious day and at an auspicious time. At the time of that marriage divine drums were sounded, and the best gods dropped showers of flowers. Vasudeva, Ugrasena, so also Akrūra, the best Yadu Balabhadra of a great lustre, so also other principal Yadus married Kṛṣṇa to Rukmiṇī with great pleasure. The cowherd Nanda came (there) with young cowherds and hosts of (other) cowherds. Yaśodā also came there with well-decorated ladies.

7-10. All the wives of Vasudeva led by Devakī, Revatī, queen Rohiṇī, and other ladies from the city performed all the marriage-rites with great joy. Devakī there affectionately honoured all gods. She got done the entire nuptial rite properly with (the help of) old ladies, and also a celebration through best brāhmaṇas. She fed the brāhmaṇas and kings like Ugrasena were well honoured with auspicious garments and ornaments.

11-14. Cowherds like Nanda, ladies like Yaśodā were honoured with many ornaments of gold and jewels and with garments. They were also delighted in that marriage-celebration. The couple together saluted Agni. The two were congratulated with blessings by principal brāhmaṇas knowing the Vedas. On that marriage-altar the bride and the bridegroom shone. The kṣatriya (viz. Kṛṣṇa), the son of Devakī, with his wife saluted old brāhmaṇas, so also his elder brother.

15-19. Kṛṣṇa, having thus completed the entire nuptial rite dismissed all kings that had come there. The best kings honoured by Kṛṣṇa proceeded (homewards). The very noble brāhmaṇas went to their respective abodes. The pious, immutable son of Devakī, quite happily lived in that divine mansion. He, being praised by sages and hosts of gods in heaven, amused himself with her as Viṣṇu with Lakṣmī. The eternal Viṣṇu, with his mind pleased day by day lived in the very beautiful Dvāravatī.

CHAPTER TWO HUNDRED FORTYNINE

Kṛṣṇa's Other Marriages

Śrī Rudra said:

1-6. The glorious daughter of Satrājit, named Satyā, born with a portion of the Earth, was another wife of Kṛṣṇa. The glorious daughter of the Sun, named Kālindī, was his third wife. She had come up as a portion of Līlā. Kṛṣṇa married Vindānuvinda's daughter Mitravindā of a bright smile, who had stood for self-choice marriage. He whose eyes were large like lotus-leaves, having bound with one noose the seven maddened bulls, took her with the dowry of his valour. King Satrājit gave to his younger brother, the noble Prasena, a great jewel called 'Syamantaka'[1]. Sometime Kṛṣṇa asked for that excellent gem. Then Prasena violently said to Vāsudeva:

Prasena said:

7. This gem everyday produces eight bhāras of gold. There-

---

1. Syamantaka—A kind of gem said to yield eight bhāras of gold and to protect the owner from all kinds of dangers and portents. Satrājit, son of Nighna, got it from the Sun, and always wore it round his neck. He afterward gave it to his brother Prasena, from whom it passed into the hands of the monkey-chief Jāmbavat who got possession of it after having killed Prasena. Kṛṣṇa, however, overtook Jāmbavat and vanquished him in fight after a long struggle. The monkey-chief thereupon presented it along with his daughter to Kṛṣṇa; Kṛṣṇa then gave the jewel back to its proper owner Satrājit who out of gratitude presented it along with his daughter Satyabhāmā to him. Afterwards when Satyabhāmā was at her father's house with the jewel, Śatadhanvan at the instigation of a Yādava named Akrūra who desired the jewel for himself, killed Satrājit and gave it to Akrūra. Śatadhanvan was afterwards killed by Kṛṣṇa, but when he found that the jewel was with Akrūra he allowed him to retain it with himself after having once shown it to the people.

fore, this gem called Syamantaka is not to be given to anyone by me.

Mahādeva said:

8-12. Having understood his intention, Kṛṣṇa remained silent. Sometime with all the best Yadus like very powerful Prasena, Kṛṣṇa went ahunting, and entered a great forest. Many in thousands followed, each one to hunt beasts. Prasena alone went far in the great forest. A lion on seeing him approached him, killed him, and snatched the gem. The very mighty Jāmbavat also killed the lion, seized the gem and quickly entered a cave resorted to by the divine women. When the sun had set, Kṛṣṇa along with his followers, entered his own city on seeing the moon risen on the fourth day.

13-18. Then all the citizens said to one another about Kṛṣṇa: "Kṛṣṇa having killed Prasena in the forest under the pretext of hunting, has definitely taken the Syamantaka gem." Kṛṣṇa, having heard those words of the people of Dvārakā, went to a dense forest through the fear of ignorant people. He showed to all of them (Prasena) killed by a lion. Having proved his innocence and having placed a great army there only, Kṛṣṇa alone went to a dense forest with Śārṅga-bow and his mace in his hand. Seeing a great cave, Kṛṣṇa entered it with a doubt. In it, in a clean house brightened with various excellent jewels, a maid having placed Jāmbavat's son on a swing and sportively holding the (Syamantaka) gem on its top, was oscillating the swing and singing with joy:

19-25a. "A lion had killed Prasena. The lion was killed by Jāmbavat. O good boy, do not cry. This Syamantaka belongs to you (only)." Hearing it, the brave Kṛṣṇa blew his conch. Due to that great sound Jāmbavat came out to the place. Continuously for ten (days and) nights a fierce fight, with fists like the thunderbolt, and frightening all beings, took place between the two. Jāmbavat, seeing the increase in Kṛṣṇa's might, and decrease in his own, realised the former words of the Supreme Being. 'This is that Rāma that has again descended for the protection of Dharma. That my master has come to grant me (the object of) my desire.' Knowing like this the lord of the bears desisted from the fight, and with great amazement, he, with his palms joined, asked Śrī Kṛṣṇa: "Who are you?" Kṛṣṇa, stopping fighting said with a grave voice:

Śrī Kṛṣṇa said:

25b-26 I am Vasudeva's son, called Vāsudeva. You very fearless, have taken away my gem called Syamantaka. Give it (back) to me quickly. Otherwise you will be killed.

Mahādeva said:

27. Hearing those (words), Jāmbavat was delighted. He saluted (Kṛṣṇa) by (prostrating himself before him) like a staff. Having taken himself round Kṛṣṇa, and saluting him, he spoke to him politely:

Jāmbavat said:

28-29. I am lucky, I am satisfied after seeing you, O lord. O you son of Devakī, I am your servant due to (my being your servant in) the former existence. O Govinda, you have given the battle desired before. O you lord of the world, mine of pity, eternal one, forgive me this battle that I had with you through delusion.

Mahādeva said:

30-36. Speaking like this, and bowing and repeatedly saluting the lord he politely seated him on a seat full of (i.e. decked with) many gems. He washed his feet resembling fresh lotuses with auspicious water; worshipped the descendant of Yadu with a (respectful offering called) madhuparka; properly honoured him with (i.e. by giving him) divine garments and ornaments; he gave him, of unlimited lustre, as his wife, his daughter endowed with beauty, named Jāmbavatī, a gem among girls. He also gave him the great gem called Syamantaka, along with other gems. Kṛṣṇa, the delighted killer of his enemies, having married the girl there only, affectionately gave that Jāmbavat final beatitude. Gladly taking that girl, his (i.e. Jāmbavat's) daughter, he went out of the cave and from it went to the city of Dvārakā. The best Yadu gave the gem called Syamantaka to Satrājit; and to that daughter (of Jāmbavat) also he gave an excellent gem.

37-47. They say that seeing the moon on the fourth of the

bright half of Bhādrapada (leads to) a false charge. Therefore, one should avoid it. If a man sees the moon on that fourth day (i.e. of the bright half of Bhādrapada), he is freed from the false charge by listening to the account of the Syamantaka. The three beautiful bright daughters of the king of Madra, viz., Sulakṣmaṇā, Nāgnajiti, and glorious Suśīlā, standing for self-choice marriage, chose Kṛṣṇa (as their husband). On one day the descendant of Yadu married them. All these, beginning with Rukmiṇī, were thus the eight queens of the noble one: Rukmiṇī, Satyabhāmā, Kālindī of a bright smile, Mitravindā, Jāmbavatī, Nāgnajiti, Sulakṣmaṇā and Suśīlā, of a slim body, said to be the eighth one. A very powerful demon, the Earth's son, named Naraka, having conquered in a battle, Indra, the lord of gods, and all (other) gods, forcibly took away the very bright ear-rings of Aditi, the mother of gods, so also the various gems of gods. So also (he took away) the Airāvata elephant of Indra and his horse Uccaiḥśravas; and rubies etc. of Kubera, and his treasures Śaṁkha[1] and Padma. The Earth's son also kidnapped the (divine) and the celestial nymphs; so also he forcibly took away the gods' weapons like the thunderbolt; and with them only, he, having struck the gods remaining in the heaven, lived in the assembly-hall fashioned by Maya in that city in the spotless sky.

48-58. Then all hosts of gods led by Indra and overcome by fear, sought the rufuge of Kṛṣṇa, non-tormenting (one). Kṛṣṇa too hearing all those acts of Naraka, granted exemption from fear to gods and thought of Garuḍa. At that moment the very powerful Garuḍa, saluted by all gods, stood with his palms joined in front of that Viṣṇu. Keśava (i.e. Kṛṣṇa), having mounted on the best bird along with Satyā, and being praised by the sages, went to the demon's abode. It was shining in the sky like the orb of the sun. It was full of many demons and had many divine ornaments. Kṛṣṇa saw that city difficult to be broken through even by gods. The powerful lord, having observed its covers, cut them off with his disc, as the sun (removes) the darkness. Then all the demons, having raised their lances, went, in hundreds and

1. Śaṅkha and Padma are two of the nine treasures of Kubera. The names of the nine treasures are: Mahāpadma, Padma, Śaṅkha, Makara, Kacchapa, Mukunda, Kunda, Nīla, and Kharva.

thousands to fight. Then with divine iron clubs, small javelins thrown with the hand, and good spears with a sharp edge they struck Keśava, as fire with straws. Then the eagle-bannered lord took his Śārṅga bow, and with arrows resembling the flames of fire, he cut off the divine weapons. The powerful Supreme Being cut off, with his disc only, their necks, elephants and speedy horses also. Some were cut off with the disc; others were struck with arrows.

59-65. In that battle some demons were struck with the mace. Thus all the demons were knocked down on the ground, as the mountains are pierced with thunderbolt discharged by Indra. The lotus-eyed Viṣṇu, having struck down all the demons, blew his great conch called Pāñcajanya. Then that brave Naraka, taking a bow and getting into a divine chariot came to fight with Keśava. The battle between the two was terrific, piercing and thrilling with many thousands of arrows like two showering clouds. Then the ancient, powerful son of Vasudeva cut off the bow of the chief of demons with a crescent-shaped arrow. He discharged a very divine missile on the great chest of Naraka. The great demon, with his chest pierced with it, fell on the ground roaring like a great mountain pierced by Indra with his thunderbolt.

66-68. Then Kṛṣṇa, having gone near the demon (lying) on the ground, and entreated by him, said to the demon: "Choose a boon." The demon said to Kṛṣṇa seated on Garuḍa: "I have nothing to do with a boon, though I am Naraka. For the good of other people I am asking for an excellent boon. O lord of the lord of all beings, O Madhusūdana, O you who remove the fear (of your devotees), those men who take an auspicious bath on the day of my death (will) not obtain (i.e. go to) hell."

Mahādeva said:

69-75. Lord Govinda gave him the boon: "Let it be so." Then actually seeing Viṣṇu's feet resembling the autumnal lotuses, and decorated with diamonds and lapis lazuli, honoured by Brahmā, Rudra etc., so also by (other) gods and sages, the Earth's son gave up his life and obtained absorption into Viṣṇu. Then all the hosts of gods, with their minds full of joy, dropped showers of flowers, and the great sages praised (him). The lotus-eyed Kṛṣṇa entered his city. He gave to Indra, the wielder of the thunderbolt, the various gems of the gods forcibly snatched away by him, so also the ear-rings of the mother of gods, and the horse Uccaiḥśravas, the best elephant Airāvata and the blazing Maṇiparvata (literally, the mountain of gems). All this the best Yadu gave to Indra. The powerful Naraka had, after vanquishing kings from all countries, taken away sixteen thousand maidens.

76-80. All of them were then confined in the harem of Naraka. Seeing Kṛṣṇa of great might, and resembling a hundred Cupids, all of them chose him, the omnipresent lord of the universe, as their husband. At this time only Govinda, of endless forms, and the Supreme Being, duly took their hand (in marriage). All the sons of Naraka, led by the Earth, sought the shelter of Govinda. He, the treasure of pity, protected them. Due to (his giving) importance to the words of the Earth, he installed them all on his kingdom. He, putting all those excellent women into the aeroplane of Indra, took them to Dvāravatī through noble messengers of gods.

81-90. Having mounted upon Garuḍa, Keśava, along with Satyā quickly went to heaven to see the mother of gods. Janārdana, the very powerful one, having entered the city of the king of gods, got down from the best bird along with his wife. There he saluted the mother of gods fit to be saluted. Aditi, affectionate towards her son, embraced him with her arms, and having seated him on the chief seat honoured him devoutly. Ādityas, Vasus, Rudras, led by Indra, then worshipped the highest god as he deserved. The glorious Satyabhāmā came to the house of Śacī. Honoured duly by her she sat on a comfortable seat. At that time, her servants, directed by Indra, affectionately gave her the flowers of the Pārijāta (trees). Taking those flowers that slender-waisted goddess Śacī tied them on her own dark, clean hair on her head, insulting the glorious Satyabhāmā. 'This human female does not deserve the auspicious flowers fit for gods.' Thinking like this, she did not give the flowers to her. Going out of the city, Satyā, full of anger, went to her husband Kṛṣṇa, and the lotus-eyed one said (to him):

Satyā said:

91. O Govinda, O best of the Yadus, this Śacī being proud

of the Pārijāta put (the flowers) on her own head without giving them to me.

Mahādeva said:

92-100. Having heard the words of Satyā, the very strong Vāsudeva, Devakī's son, uprooted the Pārijāta tree, put it on Garuḍa, and having quickly mounted, along with Satyā, on the strong one (i.e. Garuḍa), he went to the charming city of Dvārakā. Then Indra, the king of gods, full of anger, got on the Airāvata, and along with Rudras, Vasus, Ādityas, Sādhyas and hosts of Maruts went to fight with Keśava. Then all the hosts of gods, having surrounded Viṣṇu (i.e. Kṛṣṇa), dropped showers of weapons on him as clouds drop showers of water on a great mountain. With his disc Kṛṣṇa cut off those missiles of gods. The angry Garuḍa made the gods fall down with the movement of his wings as the wind makes the straws (to fall down). Then lord Indra, the master of the gods, suddenly discharged his blazing thunderbolt to kill Kṛṣṇa. Kṛṣṇa easily caught that thunderbolt with one hand. Then the frightened Indra, getting down from his best elephant (Airāvata), stood, with the palms of his hands joined, before (Kṛṣṇa) and having saluted him, and after praising him with hymns, said in a faltering tone:

Indra said:

101. O Kṛṣṇa, this Pārijāta (tree) fit for the gods was formerly given to me and the gods. (Now) how can it remain in the human (world)?

Mahādeva said:

102-107a. Then the lord said to Indra standing by him: "O lord of gods, in your house Satyā was insulted. Your dear wife Pulomajā, instead of giving the Pārijāta (flowers) to Satyā, wore them on her own head. For her (i.e. Satyā) I took away the Pārijāta (tree) to give it to her as promised, O lord of the hosts of gods. I shall place the Pārijāta (tree) in your house. Therefore; O lord of gods, let the Pārijāta be not given today. For the good of the deities I shall send the Pārijāta to the earth.

Let it remain in my house till then. O Indra, when I go to heaven take it (back) as you like."

Mahādeva said:

107b-111. Speaking like this, the best of the Yadus, gave the thunderbolt (back) to him. Saying, "Let it be so", that wielder of the thunderbolt (i.e. Indra), went, surrounded by hosts of gods, to his divine city. Kṛṣṇa too, having mounted, along with Satyā, Garuḍa, and being praised by sages, entered Dvāravatī. (Then that) omnipresent Viṣṇu, having placed that divine tree, Pārijāta, near Satyā, enjoyed with all wives. That glorious Viṣṇu, taking all forms, and giving happiness, lived in the abodes of all of them during nights.

CHAPTER TWO HUNDRED FIFTY

Aniruddha's Marriage

Śrī Rudra said:

1-3. On Rukmiṇī was born Pradyumna, Madana's (Cupid's) portion, from Kṛṣṇa. He, the very mighty one born of Cupid, killed Śambara. Aniruddha was born from him on Rukmin's daughter.

4-10. He too married Bāṇa's daughter by name Uṣā. In her dream she, aged sixteen, having enjoyed properly (Aniruddha), dark like the petals of a dark lotus, having lotus-like eyes, of large arms, wearing beautiful ornaments, got up. Not seeing him after being awake, she, tormented by passion of love, with her mind confused, saying "O you having a face like a red lotus, where are you going?" lamented in many ways. Then her friend, named Citralekhā, seeing the girl reduced to that condition, asked her, "Why is your mind confused?" She too told her about the husband obtained in her dream. She too drew the pictures of all the best human beings and gods on a piece of cloth and showed them to her. She even properly showed her (the pictures of) Kṛṣṇa, Saṁkarṣaṇa, Pradyumna, Aniruddha, born in the Yadu family. Having approved out of the pictures that of Kṛṣṇa, she, seeing Aniruddha after Pradyumna, embraced it, saying: "This is he."

11-15. Then with many illusory demonesses Citralekhā at night went to Dvāravatī. She saw Aniruddha sleeping in the harem. She enticed him, seized him, and put him on the bed of Bāṇa's daughter in the harem of Bāṇa, full of many sanctuaries and mansions. He too became awake and on seeing Uṣā who lay on the soft couch, was marked with all (good) characteristics, adorned with beautiful ornaments, garments, sandal, flowers, who had a golden complexion, fine hair, well-developed breasts, embraced her who was full of love, and happily dallied with her. Old demonesses residing in the harem, having come to know about Aniruddha thus confined and continuously dallying (with Uṣā) for just a month, reported it to the king. The king, with his eyes red with anger, being very much amazed, sent the city-servants ordering them: "Bring him here". They too quickly went up the king's palace to arrest Aniruddha lying on the bed of the princess.

16-20. He, seeing them agitated, easily took out a pillar of the palace and in a very short time only smashed the servants numbering a million with the pillar. Then the lord of the demons, seeing his servants destroyed, became curious, and deciding 'This is Śrī Kṛṣṇa's grandson as told by the divine sage', he took his bow and himself came near Aniruddha to arrest him. Aniruddha too, seeing the king with a thousand arms having come to fight, whirling his iron club, hurled it at Bāṇa. He cut off that iron club with an arrow discharged from his bow. Then having tightly bound Aniruddha with the missile of serpent he placed him in his own harem.

21-25. Then Kṛṣṇa too, having learnt through the royal sage that it was just like that, mounted upon the best bird (i.e. Garuḍa), and along with Baladeva, Pradyumna and his army came to cut off the cluster of Bāṇa's arms. Formerly Bali's son (Bāṇa) had adored Śaṅkara. He had said to (Bāṇa): "Choose a boon." Bāṇa had asked for this boon from that lord: "Always be seated at the gate of my city for (its) protection, and kill the army of the enemy that might come there." Śaṁkara too, saying, "All right" to him, remained at the gate of his city with weapons, his sons and attendants. Just at that time, seeing Kṛṣṇa to have angrily come along with his army, he got on his bull, and equipped with all weapons, and surrounded by his sons and attendants went out to fight (with Kṛṣṇa). Kṛṣṇa too seeing that lord of beings, who had held elephant's hide, a skull, who was decorated with blazing serpents, was tawny, had three eyes, had held the trident, was (capable of) destroying the entire host of beings, caused fear to all beings, resembled the fire of destruction, who was accompanied by his two sons, was surrounded by all his attendants, and who had destroyed Tripura, kept his army far behind, and accompanied by Balabhadra and Pradyumna started with a smile to fight with Rudra.

26-38. First a fierce (battle) took place between Kṛṣṇa and Śaṁkara, with arrows resembling the fire of destruction discharged from (Śaṁkara's bow called) Pināka and (Viṣṇu's bow called) Śārṅga. Rāma too had (a fight) with Bāṇa, and Pradyumna with Kārtikeya. The two great heroes fought like two haughty lions. Gajānana struck Yādava on his chest with his tusk. Rāma took a pestle and struck at his tusk. (Gajānana) having the rat as his vehicle, with his tusk broken, suddenly fled. Since then the lord of the attendants has his tusk broken in the world. He is called *Ekadanta* by gods, demons and gandharvas. (Kārtikeya) having the peacock as his vehicle fought with Pradyumna. Balarāma caused (Śiva's) attendants to run away. Śaṁkara, with his eyes very red, having fought with Kṛṣṇa for a very long time, put on his arrow a very blazing great fever, and discharged it. Kṛṣṇa by means of cold fever warded off that missile. The two fevers discharged by those two, Kṛṣṇa and Śiva, speedily entered the human world by their order. Those men who listen to (the account of) the battle between Kṛṣṇa and Śiva, are free from fever (or torment) and reach (Viṣṇu) the infallible one. Then that Hṛṣīkeśa (i.e. Kṛṣṇa), putting the deluding weapon on his arrow, discharged it at Śiva. Deluded by that missile, he yawned again and again; and he, Śaṅkara, the lord of gods, fell down on the ground in a swoon. Seeing his father unconscious, the powerful Kārtikeya, Ṣaṇmukha (literally, having six faces), raised the (missile called) Śakti and went to fight with Kṛṣṇa. Merely by the 'hum' sound, Kṛṣṇa turned him away.

39-45. Having thus vanquished the three-eyed god Śiva,

having the trident in his hand, the brave and the best of the Yadus blew his loud-sounding conch. Hearing that Śaṁkara, along with his sons, was vanquished by Kṛṣṇa, Bāṇa, getting into a chariot, himself came to fight with Kṛṣṇa. Suddenly seeing Kṛṣṇa seated on Garuḍa, he covered him with showers of many weapons and missiles, with maces, iron bars, lances, (missiles called) Śakti, iron clubs, swords, and discs continuously. Kṛṣṇa cut them off with his disc only. He discharged his (disc) Sudarśana to cut off his arms. The Sudarśana having a thousand spokes discharged at the king of demons quickly cut off the forest (i.e. the large number) of his arms in a thousand ways. In the meanwhile, O goddess, Pārvatī who had fulfilled her vow, came near Kṛṣṇa, and with the palms of her hands joined, said:

Pārvatī said:

46-49. O Kṛṣṇa, Kṛṣṇa, O lord of the world, O Nārāyaṇa, O treasure of compassion, O best of the Yadus, O lord of gods, I was your female servant in a former existence. At that time you, the pleased noble one, had granted me a boon about the perpetual state of having my husband living, O gentle one. O lord, the sages have declared that one principal name of your thousand names has given good fortune to Gaurī. O Govinda, O eternal one mounted on Garuḍa, make it true. Therefore, please give life to my husband.

Rudra said:

50-51. Thus addressed by the goddess the lotus-eyed Kṛṣṇa withdrew the missile with which her husband was made unconscious. Freed from the missile of Kṛṣṇa, Śiva, the lord of all beings, got up and joining the palms of his hands, praised the lord of the worlds.

Śaṅkara said:

52-56. O Kṛṣṇa, O Kṛṣṇa, O lord of the world, O Supreme Being, O highest god, O highest lord, O you without a beginning and an end, O you immutable one, in the human beings there is a strong power. The action of taking up a body is due to you. It is the sign of honour. Be pleased with me. Salutation to you. O eternal one, be pleased with me. O lord of the world, favour me.

Be gracious to me, O Acyuta, Keśava. You are the creator, the supporter, the destroyer of the worlds. You are the father of the worlds. O lord of gods, you alone are the Brahman of the nature of intelligence and the lack of it. You are the origin. You are without an origin. You are the lord and Śeṣa also. You are Mahat; you are the highest Brahman; you alone are the individual soul.

57-61. O best of all gods, you are immortal; O lord of gods you are the lord of the mortals. Due to your extremely good character you have an origin. The two eternal highest souls have come up from your breath. So also the five elements (have come up from you) due to your great affection. You put yourself in the work of service (i.e. as a servant) in the perishable and the imperishable, in the highest abode resorted to by gods and the place of lustre, and in the universe. This is not otherwise. He who does not know you in the world, is a fool. You are the cause of everything. The wise ones know the abode of the lord of the low and high (to be good) for service (*obscure*!). They, the diligent ones rest at the position equal to the gods. The common man remains away to bow down to your eternal position.

62-69. That fourth stage (Turyā: the state of liberation of the soul) of charming rays of light is possible in your case. O you eternal superintendent, the couples talk about you. These best ones, O you beyond qualities, narrate your names, deeds, eternal qualities and grandeurs. O Keśava, in the former and latter learning full of action and knowledge, the two, along with their sons are singing the praise of you, the lord of young ladies (*obscure*!). You are wisdom; you are the highest Brahman; with your great knowledge only, O eternal one, you yourself, the wise one, give (him) life. Due to your grace only, he who knows the soul, obtains, in this world and the highest heaven, wisdom, proficiency, intellect, perception, so also courage, and all desired objects. Then he would be immortal. The self having this name is the heart. O lord, these ten are the names of the Wisdom, the treasure of compassion: (Ātman, Hṛd=heart,) mind, desire, reasoning, recollection, volition, penance, sacrifices, and love.

70-80. This you are the highest Brahman; this you are the creator. This you are Indra, Rudra, and all the deities. O highest lord, you are all these beings—sons, friends, (other forms) of existence and others also, O eternal one. The viviparous, the oviparous, the beings generated by sweet sweat, plants, horses, cows, men, elephants and others, so whatever being there is, so also the movable beings, so also the immobile (objects)—all have sprung from you (only). The sacred texts describe you, Viṣṇu, as omnipresent. The people, impelled by you only act towards good or bad (things). Therefore, O ocean of pity, forgive by means of your most auspicious qualities this offence that I have committed. Salutation to you, O you lotus-eyed one, Govinda, Acyuta, Mādhava, Vāsudeva. O you fit to be saluted by the world, O Nārāyaṇa, salutation to you. O lord of the worlds, O Nṛsiṁha, O mine of pity, O lord of Lakṣmī, O omnipresent one, O glorious one, O highest soul, salutation to you. O lord, O you always worshipped by the liberated (souls) having Vaikuṇṭha as their dwelling place, O you lord of the three (Vedas), O Rāma, O you having lotus-like eyes, salutation to you. O you descendant of Yadu, salutation to you who destroy those that are a burden to the earth, who are of the form of Kṛṣṇa's mirth, who are Viṣṇu, who are Jiṣṇu (the conqueror).

Having thus praised and saluted Govinda, the lord of Umā, the lord of beings, having, joined the palms of his hands, spoke in a grave voice:

Rudra said:

81-90. O lord, this Bāṇa, Bali's son, is granted a boon by me. Formerly I had given him a boon that he had asked for, viz. immortality, O best of the Yadus. You deserve to do everything. Therefore, please protect this Bali's son, dear to me.

Saying "All right", the lord, Govinda, the ocean of compassion, withdrawing his disc, freed Bāṇa, Bali's son, who ran the risk to his life, had his arms cut off, and was covered with blood. Śaṁkara, the lord who had fulfilled his vow, after having freed Bali's son, having along with Pārvatī mounted the best bull (Nandin), went to his abode, the Kailāsa mountain. That Bāṇa, having saluted the very powerful Rāma and Kṛṣṇa, went with them to (his) city and freed (Aniruddha) Madana's son. Having honoured them, as they deserved, with divine garments and ornaments, he gave Uṣā (in marriage) to Śauri, Kṛṣṇa's grandson. Then Rāma and Kṛṣṇa got Aniruddha duly married. They, along with Pradyumna, were then worshipped by Bāṇa. Then Kṛṣṇa, having placed Aniruddha with Uṣā in a divine chariot, went to Dvāravatī. Like Indra with the gods, Rāma with Pradyumna, and Kṛṣṇa with the army, entered the charming city. Aniruddha, full of joy, enjoyed day and night many pleasures in the company of Bāṇa's daughter in a house full of many jewels.

CHAPTER TWO HUNDRED FIFTYONE

Destruction of Pauṇḍraka's Son

Śrī Rudra said:

1-6. Then Pauṇḍraka Vāsudeva, king of Kāśī, fasted in a solitary place, and worshipping Maheśa for twelve years, muttered the five-syllabled formula. At the time of the repetition of the name of the deity he worshipped Śaṁkara with (i.e. by offering) his own lotus-like eye. Then the lord of Umā having the trident in his hand, being pleased, said to him: "Choose a boon". Then he said to Śiva who had five faces, is the lord of all beings, and was pleased: "O giver of boons, give me a form similar to that of Vāsudeva (Kṛṣṇa)." Śiva (gave) him (a form with) four arms with a disc, a conch, a mace and a lotus (held in them), having eyes like lotus-petals, having charming hair with a crown (on it) resembling that of Vāsudeva. Solicited by him as "Give me also the marks like a yellow garment, and ornaments like the Kaustubha", Śiva also gave him all that. He enticed all people, saying, "I am Vāsudeva".

7-9. Sometime Nārada, having come from heaven to that king of Kāśī, who was haughty with pride and power, said: "You cannot have the status of Vāsudeva without conquering Vasudeva's son." That moment only he, having put himself into a chariot with Garuḍa-banner, reached Dvārakā with the army of four divisions, (numbering) an akṣauhiṇī. There he sent a messenger (to Kṛṣṇa to tell him) "I, Vāsudeva standing in a golden carriage at the gate of the city, have come to fight (with you). Without conquering me you cannot have the status of Vāsudeva."

10-14. Viṣṇu (i.e. Kṛṣṇa) too, having heard it, mounted upon Garuḍa and on coming out to fight with Pauṇḍraka, saw at the gate Pauṇḍraka with an army (numbering) an akṣauhiṇī, and seated in a chariot, and having a conch, a disc, a mace and a lotus in his hands. Kṛṣṇa took the Śārṅga (bow) and in a short time only completely destroyed that army (numbering) an akṣauhiṇī, consisting of horses, elephants and foot-soldiers with arrows resembling the fire of destruction in brightness. And with one arrow he easily chopped off the weapons in his hands like the conch, disc, mace etc. Having cut off his lotus-like head (adorned) with a crown, by means of his pure Sudarśana (disc), he caused it to fall into the harem in (the city of) Vārāṇasī. Seeing it all the residents of Kāśī, fearing 'What is this?' were amazed.

15-17. Daṇḍapāṇi, Pauṇḍraka's son, having heard that his father was killed by lord Vāsudeva, and directed by his mother, (as if) by Death, and told by his priest, offered a sacrifice, called Māheśvara, to Śaṅkara. He, being pleased, affectionately gave him a Kṛtyā (a female deity capable of destruction and proficient in magic) belonging to Maheśvara and capable of killing Kṛṣṇa. That Kāśī king, seeing that Kṛtyā of Maheśvara, that had a body full of a group of flames, had a blazing mass of hair, had tawny eyes, whose face was blazing and fierce, that had a trident in her hand, whose body was smeared with ash, who was adorned with the string of human heads, that caused fear to all gods, was presented by Rudra, impelled her to kill Kṛṣṇa along with his sons, wives and relations.

18-19. And she causing fear to the entire world, burning with her lustre the whole earth, and roaring with a sound strong like the fire at the time of deluge reached Dvārakā. All people staying there saw her and thinking it to be a great deluge, and wailing aloud, reported it to Kṛṣṇa.

20-24. Kṛṣṇa too told all of them not to fear, and seeing that very fierce Kṛtyā standing like that at the portal of the rampart, suddenly discharged that Sudarśana of a thousand spokes, capable of keeping off all weapons and missiles at the Kṛtyā. She, with lustre resembling that of a crore of suns at the time of the end of a kalpa, seeing that great Sudarśana, going up a hundred yojanas, possessed of a thousand blazing weapons, made of gold, full of lustre, capable of making the entire world reduced to a condition at the time of deluge, saluted by all gods, the refuge of the entire world, lost her lustre, was overcome by fear, and crying (aloud) she ran to Vārāṇasī. Sudarśana too closely pursued her. She too, overcome by fear and crying entered that city of the king of Kāśī. Sudarśana also, reaching the city of Vārāṇasī, reducing to ash Pauṇḍraka's son, Daṇḍapāṇi, along with servants and army and elephants, so also the city of Maheśvara having many palaces and mansions, and being worshipped by all gods and great sages, again reached Kṛṣṇa's hand which was very soft, like a kalpa (sacred precept?). And about this the (following) verses are sung:

25-28. Having burnt with vigour that army discharging weapons and missiles and never decaying, reducing to ash the Kṛtyā, then the city of Vārāṇasī which had many chariots and elephants, and along with horses and men and women, and all stores and granaries, which was difficult to be seen even by gods, the houses, ramparts and courtyards of which were marked with doors, that disc of Viṣṇu burnt the entire city only. That disc, with its power of movement unexhausted, having accomplished what cannot be accomplished, with its lustre blazing, came to Viṣṇu's hand.

CHAPTER TWO HUNDRED FIFTYTWO

Kṛṣṇa Goes Back to His Abode

Śrī Rudra said:

1-3. After the killing of Kaṁsa, the king of Magadha, hating Yādavas, always troubled them. They, being afflicted, told (about it) to Kṛṣṇa. Kṛṣṇa called Bhīma and Arjuna and consulted them: "He has worshipped Rudra. Due to his favour he cannot be killed with weapons. But somehow he must be killed." Then having thought he said to Bhīma: "Wrestle with him." He promised to do so.

4-8. Then Vāsudeva, fit to be saluted by all the mobile and immobile world, went along with Bhīma and Arjuna in the guise of a brāhmaṇa to his city and reached his harem. He too having vanquished in battle very powerful kṣatriyas and having confined them, killed one of them every month and with his blood only made an offering to Bhairava. Thus exerting to kill Jarāsandha who had killed many men and kings, he along with Bhīma and Arjuna entered his house in the guise of a brāhmaṇa. He, seeing them, saluted them (by prostrating himself) like a staff, seated them on proper seats, worshipped them with madhuparka, and said to them: "I am fortunate; I am blessed. Why have you approached me? Tell it to me. I shall give all that to you." Out of them Vāsudeva, smiling, said to the king: "We Kṛṣṇa, Bhīma, and Arjuna have come to fight with you. Choose one of us for a duel."

9-12. He too said, "All right." Then he chose Bhīma for the duel. Then a fierce, continuous duel took place between Bhīma and Jarāsandha (lasting for) twenty-five days. Then prompted by Kṛṣṇa only (Bhīma) the son of Vāyu, split his (i.e. Jarāsandha's) body into two, and dropped it on the ground. Thus Kṛṣṇa, getting Jarāsandha killed by Pāṇḍu's son (Bhīma), freed the kings confined by Jarāsandha. (Kṛṣṇa) the descendant of Yadu, getting Jarāsandha killed by (Bhīma) Vāyu's son, freed the kings confined in his house.

13-20. All those, protected by Kṛṣṇa, having saluted and praised Kṛṣṇa, went to their respective countries. Then, going to Indraprastha with the two (i.e. Bhīma and Arjuna), Kṛṣṇa made Yudhiṣṭhira perform the Rājasūya sacrifice. There, after the sacrifice was over, the chief honour was given to Kṛṣṇa with the consent of Bhīṣma. There Śiśupāla spoke many abusive words to Kṛṣṇa. Kṛṣṇa too cut off his head with the Sudarśana (disc). He, after three existences, was assimilated into Viṣṇu. Having heard that Śiśupāla was killed, Dantavaktra came to Mathurā to fight with Kṛṣṇa. Kṛṣṇa, having learnt about it, got into his chariot, and came to Mathurā.

21-24. On the bank of Yamunā, at the gate of Mathurā, a fight lasting a day and night took place between Dantavaktra and

Kṛṣṇa; and Kṛṣṇa killed him with (his) mace. He with his entire body smashed dropped dead on the ground like a mountain broken through with the thunderbolt. He too obtained the eternal, highest position, the absorption into Viṣṇu, obtainable by the meditating saints. Thus Jaya and Vijaya, under the pretext of the curse of Sanaka and others, descended into the mundane existence merely for the sport of the lord, and in the three existences they were killed by him alone. They obtained liberation at the end of three existences.

25. Kṛṣṇa also, having killed him (i.e. Śiśupāla), having crossed Yamunā, having gone to Nanda-vraja, having saluted his old parents, and having consoled them and embraced by them with their throats (choked) with tears, having embraced all old cowherds, having cheered them up with gems, ornaments, etc. gratified the residents there.

26-30. On the charming sandy bank of Yamunā, covered with auspicious trees. Kṛṣṇa incessantly sported with the cowherdesses. Viṣṇu, dressed as a cowherd, lived here for a couple of months with (i.e. enjoying) pleasure of charming sport and steady love. Then all the cowherds like Nanda, all people along with their sons and wives, beasts, birds, and animals took up a divine form due to Kṛṣṇa's favour, got into an aeroplane, and reached the highest world of Viṣṇu. Kṛṣṇa, having given all the residents of Nanda-vraja his own pure, highest position, and being praised in heaven by hosts of gods, entered the glorious Dvārakā. There, he taking up an omnipresent form, and along with Vasudeva, Ugrasena, Saṁkarṣaṇa, Pradyumna, Aniruddha, Akrūra etc., and everyday worshipped by his sixteen thousand wives and his eight divine queens, enjoyed on very soft beds graced with flowers in many mansions.

31-35. Then a fellow religious student of Rāma and Kṛṣṇa, a brāhmaṇa, their friend from childhood, very much oppressed by poverty, came, after having tied a handful of rice parched and flattened, obtained by begging, in an old piece of cloth, to the glorious city of Dvārakā to see Kṛṣṇa. He stood silent for a moment at the door of Rukmiṇī's harem. Kṛṣṇa too, knowing that a brāhmaṇa had come, went forth to greet him; and having saluted him and held him by his hand, seated him on an excellent seat in his house, and worshipped him who was trembling with fear with madhuparka after washing his feet with the water from a golden pitcher in the hands of Rukmiṇī. Having gratified him with food, drink etc. resembling nectar, he himself took with his hand the parched and flattened rice that he had obtained by begging, and ate it with a smile. The moment Kṛṣṇa ate the parched and flattened rice, he had great affluence due to much wealth, corn, (many) garments and ornaments.

36-39. Dismissed by Kṛṣṇa, he, thinking that Kṛṣṇa did not give him a small piece of cloth, or wealth, entered his own city. Then seeing his own house full of much wealth and corn, he said: "Due to his favour I have got this." With his mind delighted by means of the divine garments and ornaments, he, along with his wife, enjoyed all pleasures, performed many sacrifices to please Viṣṇu, and due to his favour got the happiness of heaven. Then Dhṛtarāṣṭra's son Duryodhana, (having deceived) Pāṇḍu's sons under the pretext of gambling that was deceitful, took away their kingdom, and expelled them from his country. Those—Yudhiṣṭhira, Bhīma, Arjuna, Nakula and Sahadeva—along with their good wife Draupadī, went to a great forest. Having lived there for twelve years, and (having lived) *incognito* for a year, all of them lived in the house of Virāṭa, the king of Matsya (country); and came, with Kṛṣṇa's help to fight with the sons of Dhṛtarāṣṭra.

40-43. There took place a great war, causing fear even to gods, between the sons of Dhṛtarāṣṭra and of Pāṇḍu at the very holy Kurukṣetra. Then Śrīkṛṣṇa also, acting as the charioteer of Arjuna, put his power into Arjuna, and getting all kings led by Bhīṣma, Droṇa etc. and along with an army consisting of eleven akṣauhiṇīs killed by him, he put the Pāṇḍavas on the kingdom (i.e. the throne). And having completely removed the burden of the earth, he entered his own city. After some time, on some day, a brāhmaṇa brought his five-year old dead son, and putting him at the gate of the palace, lamenting much, spoke many words of censure to Kṛṣṇa. Hearing that imprecation, Kṛṣṇa remained silent.

44-48. He (i.e. the brāhmaṇa) said: "My five sons have been formerly killed. This is the sixth one. If Kṛṣṇa does not bring him back to life, I shall die at the royal gate." At that time Arjuna had come to see Kṛṣṇa. He saw him lamenting like that due to the grief (caused by the loss) of his son. Arjuna too, seeing the five-year old boy dead, was full of pity, and granting the brāhmaṇa protection, promised him: "I shall bring your son back to life." The brāhmaṇa, thus cheered up by him, was delighted. Then having consecrated the brāhmaṇā-child with life-restoring missiles, seeing him not regaining life, and finding himself of a futile promise, he, full of great grief, desired to give up his life with that only.

49-53. And Kṛṣṇa, knowing all that, came out of his harem, and said to that brāhmaṇa well-versed in the Vedas: "I shall give (you back) all your sons." Having cheered him, mounting upon Garuḍa, he, along with Arjuna came to Viṣṇu's world. Seeing Viṣṇu, along with the goddess (Lakṣmī) there, in a part of the jewelled pavilion, Kṛṣṇa and Arjuna saluted him. He embraced them with his arms, and asked them why they had come (there). Kṛṣṇa said: "O revered one, give me the sons of the brāhmaṇa well-versed in the Vedas." Then that Nārāyaṇa gave Kṛṣṇa those sons of the brāhmaṇa, who were of that age.

54-57. Srī Kṛṣṇa too, putting them on the shoulders of Garuḍa, and being full of joy, himself also mounted upon Garuḍa, and being praised by groups of gods, entered Dvāravatī. To that brāhmaṇa he gave the six sons aged five. He (i.e. the brāhmaṇa) too, extremely joyful, gave a blessing to Kṛṣṇa: "May you prosper." And Arjuna having had his promise fulfilled, saluted Kṛṣṇa and went to his own city protected by Yudhiṣṭhira. A myriad thousand sons were born to the sixteen thousand wives of Kṛṣṇa. It is not possible to tell the number of their sons and grandsons. Here (i.e. with regard to this) also there is a verse:

58-62. There were eight hundred thousands and a myriad of sons. Of all of them, Pradyumna, Rukmiṇī's son was the first. This earth was covered with those innumerable Yādavas. Fearing a burden to the earth again, Kṛṣṇa desired to destroy them under the pretext of a sage's curse. Sometime all the young boys came to sport in Narmadā. There, seeing the great sage Kaṇva practising austerity, they made Jāmbavatī's son put on the dress of a woman, and tying an iron pestle to his belly, they approached the sage, and placing Sāmba's son in the guise of a wife (husband?), said to him: "Tell us whether in (i.e. from) her womb a female or a male would be born."

63-67. He, knowing it mentally, and not tolerating it, said to them all: "Be killed with this pestle." All, with their minds dejected, approached Kṛṣṇa, and reported to him what the sage had said, and that act (of them). Kṛṣṇa too threw the pounded iron pestle into a pool. From the seed of the iron (pestle) reduced to powder great kāśa (grass) resembling the thunderbolt came up. A fish ate a portion of the pestle, of the size of the small finger. A fisherman, catching that fish, took the piece of the pestle lying in the belly of the fish and fashioned (out of it) the point at the end of an arrow.

68-71. Sometime all the Yādavas like Rāma, Kṛṣṇa, Pradyumna became intoxicated after drinking the spirituous liquor sent by Indra. They took to fighting with one another, and shouting loud words fought (among themselves) and perished. Kṛṣṇa, tired of fighting, slept in the shade of a desire-yielding tree. A hunter, taking a bow and an arrow, took to hunting. Thus they who had fully abandoned their lives, went to their respective gods.

72-74. Having thus destroyed everything with the pestle, the god himself slept in the shade of a great tree surrounded by many clumps of trees. Thinking about himself of the nature of Vāsudeva having four forms, and putting (one) foot on (another) knee, he sat (there) to abandon his human form. In the meanwhile, the hunter, due to the urging of Death, saw Hari's very red foot marked with a disc, a vajra, a banner, a goad etc., and pierced it. Then recognising him to be Śrī Kṛṣṇa, and struck by great fear and trembling he joined the palms of his hands and saluted him (saying), "Remove all my faults."

75-77. Śrī Kṛṣṇa seeing him in that condition, made him rise with his hands full of nectar, and said to him (words) consoling him who was oppressed by great fear: "You have not committed a fault." Then he granted him the world of Viṣṇu, which is accessible to the meditating saints (only), from which there is no return, which is eternal and full of all secret things. He gave up his human form just at that moment only; and along with all his sons and wives got into a bright, divine aeroplane and went to Viṣṇu's world which resembled a thousand suns in brightness, was crowded with hosts of celestial nymphs and was golden, and which had Viṣṇu in it.

78-83. At that time, Dāruka getting into a chariot, approached Viṣṇu. Kṛṣṇa too sent him (back, telling him), "First bring

Arjuna of my nature." He, getting into a chariot having the mind's speed, came near Arjuna. O goddess, in the meanwhile Arjuna got into it, went round (Śrī Kṛṣṇa), saluted him, and with the palms of his hands joined said: "What do (i.e. should) I do?" And Kṛṣṇa said to him: "O Pārtha, I shall go to my own world. Going to Dvāravatī and bringing (my) eight wives like Rukmiṇī staying there, send them into my body." With Dāruka he came to the city.

84-86. In the meanwhile, gods seated in their aeroplanes and remaining in the sky, saw Kṛṣṇa going to heaven; and along with the sages praised him and dropped on him showers of flowers. Kṛṣṇa too gave up his human body, took up the body of the form of Vāsudeva, which was the cause of the maintenance and destruction of the entire world, which was all the individual souls, which was meditated upon by meditating saints checking their internal feelings, mounted upon Garuḍa, and being praised by great sages, went (to Vaikuṇṭha). Arjuna told it to all the queens like Rukmiṇī, along with Vasudeva and Ugrasena.

87-90. Hearing that all citizens and ladies abandoned Dvāravatī and all those ladies dear to Kṛṣṇa, went out of the harem, and along with Vasudeva and Ugrasena quickly approached Hari. All those old Yādavas like Vasudeva, Ugrasena and Akrūra, abandoned their bodies and came to the eternal Vāsudeva. Revatī also embraced Balabhadra's body and entered fire. Having obtained a (divine) body in it, she got into a divine aeroplane and went to the divine world of Saṁkarṣaṇa, the place of her husband. In the same way Rukmaputrī with Pradyumna, Uṣā with Aniruddha and all Yādava ladies honoured the bodies of their husbands and entered fire.

91-94. Arjuna performed the obsequies of all of them. At that time Dāruka also, getting into the divine chariot called Sugrīva, yoked with divine horses and full of all gems, came (there). The Pārijāta tree and the assembly of gods also came to the world of the lord of gods. At that time the city of Dvāravatī submergd in the great ocean.

95-97. Then the enemies of gods seized all the sixteen thousand wives (of Śrī Kṛṣṇa) going to Indraprastha along with Arjuna. Formerly the wives of gods and gandharvas had laughed at the great sage Aṣṭāvakra after seeing him. He cursed them:

"You will be prostitutes." Then he was propitiated and honoured by them. Due to his grace they, even after obtaining Vāsudeva saluted by all the worlds, as their husband, got into the hands of the enemies of gods due to that (curse) only. Arjuna too, vanquished by the enemies of gods was overcome by grief. He thought: "The strength of my arms and all my glory have gone away with Kṛṣṇa." And saying (to himself): "Today my fortune has perished", he, with his lustre entirely perished like that of the evening sun, came to his own city.

98. Thus, for the good of all gods, for destroying the burden of the entire earth, Vāsudeva descended into the Yadu-family. He destroyed all demons and removed a great burden of the earth. He freed all the residents of Nandavraja, Dvārakā and Mathurā and all the mobile and immobile from the bonds of death and mundane existence, and settled them in (Vaikuṇṭha) which is full of great splendour, is eternal, which is accessible (only) to the meditating saints, is golden, charming and pure, and always being waited upon by divine queens etc. he lived (in Vaikuṇṭha). In this connection there are these verses:

99-107. There might be all other incarnations. (But) the deeds of Kṛṣṇa are great. The lord of Ramā appeared for destroying those who caused burden to the earth. These deeds of Kṛṣṇa were for destroying the wicked. Śrī Kṛṣṇa, the ocean of pity, always delights in Vaikuṇṭha. O goddess, these auspicious deeds of Kṛṣṇa are very wonderful. I told them to you in brief. They give all fruits. He who would recite, remember or listen to this life(-account) of Vāsudeva with devotion near (the image of) Hari, goes to the highest position. Even he who has (committed) major sins or minor sins, is freed after listening to the deeds of young Kṛṣṇa. He who remembers Hari seated with Rukmiṇī in Dvāravatī, undoubtedly acquires great power. He, after meditating upon him, the leader of all gods, while in a battle, a danger, a difficulty or while surrounded by his enemy, would be highly successful. He who would remember him sporting with the young cowherdesses in the auspicious Govraja, gets all the desired (objects) and also good fortune. So also he who, suffering from great misfortune and diseases etc., would remember the eternal one, the vanquisher of the very fierce Kṛtyā living in the city of Kāśī (would be happy).

108-115. O you desiring the fruits of all times, what is the use of speaking much in this regard? A wise man should only utter the formula: 'Salutation to Kṛṣṇa'. 'Repeated salutations to Kṛṣṇa, Vāsudeva, Hari, the highest soul. I, bowing down repeatedly salute Govinda for the destruction of my affliction.' O goddess, a man should, everyday, with devotion, mutter this formula. Being free from all sins, he would obtain Viṣṇu's world. This lord Janārdana assumes different form(s) for the protection of all gods and of the worlds. I, with a desire to kill Tripura, worshipped Viṣṇu. The glorious one, taking up the form of Buddha, deluded his enemies. Those who were deluded by that teaching gave up all religious practices. (These) enemies of gods were killed by me with Viṣṇu's missile. Viṣṇu, descending in a brāhmaṇa's house at the end of Kali, will kill all the cruel Mlecchas. I have described along with all those appearances, all the forms of the lord of the world. O you of an auspicious face, what else do you want to listen to? I shall narrate it.

CHAPTER TWO HUNDRED FIFTYTHREE

Modes of Viṣṇu's Worship

Śrī Pārvatī said:

1-3. O venerable one, you have told me the very wonderful acts of Rāma and Kṛṣṇa in this (narration) of Kṛṣṇa's (deeds) in the state of grandeur. Oh, my heart, listening to the nectar of the tale of Hari—the acts of the noble Rāma and Kṛṣṇa—is not satisfied even for crores of kalpas, O lord of good, O lord of beings. Now I desire to listen to the excellent (account of the) greatness of Viṣṇu. O god, I also desire to hear about the manner of his worship.

Śrī Rudra said:

4-9. O goddess, listen. I shall tell you (the account) of the very noble Viṣṇu. The installation (of his idol) and his self-manifestation—these are the two aspects which it consists of. The installation with (the accompaniment of) the rites as told in the Śrauta and Smārta texts, of the representation of Viṣṇu of a stone, clay, wood, iron etc., is said to be *Sthāpana.* Listen (as) I (tell you) to that which is called self-manifestation. That representation of Viṣṇu of stone or wood in which the lord of souls has placed himself for men is said to be self-manifest on the earth. One should worship Viṣṇu (whose representation is) either self-manifest or installed. Keśava, the lord of the world, the eternal one, himself approaches (the deities and the great sages) for their worship. Just that which was to be enjoyed in a (particular) body became manifest. One should always worship that only and take delight in that only.

10-16. Viṣṇu, the lord of gods, should be properly worshipped. Due to the penance of the Ikṣvāku lords, he himself appeared on the earth. That Mādhava, removing sins, is to be worshipped by me at Kāśī. I settling myself properly take delight in the charming house, after visiting it, where the old one is self-manifest. The lord of sacrifices is not obtained by men by means of Yoga of eight constituents, but in worship. Being the object of the eyes he gives the desired boon. Men easily attain him in (i.e. by means of) worship in all conditions. In the very meritorious, auspicious country of Bhārata, in Jambūdvīpa, on the earth, he is always present near even the ignorant. Viṣṇu is always near in a worship and never in other (modes of reaching him). Therefore, in the country Bhārata, he is, O goddess, always waited upon by sages and even by gods with rites like penance, sacrifice etc. In this country of Bhārata Viṣṇu is always near.

17-21. One should get rid of sin by purifying (oneself) at the Indradyumna (lake), Kaurmya, the Siṁha mountain, Karavīra, Kāśī, Prayāga or (the division of Bhārata called) Saumya, or the Śālagrāma mountain, Dvāravatī, Naimiṣa (forest), so also in Badarikāśrama, Pauṇḍarika and Daṇḍaka (forest), Mathurā, Veṅkaṭa-giri, Śveta mountain, Garuḍa mountain, Kāñcī, Anantaśayana, Śrīraṅga, Vāsava mountain, Nārāyaṇa mountain, Saumya, Varāha, Vāmanāśrama. These and others are self-manifest, and give all desired fruits. The good sages say that in that in which Viṣṇu himself is near, he is self-manifest.

22-26. The best among the great devotees of Viṣṇu should install the (idol of) Keśava according to the precept, and should bring about his proximity by (muttering) a (sacred) formula. That installation is excellent. He should worship the god (installed) in it in villages and houses. The good recommend the worship in the house on a Śālagrāma stone. Praising, repeating the formula, sacrifice, abstract meditation on the magnanimous one, repeating his name, serving him, being marked with his signs (like the disc etc.) would be his worship. O auspicious one, it is divided into nine kinds. For a brāhmaṇa doing every act for him, is always laid down. A brāhmaṇa, a great devotee of Viṣṇu is the greatest teacher of men. He is venerable to all people as Viṣṇu is.

27-35. A brāhmaṇa who has gone through the five purificatory rites like being heated (with the Vaiṣṇava marks) and having five motives is said to be a great brāhmaṇa. The worship for a kṣatriya is laid down through the performance of the various acts. For vaiśyas the six types of worship are said to be: Marking (his body) with his (i.e. Viṣṇu's) marks, service, honouring those who belong to him, repeating the letters of the formula, repeating viṣṇu's names, and salutation to him. The worship for a śūdra (consists of) five (types): Repeating his names, service to him, worshipping and saluting him and honouring those who belong to him. O dear one, mental worship is common to all men. The worship of the lord of the world should be done according to one's fitness. Viṣṇu should always be worshipped by brāhmaṇas and others who are devoted to no other deity (than Viṣṇu), who do not wish to accomplish any other fruit (than securing him), who know the Vedas and the truth about Brahman, who are free from attachment, who desire salvation, who possess devotion for their preceptors, who are well-pleased, who are very good. Men should perform Viṣṇu's proper worship (i.e. the worship fit) for their castes. The good devotees of Viṣṇu should do (acts) proper for their castes and stages of life. An intelligent man should always properly perform the rites told in the holy texts and codes of law. He should never transgress the acts prescribed in the holy texts and codes of law.

36-39. That devotee of Viṣṇu, who does not practise the acts prescribed in the Śrutis and Smṛtis, becomes a heretic, and would stay in the Raurava hell. Therefore, a man should offer to the lord of the world a worship fit for his caste. One should always practise acts prescribed in the codes of law. O auspicious one, the mental worship is common to all men. Only after considering his own fitness a man should carefully perform his duty. The means for all to acquire piety are: Tranquillity, control, austerities, purity, truthfulness, avoiding (eating) flesh, non-stealing, and harmlessness.

40-50. Therefore, one should worship Viṣṇu according to his caste and stage of life. Getting up at the end of night and having properly rinsed his mouth, and having saluted the elderly persons he should remember Viṣṇu in his heart. He being pure and controlled in his speech, should devoutly repeat the thousand names (of Viṣṇu). Having evacuated the bowels and discharged the urine[1] on the outside of the village, and having properly purified[2] himself, he, the restrained and pure one, should properly sip water and should properly bathe after having brushed his teeth. O auspicious one, taking the earth at the root of a tulasī along with its leaf, and having consecrated it with the principal formula and having smeared his body along with (the repetition of) the Gāyatrī hymn only, he should bathe after offering the expiatory formula. O you very pure one, having invoked there Gaṅgā rising from the feet of Viṣṇu, and having quickly dipped (into the water) he should repeat the excellent expiatory formula. Having sipped water, he should sprinkle his person with water in the order prescribed in the formula of (i.e. sacred to) Viṣṇu. Then the wise one having quickly dipped himself, should repeat the primary formula twenty-eight times or one hundred and eight times. The devotee of Viṣṇu having consecrated himself with the formula (to be repeated) in water, should offer his prayers. Having sipped water, he should gratify deities, sages and dead ancestors. Having pressed his garment, having sipped water, he, the alert devotee of Viṣṇu, and the best brāhmaṇa, having put on a washed garment should take pure, charming clay and having consecrated it with a formula only, have on his forehead etc. the proper number of the upright sectarian marks. The wise one should then perform (i.e. offer) the sandhyā prayer and recite Sāvitrī (hymn).

1. The reading is definitely 'Mala-mūtra' and not 'Mūla-mantra'.

2. Aghamarṣaṇa: Lit. expiatory, removing or destroying sin; usually applied to a prayer repeated by brāhmaṇas (the 190th hymn of the tenth Maṇḍala of the Ṛgveda).

51-55. He controlled in speech and mind, should go home and wash his feet. Having sipped water with a concentrated mind, he should enter the hall where worship is offered. Having placed (the idol of) the lord, the god Lakṣmī-Nārāyaṇa on a charming, very bright seat, adorned with a heap of flowers, he should worship him properly with sandal, flowers and sacred rice grains. The brāhmaṇa, with his mind controlled, should worship (the idol of) Viṣṇu—either installed or self-manifest—devoutly, properly and as deserved, according to the way told in Śrutis and Smṛtis. The devotee of Viṣṇu should do what is advised by his preceptor. The Śrauta way is Vaikhānasa and the Smārta is that of Vasiṣṭha.

56-59. What is laid down in Pañcarātra is called divine text. The rite should not be dropped; (for) the propitiation of Viṣṇu is the highest. He should gladly and according to his ability offer worship to Viṣṇu with invocation, seat, (offering) materials of worship etc., sandal, flowers, sacred rice grains, incense, lamps, offerings of eatables, tāmbūla etc. and salutations. The devotee of Viṣṇu should propitiate the deity with sixteen modes of paying homage to the accompaniment at every ṛc of the two hymns Puruṣa sūkta and the principal hymn. Again during the various modes of worship he should offer a handful of flowers.

60-70. With the (various) positions of fingers the devotee of Viṣṇu should invoke the lord of the earth. So also he should offer a seat with a flower and the finger-position. With the two principal hymns he should offer at every mode of worship lamp, materials of worship, (water for) sipping, a bath with pure water in vessels, and auspicious substances mixed with tulasī-leaves. Then with fragrant oil he should smear the idol. He should also rub and clean his body with musk and sandal. Having bathed with auspicious, fragrant water with (the accompaniment of) hymns, and having properly decorated (himself) with divine ornaments and garments, he should then offer madhuparka, so also sandal made fragrant. He should devoutly and properly offer fragrant, good flowers, incense, and very beautiful lamp having eight or ten limbs (i.e. wicks). He should also give various kinds of eatables, mixed with rice boiled with milk and cakes. He should also devoutly offer camphor with tāmbūla.

Having waved the lamps he should worship (i.e. offer) a garland of flowers. Having taken himself round (the idol) and having saluted and praised (it) with excellent hymns, he should offer auspicious materials of worship after making (the idol) lie on the lap of Garuḍa. Having repeated auspicious names, he should then perform a sacrifice. He should make an offering into the fire-circle with the remaining of eatables offered to Viṣṇu. He should (repeat) every ṛc (of) the Puruṣa-sūkta and the Śrīsūkta invoking auspiciousness. He should offer into the Vedic fire oblation mixed with ghee. He should devoutly offer (it) with the gem of a hymn as (already) mentioned.

71-81. Meditating upon great Viṣṇu of the form of sacrifice one hundred and eight times or twenty-eight times, he should offer the oblation. After meditating upon the lord (i.e. Viṣṇu) resembling pure gold, holding a conch, a disc and a mace, consisting of the entire Vedas, Vedānta, Aṅgas and Upāṅgas, seated with goddess Lakṣmī, he should perform a sacrifice. He should offer the oblation with (Viṣṇu's) names (uttered) after each offering. The best devotee of Viṣṇu should assign (offerings) to the eternal devotees. Then in due order, he should offer oblations to and particularly worship the Śaktis like Bhū, Līlā, Vimalā etc. first and then the deities like Ananta, Garuḍa etc. Then Vāsudeva etc. and deities like Śakti, so also images like that of Keśava, Saṁkarṣaṇa etc., Matsya, Kūrma etc. and the weapons like the disc, so also gods like Viṣṇu, and deities like the Moon, the guardians of the quarters like Indra, so also deities like Dharma should be offered oblations to and worshipped. The best devotee of Viṣṇu, being calm, should everyday, in his daily rite of worship offer the sacrifice to Viṣṇu. In the worship in the house, he, by offering properly the five sacrifices, should duly offer the oblation and then sip water. Seated on the white seat with the skin of the black antelope and darbhas placed on it he should bring about comfort for (being able to enjoy) pleasures by the use of hymns. Properly seated in the position of Padma he should purify the elements of the body.

82-90. With his senses controlled, he should, with a hymn, practise the three (kinds of) breath-control. Then facing the north he should bring about the expansion of the heart-lotus by means of the Sun of knowledge. The best devotee of Viṣṇu should one by one, imagine in its pericarp, full of the three, the triad of the orbs of the sun, the moon, and the fire. On them he should imagine a seat full of many gems. He should (mentally) arrange at the end of the root of the heart-lotus a lotus with eight (kinds of) grandeur, having brilliance like that of the young sun, and full of the syllables of the mystic formula. Then the pure devotee, of a calm mind, should meditate upon lord Viṣṇu who is seated on it with goddess (Lakṣmī), who resembles a crore of moons, who has four hands, a beautiful body, who holds a conch, a disc and a mace, whose eyes are large like lotus-petals, who is distinguished with all (auspicious) marks, on whose chest are Śrīvatsa and Kaustubha, who has put on a yellow garment, beautiful ornaments, who is adorned with divine ornaments, whose body is smeared with divine sandal, who is graced with divine flowers, is adorned with the garland of wood-flowers and delicate leaves of tulasī, who resembles a crore of suns in lustre, whose body is embraced by Lakṣmī having all (good) marks, who is auspicious; having thus meditated, he should repeat the hymn.

91-96. Having with devotion mentally worshipped (Viṣṇu) a thousand or hundred times, or according to his capacity, he should stop. He should devoutly honour those who belong to him (i.e. his devotees), that have come at that time, and having pleased them by (giving them) food, drink etc., he should dismiss them after following them (a few steps). Having worshipped the dead ancestors he should duly gratify the deities. Having honoured the guests and servants, the couple should eat. He should always avoid the worship of yakṣas, demons and spirits. A brāhmaṇa who through folly worships them, would certainly become a cāṇḍāla. Resorting to yakṣas, goblins and deities enjoying liquor and flesh is said to be equivalent to drinking liquor. The worship of ghosts of brāhmaṇas, vampires, yakṣas and spirits is the means for men of reaching the very fierce hell, Kumbhīpāka.

97-106. Due to the worship of yakṣas and spirits all the religious merit earned during crores of existences by (performance of) sacrifices and (giving) gifts, is lost instantly. Due to the worship of yakṣas and spirits, a woman or a man becomes an insect for thousands of crores of kalpas and hundreds of crores of kalpas and sinks in feces along with his dead ancestors. He who eats the food offered to yakṣas, goblins or vicious deities would be the eater of pus and blood. The brāhmaṇa (who eats food) assigned to yakṣas, hosts of spirits, cruel ghosts of brāhmaṇas, (would instantly become) a cāṇḍāla only. That woman who would worship yakṣas, goblins, serpents, demons, goes with her face turned down to the fierce Kālasūtra hell. One having lived there along with one's dead ancestors, and licking urine and feces till deluge, and with one's body being eaten by insects, is then born within ten days in hundred (śatasaṁkhyayā?) on the earth. Therefore, one should avoid the worship of yakṣas etc. and of (vicious) deities. One should even avoid an independent worship of brāhmaṇas well-versed in Vedas. Having worshipped god Nārāyaṇa Hari, venerable to the world, a man should worship the installation of the god covered on all sides. With the remnant of what is enjoyed by Viṣṇu, he should throw an offering to them.

107-115. The devotee of Viṣṇu should also perform a sacrifice with (materials) that have remained after it (i.e. Viṣṇu's worship). He should offer an oblation to the deities after having properly made an offering to Viṣṇu. He should also offer everything to his dead ancestors and should secure immortality. Harassing beings leads wise men to hell. O daughter of the (Himālaya) Mountain, know that which, without being given, is taken by men to be a theft and is the cause of hell. A man who eats prohibited articles of food like garlic, (drinks) liquor etc., (eats) radish, red garlic, sesamum-flour, pot-herb, bilva, kośātakī-fruit, bottle-gourd, egg-plant, bījāli-fruit, kavaca fruit, and other prohibited articles of food as noted in the holy texts, reaches a strange, inauspicious hell. The food of the non-devotees of Viṣṇu, that of the fallen, that which is not offered to Viṣṇu would be like the flesh of a dog. He who eats the food of (i.e. offered to) yakṣas, demons and spirits, so also (he who enjoys) wine, liquor and onion goes to a hell where the food is pus and blood. A man (goes to hell) by means of these—installing, touching or coming in contact with them. They too just go to a hell where the food is feces, urine and insects. So also a man (goes to hell) due to contact with the fallen and the heretics.

116-117. Knowing the ancient best Puruṣa (i.e. Viṣṇu), the

entire enjoyer of all sacrifices, a man should perform his daily and occasional obligatory rites, so also those that are performed through the desire for some object (optional). O goddess, those who desire heaven, should never worship yakṣas, demons, spirits, goblins and Bhairavas.

118-124. A brāhmaṇa should avoid worshipping yakṣas, demons and spirits. (For by doing so) for three hundred crores of kalpas he remains in the state of a goblin. Therefore, the worship of demons and spirits is prohibited. Due to the worship of yakṣas and groups of spirits he goes to the Raurava hell (and stays there) for thousands of crores of kalpas and hundreds of crores of kalpas. He, being without the marks like the conch, the disc and other marks most dear to Viṣṇu, and fallen from all pious acts would go to hell. By means of illicit intercourse, harm (to others), snatching another's wealth, by eating prohibited articles of food, he would instantly reach hell. (If) a man abandoning the woman whose hand he has sought, goes to another woman, that is illicit intercourse; it is the cause of instantly going to hell. A man similarly goes to hell only due to the contact with the fallen, the heretics and also those who do impious deeds. He should even avoid the contact of those who come in contact with such persons.

125. The devotee of Viṣṇu should avoid a family full of sins. Seeking solitude, he should abandon the village mixed with (i.e. full of) great sins.

126-131. Similarly, he who desires absolute solitude, should even abandon that region. The means to attain Viṣṇu is said to be doing one's own duty, having knowledge, devotion etc. That brāhmaṇa who practises his duties and knowledge in accordance with Viṣṇu's order, and is highly devoted to Viṣṇu, would be the one who solicits solitude. The devotee of Viṣṇu should properly avoid a prohibited act with a sinful thought (i.e. by looking upon it as a sinful act). Soliciting solitariness he should even mentally abandon (acts according to) the holy text due to blemish. Similarly he who desires absolute solitude, should avoid (acts) looking upon them as fit to be abandoned. Acts are said to be of three kinds: daily, occasional (both obligatory) and (those which are) performed through the desire for some object (i.e. optional).

The sages have declared knowledge also to be like that in the world: the discrimination between what ought and ought not to be done; thinking about the other world; the means to accomplish it; the knowledge of Viṣṇu's nature only. A devotee should be full of devotion. It is said to be of nine kinds:

132-140. The auspicious marks of Sudarśana (disc); the upright sectarian mark on the forehead; repeating the formula of (i.e. taught by) the good preceptor; worshipping Viṣṇu properly; recollection of Viṣṇu; glorification of Viṣṇu; service of the highest soul; salutation before him; and honouring those who belong to him; resorting to his favour and a holy place. (Thus) devotion is said to be of nine kinds. That with which the devotee of Viṣṇu seeks the shelter of god Viṣṇu, should be known as pious resignation. It is declared to be of three kinds: It is said to be of three types in the world: tāmasī (vicious), rājasī (passionate) and sāttvikī (sincere). Fulfilment is also divided into three (kinds); it is common to all (human) beings. Looking upon these four as fit to be abandoned(?), the devotee of Viṣṇu should give it(?) up. Brahman only, being the means, would cling to Viṣṇu's devotee(?). The best among the great devotees of Viṣṇu should practise acts, knowledge through love for the lord, and abandoning (i.e. not looking upon) them as means. With devotion he should worship Viṣṇu three times (a day). O you auspicious one, he should especially worship him at the time of an occasional obligatory (rite). On everyday of the month of Kārtika he should worship him (i.e. Viṣṇu) with jasmine flowers. He of a controlled mind and a firm vow, should continuously offer a lamp. Having fed brāhmaṇas he would, in the end, attain absorption into Viṣṇu.

141-145. O goddess, in Dhanu-month, he should every morning continuously worship the lord of gods with lotuses and white and black karavīra flowers. He should offer incense, lamps and eatables according to his capacity. At the conclusion he should feed brāhmaṇas who are the best among the great devotees of Viṣṇu. He undoubtedly gets the fruit of a thousand horse-sacrifices. In the month of Māgha, (every morning) when the sun has risen, he should particularly bathe in a river, and worship Viṣṇu with flowers and lotuses, O you of an auspicious face. He should offer rice cooked in milk and eatables with ghee (to Viṣṇu). Having bathed (every morning) he should continuously worship Viṣṇu (everyday) for a month. In conclusion he should offer sugar with water.

146-151. O you of an auspicious appearance, he should devoutly honour Viṣṇu's devotees at the end of the month. Similarly in the month of Caitra he should daily worship the lord of the world with campaka flowers and also with bakula flowers; and should offer food prepared in jaggery. Being well concentrated, he should feed brāhmaṇas at the end of the month. He would (thus) obtain (the fruit of) the worship performed for a thousand years. In Vaiśākha he should worship the god with great lotuses having hundred petals. O goddess, having worshipped him in the proper manner, he should devoutly offer him water mixed with molasses along with curd, food and fruits. O Pārvatī, the lord of the world, along with Lakṣmī, is pleased. In the month of Jyeṣṭha, he, having worshipped Hṛṣīkeśa with white lotuses, trumpet(-flowers), and blue lotuses, and having devoutly offered him food with mangoes, he would be the giver of a crore of cows.

152-157. Having fed Viṣṇu's devotees, he would obtain complete immortality. In (the month of) Āṣāḍha he should everyday worship devoutly Acyuta, Lakṣmī's husband, and the god of gods with clove-flowers, and offer him rice boiled in milk. At the end of the month he should feed brāhmaṇas, the best among great devotees of Viṣṇu. Undoubtedly he obtains (the merit) of the worship for sixty thousand years. In the month of Śrāvaṇa he should worship Viṣṇu with punnāga flower, and ketakī petals. Having worshipped Viṣṇu with devotion, he would not obtain birth again. Devoutly he should give cakes mixed with sugar and ghee. He should feed brāhmaṇas; similarly he would obtain full immortality. In Śrāvaṇa he should worship the lord with kunda and kurabaka (flowers). He should devoutly offer milk and food mixed with jaggery. Everyday he would obtain the fruit of the gift of a crore of cows.

158-170. In the month of Āśvina he should worship Viṣṇu with blue lotuses. He should devoutly offer him milk mixed with cakes. Being delighted and surrounded by his own people, he reaches Viṣṇu's world for thousands of crores of kalpas and hundreds of crores of kalpas. O goddess, in the same way, in the month of Kārtika he would obtain absorption (into Viṣṇu) on devoutly worshipping Acyuta with tender tulasī-leaves. With devotion, and in due order, he should devoutly and duly offer food with milk, ghee and sugar, so also rice boiled in milk and cakes. O you of an excellent face, one should, according to one's capacity, particularly worship Viṣṇu on the new-moon day, Saturday, constellation sacred to Viṣṇu, the Sun's passage, portentous calamity, and lunar or solar eclipse. The best brāhmaṇa should offer a sacrifice to Viṣṇu according to his capacity on the day of Jupiter's passage (from one to another constellation) and constellations of Viṣṇu's birth. He should offer a handful of flowers, approved by the Vedas, for every ṛc. He should also break the fast with the oblation of rice,[1] barley and pulse boiled for presentation to the gods and the manes, or with rice cooked in milk. He should feed Viṣṇu's devotees and give them presents according to his capacity. Having emancipated a crore of (the members of) his family, he would obtain Viṣṇu's position. If the best devotee of Viṣṇu is unable to worship Viṣṇu, he should, along with the repetition of hymns sacred to Viṣṇu,[2] everyday offer a sacrifice with a thousand handfuls of flowers. Or the wise man should worship the lord to please him (offering a handful of flowers) with every verse. Or continuously for seven nights he should (recite) the gem of a hymn one thousand and eight times, and should worship him with an offering. The wise man should especially honour the best among the great devotees of Viṣṇu. At the end he should, according to his wealth, take an ablution. A brāhmaṇa should take an ablution to the accompaniment of the repetition of hymns sacred to Viṣṇu.

171-174. The best brāhmaṇa, having duly and according to his capacity, bathed here, and having devoutly washed his feet in another vessel, should worship (Viṣṇu) with incense, flowers etc. and garments, ornaments etc; so also he should worship him with a tāmbūla, fruits according to his capacity. Having fed (a brāhmaṇa) with food, drink etc. and having repeatedly saluted him, he should follow him to the boundary (of the village), and having saluted him who is dismissed, he should again salute him

1. Caru: An oblation of rice, barley, and pulse boiled for presentation to the gods and the manes.

2. (Vaiṣṇava) anuvāka: repeating (hymns) sacred to Viṣṇu,

devoutly, and slowly return. With his mind controlled, he, having entered his house, should again worship the lord of beings.

175-179. Thus till he is alive, he should diligently worship Viṣṇu. O auspicious one, he should especially always honour those that belong to him. O goddess, of all worships that of Viṣṇu is the best. Therefore, honouring those that belong to him, is the best. He who would worship Viṣṇu, but would not honour those who belong to him should not be reckoned as Viṣṇu's devotee, but is known to be a hypocrite. Therefore, a man should always with (i.e. making an) effort honour those that belong to him. By means of honouring the best devotee of Viṣṇu, he overcomes the entire stream of difficulties. O goddess, thus I have described the excellent daily and occasional (obligatory) worship of Viṣṇu, so also that of those who belong to him.

180. O goddess, I have also described to you, his valour, nature, the accomplishment of the fruit, his residence, body so also the group of the four (kinds of) acts etc. What else do you desire to hear?

CHAPTER TWO HUNDRED FIFTYFOUR

One Hundred and Eight Names of Rāma

Vasiṣṭha said:

1. That goddess, thus addressed by her lord, the Trident-holder, saluted the noble one. and with the palms of her hands joined, then spoke:

Pārvatī said:

2-3. O lord, you have well described the excellent practices of (i.e. sacred to) Viṣṇu, and the nature of the highest lord Viṣṇu, which is the greater secret than a secret (i.e. the greatest secret). O you saluted by all gods, I am fortunate; I am blessed. Due to your favour I (shall) worship the eternal lord of gods.

Vasiṣṭha said:

4. Then hearing her words Śiva, the destroyer of Tripura, with his heart pleased, embraced the goddess (and said):

Rudra said:

5-7. Well (said), well (said), O great goddess, O you of an excellent face. Worship Hṛṣīkeśa, Acyuta, the lord of Lakṣmī. O good one, with you as my wife, devoted to Viṣṇu, I am fortunate. O you of a beautiful body, permitted by your intelligent preceptor, Vāmadeva, worship the ancient lord, Viṣṇu. O you daughter of the (Himālaya) Mountain, by worshipping Viṣṇu in the way of (i.e. according to) the advice of the preceptor, a man obtains every desire (object), not otherwise.

Vasiṣṭha said:

8-9. The goddess, thus addressed, and being delighted and desirous of worshipping Viṣṇu, then suddenly approached Vāmadeva, O king. The goddess, after approaching, honouring the preceptor and saluting the best sage with the palms of her hands joined, said (to him):

Pārvatī said:

10. O revered one, O best brāhmaṇa, by your grace I shall properly worship Viṣṇu. Please permit me.

Vasiṣṭha said:

11-12. Thus addressed by the goddess, the preceptor, the great sage Vāmadeva, duly gave her an excellent mystic formula. The best sage told (her) the thousand names of Viṣṇu. The preceptor, after telling her the manner of worship, also spoke with great love to Pārvatī who had fulfilled her vow.

Vāmadeva said:

13. O you of an excellent face, having everyday worshipped Viṣṇu in the morning, repeat the thousand names of Viṣṇu after that.

Vasiṣṭha said:

14-16. Pārvatī who was advised by that preceptor Vāmadeva, thus addressed by that preceptor, worshipped (Viṣṇu) with her mind delighted, saluted (him), and again came to her abode. Then after a few days, the bull-bannered Śaṅkara, having worshipped Viṣṇu on a Dvādaśī-day, was seated on a charming peak of Kailāsa. He then spoke to Pārvatī to take food.

Śaṅkara said:

17a. O Pārvatī, saluted by the world, come to eat with me.

Vasiṣṭha said:

17b-18. Goddess Pārvatī said to him: "O god, I shall eat after I repeat the thousand names (of Viṣṇu). O lord, you may eat food." Then the highest lord, smiling, said to her:

Śaṅkara said:

19-22a. O Pārvatī, you are fortunate; you are blessed. You are Viṣṇu's devotee. O goddess, without good luck, devotion to Viṣṇu is difficult to have. O you charming one, O you of an excellent face, I, saying 'Rāma, Rāma', am interested in Rāma. Rāma's name is equal to the thousand names (of Viṣṇu). O Pārvatī, my mind, hearing the names beginning with (the letter) 'ra', becomes pleased, due to the expectation of their being Rāma's names. O great goddess, uttering (the word) *Rāma*, now eat with me.

Vasiṣṭha said:

22b-23. Then uttering the name *Rāma* Pārvatī ate with (Śaṅkara). Then the great goddess Pārvatī, seated with Śaṅkara, uttered the name *Rāma*, and with her mind disposed to love, asked god Śaṅkara:

Pārvatī said:

24. You said Rāma's name is equivalent to the thousand names (of Viṣṇu). The enemy of Rāvaṇa has other names (also). O lord of gods, tell them to me. Devotion (for them) has arisen in me.

Śrī Mahādeva said:

25-29. O Pārvatī, listen. I shall tell the names of Rāma. O

Pārvatī, whatever common and Vaidika words are there, they are Rāmacandra's names. Among them the (Viṣṇu-)sahasra (-nāma) is superior; and among them the hundred and eight names (told) below are chief. Just one name of Viṣṇu is said to be superior to all Vedas; so also are the thousand names equal to Rāma's names. O dear one, that fruit which one who recites the hymns of all Vedas, gets is obtained crorefold by Rāma's name only. O you of an auspicious appearance, listen to the principal names of Rāma. O dear one, I shall tell you those which are sung by the sages:

30-47. Om, Śrīrāma; Rāmacandra; the eternal Rāmabhadra; the lotus-eyed one; the glorious lord of kings; the best among the Raghus; the lord of Jānakī; the conqueror; the victorious one; Janārdana; the one dear to Viśvāmitra; the controlled one; the one who is exclusively devoted to the protection of those who have sought his shelter; the destroyer of Vālin; the eloquent one; the truth-speaking one; the one of genuine valour; the one true to his word; the one getting the fruit of his vow; always the resort of Hanūmat; the son of Kauśalyā; the destroyer of Khara; skilled in killing Virādha; the protector of Bibhīṣaṇa; the one who cut off the head of Rāvaṇa; the breaker of seven tālas; the one who broke Śiva's bow; the one who broke down the great pride of (Paraśurāma) the son of Jamadagni; the one who killed Tāḍakā; the one who mastered Vedānta; the soul of the Vedas; the only medicine for the bondage to the mundane existence; the enemy of Dūṣaṇa and Triśiras; the one having three forms; having three qualities and (of the form of the) triad (i.e. the three Vedas); the one having three strides; the soul of the three worlds; the one whose acts are said to be meritorious; the protector of the three worlds; the archer; the one who lived in Daṇḍaka forest; the one who sanctified Ahalyā; the one devoted to his parents; the one who grants boons; the one who has controlled his senses and anger, his greed; and who is the preceptor of the world; the one who associated himself with bears and monkeys; the one who resorted to Citrakūṭa; the one who gave the boon of protection of Jayanta; and the one who was served by Sumitrā's son; the one who is the superior lord of all gods; the one who brought the dead monkeys back to life; the killer of the deceitful Mārīca; the one who is illustrious; and who has large arms; the one who is praised by all gods; who is gentle; who is friendly; who is the best sage; who is a great meditating saint; who is very generous; the one who gave a stable kingdom to Sugrīva; the one who is said to give greater fruit than (one due to) all religious merit; who destroys all sins; the one who is the first god; and also the greatest god; the one who is the dawn of good fortune; who has great strength; who is the ancient and best Puruṣa (the Supreme Being); the one who has a smiling face; who speaks measured words; who speaks first; (who is called) Rāghava; the one who is grave with infinite virtues; who is wise and uncommon due to the quality of control; who does human acts due to his Māyā (illusory power); the one who is honoured by Mahādeva (i.e. Śiva); the one who constructed the bridge; the one who vanquished the Ocean; who is full of all holy places; who is Viṣṇu; whose body is dark, handsome, brave; who wears yellow garments; who is an archer; who is the lord of all sacrifices; who (himself) is the sacrifice; who is free from old age and death; the one who installed Śiva's Phallus; who is free from primitive qualities; the one who is the highest lord; who is the highest Brahman; who has the body of consciousness and joy; who is the highest light; the one who is the highest abode; the highest sky; and the higher than the high; who is the highest lord; who has gone to the other side; who is the opposite bank; who is of the nature of all souls; is auspicious. These are the hundred and eight names of Śri Rāmacandra.

48-51. O goddess, I have told you this secret of secrets through love for you. He who would recite or listen to these (names) with a devoted heart, is freed from all sins (committed) even during crores of kalpas. Watery places turn into dry grounds, and foes become friends. Kings become servants, and fires become mild. Spirits become favourable, and unstable wealth becomes stable for the man who recites them devoutly; so also planets become favourable; calamities are removed, of the man who recites (them) devoutly, O daughter of the (Himālaya) Mountain.

52-57. He who would recite it with great devotion, has the three worlds under his control. By narrating (them) he obtains whatever object he desires. With five ancestors and five successors, he always delights in Vaikuṇṭha for thousands of crores of kalpas, and hundreds of crores of kalpas. Those men who praise Rāma who is dark like dūrvā-blades, who is lotus-eyed, who has put on yellow garments, with divine names, are not worldly spirits. Salutation to Rāma, Rāmabhadra, Rāmacandra, the Creator, to Raghunātha, to the lord, and the husband of Sītā. O goddess, a man, repeating this hymn day and night, is free from all sins, and would obtain absorption into Viṣṇu. O you having beautiful brows, through love for you I have thus told you Rāma's greatness contained in the Vedas and called auspicious.

Vasiṣṭha said:

58-59a. Having heard that greatness of the highest lord told by Śaṅkara, she, with her eyes full of tears of joy, obtained incomparable delight. Having saluted her husband, the bull-bannered, lord of gods.

Pārvatī said:

59b-60. Oh, matchless is the greatness of Rāma, the highest soul. Even (after hearing it) for hundreds of kalpas my ears would not be satisfied. I am fortunate: I am blessed. O sinless one, you have told me everything. May I have, through your grace, devotion for Rāma in every existence.

Vasiṣṭha said:

61-69. Speaking like this, Pārvatī, the best devotee of Viṣṇu, lived happily in all conditions with her husband on the Kailāsa mountain, repeating the formula: 'Salutation to Rāma, Rāmabhadra, Rāmacandra, the Creator, to Raghunātha, the lord, the husband of Sītā.' O king, I have told you all this topmost secret. O king the religious treatises proclaimed by Rudra are vicious (*tāmasa*). The bull-bannered (god) narrated them for deluding people. Lord Śiva told this one in private to the goddess. The lord, highly devoted to her, told the goddess this significant gist of the hymn, with a hidden meaning, through love for her, O king. He who would listen to or recite with a mind full of devotion, this wonderful dialogue between Umā and the great Lord, would be an omniscient and great devotee of Viṣṇu. Being free from all practices, he obtains the highest position. O very mighty lord of kings, in your dynasty Viṣṇu, the propitious highest lord will be born as Daśaratha's son for the good of all people. Therefore, the Ikṣvākus, among whom lord Rāma, of lotus-like eyes, is born, are honoured even by gods, O king.

CHAPTER TWO HUNDRED FIFTYFIVE

The Three Gods Subjected to Test by Bhṛgu

Dilīpa said:

1-6. O brāhmaṇa, you have fully told (me) about all the practices, and about the general and particular nature of the highest (lord) and the individual soul. O best brāhmaṇa, through curiosity I am asking you one other (question). Due to your great love (for me) properly tell (i.e. answer) that also. Rudra, the destroyer of Tripura, is the best among the great devotees of Viṣṇu. Due to what did he, along with his wife, have a condemned form? How did the very illustrious one have the form of clitoris? O best brāhmaṇa, how did the five-faced one, four-armed one, trident-holder and three-eyed one have a condemned form? O son of Mitra-Varuṇa, tell all this (to me).

Vasiṣṭha said:

7-13. O king, listen; I shall explain to you what you have asked me respectfully. In the pure hearts of men a thought for bliss is produced. Formerly on the best mountain Mandara Svāyambhuva Manu performed, along with sages, an excellent prolonged sacrificial session. There came all sages who had fulfilled their vows, who were proficient in various holy texts, whose lustre was like that of the young sun and fire, who, the brāhmaṇas, were well-versed in all Vedas, and who had mastered all religious practices. When the great sacrificial session took place, the sages whose sins had been exhausted, and who had penance as their wealth, spoke among themselves in order to find the truth about the deity. Which excellent deity should be honoured by brāhmaṇas proficient in the Vedas? Who, out of Brahmā, Viṣṇu and Śiva, being praised, gives salvation to men? Water of (i.e. flowing from) whose feet should be resorted to? So also the purifying remnant of whose food should be enjoyed? Who, the immutable one, is the highest abode, the highest soul and who is eternal? Whose favour and holy place would gratify the manes?

14-20. Such a great discussion took place among those who were seated. Some great sages said: "Rudra alone (is the greatest deity)." Other best sages said: "Brahmā alone is fit to be worshipped." Other best one said that the Sun alone was fit to be worshipped among the souls. Other brāhmaṇas said: "The immutable lotus-eyed Vāsudeva, the highest one, the one without a beginning or an end (viz.) Viṣṇu alone is the highest lord. He, the best among the deities, deserves to be worshipped." To them, who were discussing, Svāyambhuva Manu said: "He, the lord, who is full of good nature, who has auspicious qualities, who is lotus-eyed, who is glorious, who is the lord of Lakṣmī, who is the highest Brahman, is the only lord adored by brāhmaṇas, proficient in Vedas. Others mixed with passion and vice are not fit to be worshipped." Having heard these words of him, all the great sages, joining the palms of their hands, said to the brāhmaṇa, Bhṛgu, the treasure of penance:

The sages said:

21-25. O you of a good vow, you are able to remove our doubt. Approach, O you of a good vow, Brahmā, Viṣṇu and Maheśa. O sage, go near them and observe their bodies. Out of them, he who possesses the pure sattvaguṇa, is alone fit to be worshipped, and never anyone else. He, full of pure sattva, will be friendly to brāhmaṇas. To brāhmaṇas he will be a holy place and a favour. Even to deities and manes the remnants of his food will be purifying. Therefore, O best sage, go to the residence of gods. O lord, O best sage, quickly bring about the welfare of all people.

26-27. Thus addressed, the best sage, along with Vāmadeva, quickly went to Kailāsa where the bull-bannered (god) lived. Having gone near the door of the house of the magnanimous Śaṅkara and seeing very fierce Nandin with a spear in his hand, he said (to him):

28-34. "I, the brāhmaṇa Bhṛgu, have come to see Hara, the

best god. Quickly announce me (i.e. my arrival) to the magnanimous Śaṅkara." Hearing the words of him, Nandin, the lord of (Śiva's) attendants spoke harsh words to the great sage of an unlimited splendour: "The lord is not in the vicinity. Śaṅkara is sporting with goddess (Pārvatī). O best sage, go back if you desire to live." Thus repudiated by him the (sage) of a great penance remained there, at the door of the great lord, for many days. "Since he, arrogant due to the company of a woman, thinks lightly of me, he shall have the form of clitoris. Approached (i.e. overcome) by vice he slights me, a brāhmaṇa! Reduced to an impious state, he will not be adored by brāhmaṇas. Therefore, all the food, water, flowers and oblations offered to him will undoubtedly be useless."

35-40. The very lustrous one, having thus cursed Śaṁkara honoured by the world, said to the very fierce attendant, Nandin, holding a spear, O king: "May Śiva's devotees, having ash, phallus and bones be impious and out of the Vedic fold." The sage, having thus cursed Rudra, Tripura's killer, went to Brahmā's world, respected by all people. The very intelligent one, having seen Brahmā, saluted him by joining the palms of his hands. The great ascetic, having saluted him, remained silent before him. Seeing the best sage, Brahmā, possessed of an abundance of rajas did not honour him, the great sage that had approached him. He also did not rise to honour him, nor did he speak pleasing words.

41-45. The lotus-seated (Brahmā) remained there with great majesty. Seeing him with preponderance of rajas, the great sage, the grandsire of all worlds, who was very lustrous, said (these) words to Brahman: "Since you, having preponderance of rajas, are slighting me, therefore, be dishonoured by all people." Bhṛgu, the brāhmaṇa, having thus cursed the magnanimous Brahmā, respected by the world, suddenly went to Viṣṇu's residence. The brāhmaṇa, having entered Viṣṇu's world on the northern coast of the Milky Ocean, and being properly honoured there by the glorious ones remaining there, and not being stopped there, entered the inner apartment.

46-52. Having entered that spotless palace, resembling the sun, he saw Lakṣmī's lord lying on the bed of the serpent. Both his feet were being rubbed by the lotus-like hands of Lakṣmī.

Seeing him, the best sage Bhṛgu, full of anger kicked with his left foot Viṣṇu's chest. The lord, getting up quickly, and gladly saying, "I am fortunate", joyfully pressed his foot with his hands. Slowly stroking his feet he spoke (these) sweet words: "O brāhmaṇa-sage, I am fortunate. I am always blessed. Due to the contact of your foot, there will be propitiousness in my body. May the dust-particles from the foot of a brāhmaṇa, which are the cause of the acquisition of affluence, which are the comets to the host of calamities that have come up, which are bridges over the boundless ocean of the mundane existence, purify me. All the holy places like Gaṅgā etc. undoubtedly remain in the body of him, on whose body dust-particles from a brāhmaṇa's foot always remain."

53-54. Saying so and quickly getting up with goddess (Lakṣmī), Viṣṇu devoutly honoured him with divine garlands, sandal etc. Having seen him, the best sage, with his eyes full of tears of joy, got from the best seat, and saluted that treasure of compassion. The great ascetic, having joined the palms of his hands, gladly said:

Śrī Bhṛgu said:

55-64. Oh, what a (handsome) form! Oh, (great) tranquillity! Oh, (great) knowledge! Oh, (great) pity! Oh, his patience is spotless! Oh, the goodness of Viṣṇu! Similarly the ocean of virtues has natural, auspicious, goodness. It is not at all present in all other gods. You alone are hospitable to the brāhmaṇas. You alone are the protector. You alone are the highest Brahman. You alone are the lord of brāhmaṇas. No other god is respectable. O Puruṣottama, those who worship any other god than you, have become impious, and are censured by all the world. You, Janārdana, are alone fit to be worshipped by brāhmaṇas, well-versed in the Vedas. None else among the gods is ever venerable. Brahmā, Rudra and others, mixed with rajas and tamas are not fit to be worshipped. You, having pure sattva, are fit to be worshipped by brāhmaṇas. The water (flowing) from your feet should be resorted to by manes, gods, and all brāhmaṇas. It gives salvation, and destroys sins. Manes, gods, brāhmaṇas should take what is left over after you have eaten, and not what is left over after others have eaten. The food, flowers, so also water of (i.e. offered to) other gods, would all be unfit to be touched. It is useless like liquor. Therefore, a wise brāhmaṇa should constantly worship you, the eternal one, everyday and should take water of (i.e. sanctified by) you and food eaten by you.

65-68. A brāhmaṇa should not see another god; should not worship him. He should not partake of another god's favour; should not enter the sanctuary of any other (god). (If) a man does not give in this world the food and holy water enjoyed by you in the rite of śrāddha offered to his ancestors, all that would be fruitless. His dead ancestors fall into (and live in) the hell of pus and blood for thousands of crores of kalpas and hundreds of crores of kalpas. O master, when one offers an oblation (into fire) or gives (offerings) to deities and manes after offering them to you, there is satisfaction (of deities and manes), (i.e. he satisfies them) and he gets immortality.

69-78a. Therefore, you alone are adorable to gods, and none else. He who, through folly, would worship other (deities) will be impious. You are Nārāyaṇa; you are glorious; you are the ancient Vāsudeva. You are omnipresent Viṣṇu. You are eternal, highest soul and the great god. You alone are fit to be worshipped by brāhmaṇas. You are hospitable to brāhmaṇas. You possess pure sattva. Due to your being venerable to brāhmaṇas and due to your virtue of having pure sattva, obtain the status of a brāhmaṇa among all the gods themselves; for all brāhmaṇas will resort to you, the highest Brahman, alone. They were brāhmaṇas and not others. There is no doubt about this. Devakī's son is holy. Madhusūdana is holy. The lotus-eyed one is holy. Viṣṇu, Acyuta is holy. Lord Kṛṣṇa is holy. Vāsudeva, Acyuta, Hari (is holy). Narasiṁha is holy. So also is the immutable Nārāyaṇa. Śrīdhara, Śrīśa, Govinda, Vāmana is holy. The Yajñavarāha, Keśava, Puruṣottama is holy. Glorious, lotus-eyed Rāma, descendant of Raghu, is holy. Padmanābha is holy. So also Dāmodara, the lord, Mādhava, Yajña, lord Trivikrama is holy. Hṛṣīkeśa is holy; Janārdana, wearing yellow garments (is holy).

78b-87. Salutation to the holy god, to Vāsudeva, holder of the Śārṅga (bow); (Salutation) to Nārāyaṇa, Śrīśa, having lotus-like eyes. Salutation to the holy god, Vāsudeva, Viṣṇu. Salutation to the highest god full of auspicious qualities. Salutation to the holy god, of the form of all gods. Salutation to you having the body of the Boar. Salutation to you, the lord of the triad (of the Vedas). Salutation to the holy god, lying on the bed of the serpent. Repeated salutations to Rāghava having eyes like lotus-petals. O lord, all gods and sages, deluded by Māyā, do not know you, the lord of all worlds and a great soul. O revered one, even all those proficient in the Vedas do not know you by your name, form and qualities and your acts difficult to be performed. I, capable of knowing your sattva, suggesting your superiority, have been sent by the great sages; (and therefore) I have approached you. O Keśava, in order to know your character and qualities, I put my foot on your chest. O Govinda, O treasure of pity, forgive it.

Speaking like this, and repeatedly saluting Viṣṇu, and being honoured there by the divine, magnanimous, great sages, Bhṛgu, with his mind delighted, again went to the place of sacrifice having an auspicious name.

88-93. The great sages, having seen the magnanimous one to have come back, rose, saluted him, and duly worshipped him. The best sage told them all that: "O best sages, Brahmā and Śiva, the best sages have preponderance of the qualities of rajas and tamas. They were cursed by me. They are not fit to be worshipped by brāhmaṇas. Śaṁkara enveloped by tamas was cursed by me on the peak of Kailāsa. Viṣṇu full of pure sattva is the ocean of auspicious qualities. Nārāyaṇa is the highest Brahman. (He i.e.) Viṣṇu is the deity of brāhmaṇas. Śrīpati, Viṣṇu, Vāsudeva, Janārdana is holy. Govinda, Hari, Acyuta of lotus-like eyes is holy. O best men, he alone is fit to be worshipped by brāhmaṇas, and none else.

94-97. He who, through folly, would worship another (god) will be impious. Even sinners get salvation just by remembering Kṛṣṇa. The water (flowing) from his feet should be taken. The remnants of the food (offered to) him are purifying. It gives heaven and salvation to men, especially to brāhmaṇas. (A man) should everyday offer an oblation which is (first) offered to Viṣṇu, to the gods. He should also offer it to his dead ancestors. (Then) he gets complete immortality. O brāhmaṇas, the dead ancestors of him who does not offer (food) enjoyed by Viṣṇu, to them at a śrāddha-rite, always eat (and drink) feces and urine.

98-101. Therefore, brāhmaṇas should always eat the remnants of the food offered to Viṣṇu. The remnants (of food offered to other gods) are useless and (therefore) condemned. A brāhmaṇa, weak in knowledge, who even once eats the remnants of food etc. offered to Śaṅkara etc., would certainly be a cāṇḍāla. For thousands of crores of kalpas he is roasted in the fire in hell. O best brāhmaṇas, the remnants of offerings to gods like Rudra, are said to be equal to food offered to demons, yakṣas, goblins and like liquor and flesh. Brāhmaṇas should not eat that food, the offering enjoyed by (these) gods.

102. Therefore, O best brāhmaṇas, leaving another god, worship diligently, till you live, the ancient Viṣṇu only.

103-109. With your doubts removed, endowed with the five purifications like imprinting the body with heated marks, with good hearts, looking upon that as the highest abode of Viṣṇu, properly worship that extraordinary Viṣṇu, O best brāhmaṇas. The brāhmaṇas marked with the disc(-impression) are good and extraordinary. Those without the disc-marks are said to be ordinary and vicious. Therefore, a man should have the heated marks of a disc and a conch at the roots of his arms, which (marks) of (i.e. sacred to) Viṣṇu burn the stream of sins due to contact with ordinary persons. Having had the upright sectarian marks on the body according to the manner prescribed in the holy texts, he should worship Viṣṇu according to the rules with the gem of the hymn (viz. Viṣṇu-sahasranāma). Being diligent he should also partake of the remnants of food offered to him. He should always worship gods at the time of finishing his worship. O brāhmaṇas, knowing him to be the highest lord enjoying all sacrifices, one should always offer (oblations into fire), give (presents to him) and mutter (his names)."

Vasiṣṭha said:

110. All the sages, thus addressed, and with their sins exhausted, saluted Bhṛgu and with the palms of their hands duly joined, said:

The sages said:

111-112. O revered best brāhmaṇa, you alone remove our

doubts. You are the refuge of the people. O brāhmaṇa, you are the highest asylum. You alone are the best piety. You alone are the highest penance. We shall exist due to your favour, and not otherwise, O brāhmaṇa.

Vasiṣṭha said:

113-117. All the great sages, having thus praised that brāhmaṇa Bhṛgu, and having got the hymn from him, worshipped Viṣṇu. O best king, I have told all this to you as the occasion has arisen. O best king, due to the touch of the lotus-like hand of Rāma the entire form condemned by the world will be spotless. Rāghava, the highest Brahman, is the purifier among all gods. Touched and seen by him all these, Śaṁkara and others, become spotless. Viṣṇu, the ocean of the virtue of affection, is the father, the mother of all gods. He is also the protector of all people. If you desire the highest position, then seek his shelter only.

118. O king, I have told you the entire Purāṇa, acceptable to the Vedas, and narrated by Brahmā in the age of Svāyambhuva Manu.

119-125. This account, (causing) liberation, of Viṣṇu should be told to the one modest due to devotion for Viṣṇu and having pure sattva, and not otherwise (i.e. to none else). The reader (or reciter) of this should have the marks of a conch, a disc, an upright sectarian mark etc. It should always be heard from his mouth. (Then only) you will have a son. Not otherwise. In him who, being well-composed, would recite to others or read (for himself) this (Purāṇa), is always produced undivided devotion for Viṣṇu. A student obtains knowledge; one seeking religious merit obtains it. One seeking salvation obtains it. One desiring enjoyment gets happiness. A man, full of devotion, should read it on the twelfth day, when the Sun is in the Śravaṇā (constellation), on a Saṁkrānti day, or at an eclipse, or on the full-moon day or the new-moon day. He who, being composed, reads half a verse or a quarter of it, undoubtedly obtains the fruit of a thousand horse-sacrifices. I have thus narrated to you this Purāṇa-text. Worship Viṣṇu if you desire the highest position.

Sūta said:

126-127. The best king (Dilīpa), thus addressed by his preceptor Vasiṣṭha, saluted and duly honoured him. Having properly received the hymn from the best brāhmaṇa, and having, till the end of his life, diligently worshipped Viṣṇu, he reached, in (due) time, the ancient position of Viṣṇu, fit to be reached by meditating saints.

VII KRIYĀYOGASĀRAKHAṆḌA

(Section on Essence of Yoga by Works)

CHAPTER ONE

A Dialogue between Jaimini and Vyāsa

Salutation to Śrī Gaṇeśa. Now is commenced the Kriyāyogasārakhaṇḍa.

1. We devoutly, constantly salute the pair of the lotus-like feet of Lakṣmī's lord, which is crowned with the bees of the heads that are bowing down, of the line of the gods like Brahmā, which very much nourishes the mass of the exquisite beauty of the lakes of the minds of the meditating saints, which has the mass of the drops of the honey of the water of Gaṅgā, and which removes the afflictions of the mundane existence.

2. Salutation to that god Viṣṇu who, the lord, taking up various forms protects the entire world, those who are highly devoted to worshipping whose feet never plunge into the universal ocean, of whom, the residence is continuously in the lotus-like hearts of all living beings, and who takes up the form of a hog.

3. I salute this (Viṣṇu) along with Lakṣmī, who, the god, spoke in the form of Vyāsa in (i.e. through) the Purāṇa the practices after having taken them out from the Vedas for the good of the world.

4-6. Once all sages, desiring the good of the world, had an interesting chat in the very charming Naimiṣāraṇya. In the meanwhile, Sūta, the very lustrous and glorious disciple of Vyāsa, came there recollecting Viṣṇu. All ascetics like Śaunaka, seeing Sūta, master of the meaning of holy texts, coming there, rose and saluted him.

7-9. He, the best among those who know religious practices, also suddenly and devoutly saluted, (after prostrating himself) like a staff on the ground, the sages, the great devotees of Viṣṇu. Surrounded by all the groups of his disciples, the very intelligent one sat among the sages on an excellent seat offered by the best sages. Śaunaka, the best sage, full of modesty and joining the palms of his hands, said these words to him, seated there:

Śaunaka said:

10-12. O Sūta, O revered one, O omniscient great sage, by what means would men have great devotion for Viṣṇu when the Kali age has arrived? In the Kali (age) all men will be engaged in doing sins; will be devoid of Vedic learning. How would they achieve their (spiritual) good? In the Kali (age) man's life is dependent on food. Similarly people are short-lived. So also they will be poor and troubled by various miseries.

13-16. O brāhmaṇa, whatever good act is told in the holy texts is accomplished with effort. Therefore, men will not at all do acts in the Kali (age). The wicked-hearted ones will, along with members of their families, meet with destruction when good acts have vanished (and) sinful acts have commenced. O best one, O son of Sūta, tell how great religious merit would be possible with very small exertion, little wealth and within a short time. It is decided in the holy texts that he, due to whose advice, men perform (acts of) sin or (of) virtue, would partake of (the fruits of) them.

17-20. The four—givers of good advice, the kind ones, those free from deceitfulness and those opposing the sinful way—are comparable to Viṣṇu. Viṣṇu of the form of knowledge does not look pleasingly at him who, having obtained knowledge in the mundane existence, does not give it to others. That man, delighting others by means of gems of knowledge and (other) gems, should be known as very intelligent and as Viṣṇu having a human form. O best sage, you have mastered the Vedas and the Vedāṅgas. There is no other teacher than you, since you are taught by Vyāsa.

Sūta said:

21-24a. O best sage, you are fortunate. You alone are the chief of Viṣṇu's devotees, since you always desire the good of the people. O Śaunaka, listen. For the good of all the people, especially for that of Viṣṇu's devotees, I shall tell you what you desired to hear. Listen to all that (Vyāsa) said when asked by

Jaimini. The great sage Jaimini, always engaged in the practice of abstract meditation, bowing his head, saluted Vyāsa.

Jaimini said:

24b-25a. O revered one, O you who know all religious practices, O son of Satyavatī, tell me from the beginning by what means salvation would be (obtained) in Kali (age).

Sūta said:

25b. O best sage, hearing the words of Jaimini, Vyāsa, with his mind pleased, commenced the propitious tale:

Vyāsa said:

26a-33a. O Jaimini, O best sage, O very intelligent one, you are fortunate, since you always desire to listen to the story of Viṣṇu. Whosoever has a mind to listen to a good story, would have knowledge; and they look upon knowledge as giving salvation. The creator has in vain made the earth to have a burden by creating him, the sinner, who does not like the story of Viṣṇu. The devotees of Viṣṇu are proud of narrating Viṣṇu's tale on the earth. O best sage, that day on which the story of Viṣṇu is not heard, is a bad day, and not that day which is covered with clouds. The lord never abandons being present there on whichever portion of the earth the story of Viṣṇu exists (i.e. is narrated). Having cursed the man who brings in an obstacle when the story of Viṣṇu is commenced, the lord, along with deities goes (away).

33b-38. Those men who are delighted on hearing the glory of Viṣṇu, should be known as portions of gods. They, the best ones, should be looked upon as fit to be honoured. Those men who on hearing the story of Viṣṇu, laugh at (it), should be known as portions of demons. They partake of (i.e. live in) hell. O best brāhmaṇa, at that place where Viṣṇu's story which removes the sinful ailments of the people that listen to it, is (told) everyday, all the holy places like Gaṅgā, the divine sages, deities, sages having penance as their wealth, stay. O sage, listen to this Essence of the Yoga by Works which is very significant and which destroys sins, along with the story of Viṣṇu and Itihāsa.

CHAPTER TWO

Characteristic Marks of a Vaiṣṇava

Vyāsa said:

1-7. At the beginning of the creation great Viṣṇu (Mahāviṣṇu), desiring to create the entire world, turned himself into three forms—creator, protector and destroyer. The Supreme Being produced from the right side of his body, himself, called Brahmā, for creating this world. O sage, then the lord of the world produced from the left portion (of his body), his portion viz. Viṣṇu, for the protection of the world. The lord who had taken his abode in a lotus, produced from the middle part of his body the imperishable Rudra for the destruction of the world. Some describe the god having the three qualities rajas, sattva and tamas as Brahmā, some as Viṣṇu and some as Śaṅkara. Viṣṇu (who is) one (only), dividing himself into three, creates, devours and protects (the world). Therefore, the best people should not differentiate among the three in the worlds. The original Prakṛti (Nature) of the great Viṣṇu, the highest soul, which is the cause of the universe of beings is described as (consisting of) Vidyā (knowledge) and Avidyā (ignorance).

8-9. She (Prakṛti), of the form of existence and non-existence, is eternal, and is the cause of the world. She suddenly had three forms, Brāhmī, Lakṣmī, Ambikā. O sage, then having appointed (this) original (Nature) to create, maintain and destroy (the world), the first Highest Being vanished there only.

10-17. By his order Brahmā then, with concentration, produced the five gross elements—earth, ether, air, water and fire. The lotus-seated one also produced (the seven worlds) like Bhūr, Bhuvar, Svar, Mahas, Jana, Tapas and Satya (above the earth). O brāhmaṇa, then Brahmā created the (nether) worlds in this order: Atala, then Vitala below it, Sutala below it, Talātala still below, Mahātala below it, then Rasātala below it, and Pātāla below it. At the centre of the earth he produced the great mountain (viz. Meru) with jewelled peaks and bright like gold for the residence of the deities. He produced Mandara, the western mountain, Trikūṭa, Udaya and also various other mountains. Then he produced the Lokāloka mountain; and the highest lord,

Brahmā, produced the seven oceans and the seven islands in between, O best brāhmaṇa. O best brāhmaṇa, (there is) Jambūdvīpa, (then there is) the dvīpa called Plakṣa. It is double (the size of) it (i.e. Jambūdvīpa). (The dvīpa) Śālmalī is double (the size of) it (i.e. Plakṣa).

18-20. These dvīpas (islands) like Plakṣa etc. have all divisions, have all qualities and are forms of deities and divine sages. O brāhmaṇa, these seven islands are surrounded by seven oceans: I shall narrate the names of the oceans. Listen: Lavaṇa, Ikṣu, Surā, Sarpi, Dadhi, Dugdha and Jala. O divine sage, these oceans are to the east and west.

21-22. The mountains like Lokāloka should be known to be double (in size). O best brāhmaṇa, then Brahmā produced in every island trees, bushes, creepers etc., so also the lower animals, and gods, human beings, nāgas, and vidyādharas also.

23-28. Then in due order he created his sons, the sages like Dakṣa, so also brāhmaṇas, kṣatriyas, vaiśyas and śūdras. The lord also produced their livelihood etc. They call that Bhārata giving auspicious and inauspicious fruits, which lies to the south of the Hema mountain and to the north of the Vindhya mountain. All the best men who obtain a birth in Bhārata country, and do religious practices are like Viṣṇu. O best one, people enjoy (or suffer) the fruit in the land of an auspicious or an inauspicious act performed in the land of actions. There is none else like him in thc three worlds, who, having come to the land of actions, is engaged in pious acts. His birth is fruitful and he has well lived his life.

29-30. He who has no inclination to the service of Viṣṇu (has lived in vain). Firm devotion to Viṣṇu, the god of gods, the only lord of the mundane existence, is produced in men by means of religious merit earned during crores of existences. He is the giver of all happiness; he is praiseworthy and fearless.

31-33. That country where a devotee of Viṣṇu does not stay should be abandoned. A small or great sin committed during previous existence, perishes that moment only when the devotee of Viṣṇu is seen. What is the use of a bath in Gaṅgā to him who would devoutly have the water (flowing) from the feet of a devotee of Viṣṇu, that removes all sins, on his head?

34-40a. He who associates himself with Viṣṇu's devotees

even for a short time is freed from all sins among which a brāhmaṇa's murder is prominent. O best brāhmaṇa, all those religious acts that are performed before a devotee of Viṣṇu are protective. That place where Viṣṇu's devotees stay for a while is, to speak the truth, a holy place, a penance-grove. O brāhmaṇa, that gift like food, water, fruit, whichever is given to Viṣṇu's devotee would be inexhaustible. The devotee of Viṣṇu is said to be of the form of all deities. If a man has pleased him, then all deities are pleased in this very fierce worldly existence, full of various afflictions. A man who is a devotee of Viṣṇu never sinks. Therefore, O best brāhmaṇa, you too, having always devoutly propitiated Viṣṇu by the Yoga in the form of deeds, go to the highest position of Viṣṇu.

Sūta said:

40b-41a. Having heard these words of the magnanimous Vyāsa, Jaimini, putting the palms of his hands on his head, said:

Jaimini said:

41b-43a. O preceptor, you have repeatedly told the greatness of Viṣṇu's devotees. Now tell me everything—what are their characteristics, and, O best sage, how should Viṣṇu's devotees be recognised? Tell me all that from the beginning, if you favour me.

Vyāsa said:

43b-45. Listen to what the lord who was asked by the creator himself, had said when Madhu and Kaiṭabha were killed. I know it. Having, in the form of Rudra, destroyed the entire world at the end of a kalpa, the lord all alone slept by his magical power born of Yoga (Yogamāyā). When the lord had, under the influence of Yoganidrā,[1] slept, the entire earth, was plunged in the mass of water.

46-49. Then Brahmā, the creator of the world, with his mind devoted to him (i.e. Viṣṇu), meditated upon that first god and remained on his lotus-like navel. O brāhmaṇa, at that very fierce time two fierce, very great demons, named Madhu and

1. Sleep personified as a goddess and said to be a form of Durgā.

Kaiṭabha were produced from the excretion of wax from Viṣṇu's ear. The two very fierce demons moving in the air, saw Brahmā on the lotus-like navel of Śrī Viṣṇu. O brāhmaṇa, the two very mighty and brave demons, with their eyes red with anger exerted to kill him.

50-51. Then Brahmā, the creator of the world, conceiving their murder, praised the revered Yoganidrā with soft words. Having heard the praise of (i.e. uttered by) Brahmā, the highest god, she spoke (these) words with affection: "Tell me what you desire."

Brahmā said:

52. These two very fierce demons have determined to kill me. Quickly delude them with trickery. Leave Viṣṇu, the protector.

53-56. Then that sleep of the lord abandoned that great Viṣṇu. Then he, affectionate to those who sought his shelter, and full of pity, fought a close fight with the two demons in the air. After having fought a very fierce fight for five thousand years, nobody became victorious or nobody was defeated. Then the two demons, who were then deluded by that great Māyā, said to Viṣṇu: "Choose a born from us." O brāhmaṇa, then Viṣṇu laughed and spoke these words:

57-60. "O demons, if you are pleased, then quickly get yourselves killed by me." Then the two fierce demons, having great wisdom, and deluded by that great Māyā said: "There is no doubt that just this boon is granted to you. O Viṣṇu, kill us at a place where there is neither water nor land." Then, O brāhmaṇa, bringing the two great demons up to his hip, he suddenly killed them with the wonderful edge of his disc. Seeing that (Viṣṇu) the Disc-holder had killed the demons Madhu and Kaiṭabha, Brahmā, with his fear gone, praised the lord of the god of gods.

Brahmā said:

61-64. Salutation to the highest god who destroys all the pains of him who submitted himself to him. Salutation to him of the nature of the three guṇas, to Nārāyaṇa of unlimited valour. Men who have resorted to your lotus-like feet, never meet with a calamity. O you of infinite fame, I have known this. You have instantly removed this great calamity of me. You are the lord of supernatural means. You are kind. O lord of the three worlds, O god of gods, O protector of those who seek your shelter, O god, though you protected me from being destroyed by the cruel host of demons, and killed these two demons, and though these two (demons) Madhu and Kaiṭabha are very ruthless, yet mentally I look upon them as our own kinsmen, since they pleased you, the god giving all auspicious (objects), by giving you the boon of the destruction of their own life.

65-69. O lord of gods, to that man, at whom you look with pity, the three worlds are charming; all his enemies along with (the members of) their families perish; his friends and all his kinsmen prosper. O bee to the lotus of the face of Lakṣmī, O god of gods, O you who destroy the fear and grief of the people in the worldly existence, always protect, with compassion, me who am resorting to the pair of your lotus-like feet. I salute you. O you lotus-eyed one, be pleased. O lord of Lakṣmī, be pleased. O lord of all beings, be pleased. O all-sustaining one, I salute you. Salutation to you who are pleased with your devotees. Salutation to you who give (i.e. produce) devotion. Salutation to you, of the form of knowledge. O faultless one, be my refuge. Salutation to you, salutation to you, salutation to you. (Repeated) salutations to you. O you full of the world, protect, protect (me).

Vyāsa said:

70. That revered god, praised with these and other hymns by Brahmā, creator of the worlds, was very much pleased.

The lord said:

71. O Lotus-seated (Brahmā), I am pleased with this hymn and devotion of you. Tell me what you desire. I shall give it to you on the earth.

Brahmā said:

72. O lord of gods, O ocean of compassion, O you full of the world, if you are pleased, then let there be no calamities to (i.e. befalling) your devotees. This is the boon of me (i.e. I ask for).

The lord said:

73-74. O best god, let it be so. I have granted this boon to you. On the earth let my devotee never face a calamity. I always live in the hearts of the devotees of Viṣṇu (i.e. me). Therefore, the devotees of Viṣṇu will never have calamities.

Brahmā said:

75-79. O lord of the world, you have undoubtedly given (me) everything, since you have knocked down these demons in a battle. O lord, you will protect him who, finding sometime, praises you with this hymn with great devotion. Oh, it is a great wonder that you who cannot be conceived by means of meditation by gods, roam in the bodies of the devotees of Viṣṇu (i.e. you). O master, what would happen when you are pleased even for a moment? (Then) it is a great wonder that such as you are, you move in the company of the devotees of Viṣṇu. O enemy of Kaiṭabha, who are the devotees of Viṣṇu? Or what are their characteristic marks? How are all of them to be recognised? O Keśava, tell that to me.

The lord said:

80-82. O best one, it is not possible for me properly to narrate the characteristic marks of Viṣṇu's devotee even for hundreds of crores of kalpas. Listen to them in brief. The mundane existence is dependent on Viṣṇu's devotees. Gods are looked after by Viṣṇu's devotees. I am also dependent on them. Therefore, Viṣṇu's devotees are the greatest. O Brahman, leaving Viṣṇu's devotee I do not stay elsewhere even for a moment. Viṣṇu's devotees are my kinsmen.

83-103. Those who are without lust and anger, who are free from harmfulness and hypocrisy, who are free from greed and folly, should be known to be Viṣṇu's devotees. Those who are not jealous, who are kind, who desire the good of all beings, who speak the truth, should be known to be Viṣṇu's devotees. Those who advise pious acts, who practise pious acts, who serve their preceptors (and elders), should be known to be Viṣṇu's devotees. Those who look upon you, me and Śaṅkara as equal, and who honour a guest, should be known to be Viṣṇu's devotees. Those who have expounded the Vedic learning, who are always devoted to brāhmaṇas, who are impotent to other women (i.e. women who are not their wives), should be known to be Viṣṇu's devotees. Those who devoutly observe the Ekādaśī-vow, who sing my names, should be known to be Viṣṇu's devotees. Those who put up temples of deities, who wear tulasī-garlands, who wear lotuses and akṣa-seeds, should be known to be Viṣṇu's devotees. O Brahman, those whose bodies are marked with (the signs of) my weapons like the conch, the disc, the mace, the lotus, should be known to be Viṣṇu's devotees. O Lotus-seated (Brahman), those around whose necks are (worn) the garlands of dhātrī-fruits, and who worship me with the leaves of dhātrī, should be known as Viṣṇu's devotees. Those who put marks (on their body) with the clay from the root of the tulasī-tree and with the mud of tulasī-wood, should be known to be Viṣṇu's devotees. Those who are devoted to a bath in Gaṅgā, to (repeating) the name of Gaṅgā, and describe the greatness of Gaṅgā, should be known to be Viṣṇu's devotees. Those in whose house the Śālagrāma-stone always remains, so also remains the holy text of Bhāgavata, should be known to be Viṣṇu's devotees. O best one, those who everyday clean my places, who offer me lamps, should be known to be Viṣṇu's devotees. Those who again make new (i.e. repair) my shattered temple, and put there decorations, should be known as Viṣṇu's devotees. O you Four-faced (Brahmā), those who grant security to the timid, who give knowledge to the brāhmaṇas, should be known to be Viṣṇu's devotees. Those whose heads are sprinkled with the water (flowing) from my feet, and who eat the offerings of eatables presented to me, should be known to be Viṣṇu's devotees. Those who offer food and water to those oppressed by hunger and thirst, and those who take to devout deeds, should be known to be Viṣṇu's devotees. Those who construct gardens and plant the pippala-trees, those who serve cows, should be known to be Vaiṣṇavas. O Brahman, those great devotees who make offering of libations of water everyday to the deceased ancestors, who serve the distressed, should be known to be Vaiṣṇavas. Those who construct lakes and put up villages, who are engaged in offering their daughters (in marriage), who serve their parents-in-law, should be known to be Vaiṣṇavas. Those who wait upon their eldest sister and eldest brother and who do not censure others, should be known to be Vaiṣṇavas.

104-111. All virtues are present in Viṣṇu's devotees. (Even) a particle of blemish is not present in them. Therefore, O Four-faced (Brahman), you now be a Vaiṣṇava. O lord of the beings, always propitiate me with the employment of devout deeds. Undoubtedly everything will be good for you. O four-faced (Brahman), those who look upon the wealth of a deity, the wealth of a brāhmaṇa, and the wealth of others as poison, should be known to be Vaiṣṇavas. Those who are free from devotion to heretics, who are highly devoted to Śiva, who are engaged in (observing) the vow of Caturdaśī, should be known to be Vaiṣṇavas. What is the use of speaking much again and again? Those who worship me, should be known to be Vaiṣṇavas. Create the world again as it was before.

Speaking like this, the highest god vanished there only. Then Brahmā created the entire world as before, and having worshipped Viṣṇu by means of the devout deeds, went to the highest position. Those who devoutly recite this chapter in front of (the idol of) Viṣṇu, become free from all sins, and in the end go to Viṣṇu's abode.

CHAPTER THREE

The Story of King Manobhadra

Jaimini said:

1. O very intelligent Vyāsa, tell me the truth about the yoga of devout deeds. From you I desire to know this yoga of devout deeds.

Vyāsa said:

2-6. It is difficult to obtain the human body (i.e. existence) on this earth, O brāhmaṇa. A wise man, after having got a body, should practise yoga for salvation. There are said to be two kinds of yoga: of acts and of meditation. The first of the two viz. that of acts, gives all desired objects to those who practise it.

Worship of Gaṅgā, of Śrī Viṣṇu, (giving) presents, so also devotion to brāhmaṇas and to the Ekādaśī-vow, similarly devotion to Dhātrī and Tulasī and honouring guests are in brief said to be the constituents of the yoga of acts, O best brāhmaṇa. O brāhmaṇa, without the yoga of acts the yoga of meditation does not succeed. One engaged in the yoga of acts goes to the highest position of Viṣṇu.

Jaimini said:

7-10. O lord, tell me the importance of those which are the constituents of the yoga of acts, if you favour me. What are the virtues of Gaṅgā? O brāhmaṇa, what is the fruit of Viṣṇu-worship? Which are the best presents? What is the devotion to the brāhmaṇas? What is the fruit of the Ekādaśī-vow? What kind of devotion is devotion to Dhātrī? What kind of devotion is Tulasī-devotion? What is honouring a guest? O sage, tell all this to me. I have got eagerness to hear all this. In the three worlds none else but you are able to tell it.

Vyāsa said:

11-16. Well, well, O best brāhmaṇa, your mind is certainly pure, since you have a strong desire and curiosity to hear this secret account. It is not possible to narrate thoroughly the merit of Bhāgīrathī. Therefore, I shall tell you in brief. Listen with an attentive mind. When one mutters the very soft couple of letters 'Gaṅgā', I think his sin would go away. It gratifies great beings. Gaṅgā is easily accessible everywhere. It is not easily accessible at (these) three places: Gaṅgādvāra, Prayāga, and at the place where Gaṅgā joins the ocean. O sage, all gods including Indra, come to the charming Gaṅgādvāra, and bathe there, offer presents etc. O sage, those human beings, animals, insects etc. that accidentally die there, obtain the highest position.

17-21. O brāhmaṇa, listen to a historical account about this, being told by me. By properly listening to it (a man) gets freed from all sins. Formerly in this world there was a powerful king named Manobhadra, who knew the entire prescribed course of conduct and who was born in the family of Soma. His queen was Hemaprabhā who was a loyal wife, who spoke pleasing words, who was very fortunate, and who was endowed with all (auspicious) marks. The very powerful king, having killed in battle one and all of his enemies, ruled over the entire earth along with the oceans and islands. That very glorious king once called all his ministers and in the assembly spoke (to them) these words with affection:

Manobhadra said:

22-25. O ministers, I have protected this entire earth. All enemies, with their sons, army and elephants have been killed by me. I looked after members of my family by means of all sacrifices with the accompaniment of presents (to brāhmaṇas). (But now) this power of me has been taken away by (this) mighty old age. I, being weak, am unable to perform certain acts. Royal glory like a lovely but an old woman, full of all ornaments, does not look splendid with a powerless person. As long as women of charming eyes do not desire a king to lose his power, all his enemies on the earth are afraid of him.

26-31a. The earth would abandon an old king, though he is endowed with all virtues, and though he has set his heart upon her, as a wanton lady (though) looked after (by a man leaves him). All virtues are obtained by means of devotion. Great glory is obtained through virtues. Bliss is obtainable through (giving) gifts. The Earth is obtainable through might. A man without might is helpless, and is not firm in taming his enemy. A king who accepts the words of a fool only, delights his enemies. Therefore, O excellent ministers, I, dividing my entire kingdom, desire to give it to my two sons, if you agree.

The ministers said:

31b-36. We agree to these words expressed by you, the wise one, O king. There is no doubt about it.

Then, by the king's order, his two young sons named Vīrabhadra and Yaśobhadra, who were the best, endowed with virtues, spoke pleasing words, were devoted to their father, always calm, strong, eagerly engaged in piety, came to the assembly. Then the king, the best among those who knew politics, suddenly divided his kingdom and gave it to them through curiosity. In the meanwhile, O best brāhmaṇas, a vulture along with his mate came there and sat in the assembly. Seeing the two (princes) to have come, the two birds were very much delighted.

37a. The king said: "Tell (me), what is your auspicious arrival due to?"

The vulture said:

37b-39. O king, O conqueror, I am a vulture. I have gladly come to see the prosperity of your sons. These two have seen (i.e. faced) a great calamity in their former birth. To see their prosperity in this birth we have come (here).

Hearing the very wonderful words of the vulture, the king, with his mind full of wonder spoke again, O brāhmaṇa.

The king said:

40-41. O vulture, I have heard these very wonderful words from you. How do you know the former account of these two? O best among birds, if you know the former account of these two, then tell it in full.

The vulture said:

42-45. O king, in the age called Dvāpara these two were cāṇḍālas. They were the sons of Satyaghoṣa, and their names were Gara and Saṅgara. O king, once they died in their house. To take them from there Yama's servants with large teeth, having nooses in their hands and numbering thousands of crores came there and fastened these two, inflated with pride, with leather-nooses. And they took them to Yama's abode along a path very difficult to tread upon. Seeing these two, Yama said to Citragupta:

46-47a. "O Citragupta, take into account the entire conduct of these two." By his order Citragupta considered their auspicious and inauspicious acts from the beginning and said to Yama:

Citragupta said:

47b-51. These two large-armed ones, are really (men) of meritorious vows and a great heart. If there is any bad act seen among all acts, it is not giving a present to a brāhmaṇa, after picking it on their own. O king, due to that act only, these two went to hell. The giver who after picking a gift does not give it to a brāhmaṇa, goes to a fierce hell causing fear to all beings. The giver would not remember the gift; the receiver does not ask for it. Both live in hell as long as the moon and the sun are (in the sky). Therefore, O lord, these two, snatching the wealth of a brāhmaṇa, are great sinners.

52. Let the servants quickly take them to a fierce hell.

53-58. O lord of the earth, then the messengers, with their lips bitten due to anger, threw these two into a fierce hell. O king, on the same day Yama's servants coming to me took me along with my spouse to Yama's abode. O king, listen to the act which I also had done. I shall tell it from the beginning. It causes amazement to the listeners. Formerly I was a brāhmaṇa named Sarvaga, belonging to a great family, living in the Saurāṣṭra country, and master of the Vedas and the Vedāṅgas. This my glorious, loyal, very fortunate wife named Mañjukaṣā, was born in a pure family. I was mad due to learning, age and means, O glorious one. I, a youth, once mentally disrespected my parents. (I thought:)

59-63. 'I am worthy of being praised in the assembly of many. I am a hermit. I perform all (good) acts. I am wealthy. I am handsome. I am wise. I am engaged in feeding my relatives. But the parents of just a man like me are attached to sinful acts. They are talkative. They are cruel, and strongly desire the company of heretics. My parents have rendered fruitless valour, life, wealth, so also the family, knowledge, fame and all (my) possessions.' O king, repeatedly thinking like this in my mind, I, through disrespect, gave up service to parents, which gives auspicious (results). Due to this act, O king, I was thrown by (Yama's) messengers, by Yama's order, into the hell where the two great sinners (lived).

64-67. O king, listen how long I, along with my wife, lived in this fierce hell with these two sinners. O best king, I experienced the great misery of hell for thousands of crores of yugas and hundreds of crores of yugas. Then, O king, my wife and I were born in the family of vultures, eating the flesh of dead bodies.

These two, O king, who desired to put an end to (their stay in) hell, were born in the family of locusts to experience the fruit of their deeds.

68-77. O king, listen to the deeds these two did in their existence as locusts. I shall tell them, which would amaze the listeners. O king, once a very mighty wind blew. It made the two fly up and dropped them into the very spotless interior of Gaṅgā. These two, of delicate bodies, having fallen into the water of Gaṅgā, instantly met with death removing all sins. Then messengers of charming eyes came to take them. So also aeroplanes endowed with all enjoyments came (there). These two, freed from all sins, and adorned with Tulasī and flowers, got into a divine aeroplane, and went to Viṣṇu's city. O king, they remained there till Brahmā's existence was manifested. Then by Brahmā's order they came to Indra's city. There they enjoyed pleasures difficult to be obtained even by gods. O king, they remained there till the time the very glorious ones were born in your family to enjoy the entire earth. For him who casts his body into Gaṅgā, there is no rebirth. Yet these two, very meritorious ones, were born to enjoy the earth. O king, these two, along with their sons and grandsons, will enjoy the earth for a long time, will meet with death in Gaṅgā, which is difficult to be had even by the meditating saints, and will be absorbed into Viṣṇu.

78-79. Due to my power of recollecting the former existences, I have told you all this former account. These two crest-jewels of the class of kings, have reached this state after having met with death in Gaṅgā. Who will protect the two of us, the wicked ones.

80-87. Disrespect for friends gives men the affliction (to be suffered) in hell. O king, it was seen just in my case. O best brāhmaṇa, absence of devotion to parents gives pain in this world and in the next. In this world it leads to the destruction of wealth and in the next world (i.e. after death) it leads to hell. O king, I think the sin like a brāhmaṇa's murder is better. There is at sometime acquittance from it. But this (misery) is eternal. On the earth men cut off, with the axe of disrespect for their parents, the tree of religious merit, destroying all afflictions, and secured with great trouble. O king, Viṣṇu himself eats whatever is presented into the mouth of the father (and mother), since, O hero,

Viṣṇu is of the form of the father (and mother). Parents are actually deities. Those who serve them day and night, have all fulfilments due to the grace of the lord of the world. Those men who remain (even) for a day without serving their parents live for a thousand kalpas in hell. Therefore, this great misery has come to me now. I do not know when I, along with my wife, go to (i.e. obtain) salvation.

Vyāsa said:

88. Having heard these words of him, and having grasped them, O best brāhmaṇa, the king became delighted and being amazed, spoke again:

The king said:

89-94. O vulture, I have heard these wonderful words from your mouth. But I and these (ministers) do not properly apprehend them.

Then, O best king (?) there was heard a loud voice in the sky: "This is true, true, true. There is no doubt about it." Then, O brāhmaṇa sage, the bird, along with his wife, became as he was before the narration of the greatness of Gaṅgā. Drums were sounded. Best gandharvas sang. Hosts of celestial nymphs danced. Shower(s) of flowers dropped down. A divine aeroplane, endowed with all enjoyments, arrived. The hosts of messengers, sent by (Viṣṇu) the enemy of Kaiṭabha, (also) came (there). Then (the bird) moving everywhere, along with his dear wife forthwith got into the aeroplane and went to Viṣṇu's abode.

95-96. O best brāhmaṇa, the king, having heard about the wonderful act, became, along with his sons and wife, exclusively devoted to the worship of Gaṅgā. In the three worlds there is no holy place like Gaṅgā, by merely uttering the name of which (one) moving everywhere would obtain salvation.

97-98. O best brāhmaṇa, I have narrated to you the greatness of Gaṅgādvāra, which destroys all sins. What else do you desire to hear? The sins of those men who listen to this chapter with great respect in a temple, and of those devotees of the class of brāhmaṇas, who listen to it, perish suddenly.

CHAPTER FOUR

Praṇidhi, Padmāvatī and Dhanurdhvaja

Jaimini said:

1-2. Through your grace I have heard about the greatness of Gaṅgādvāra. Now I desire to listen to the greatness of Prayāga. O sage, also tell me about the greatness of the union of Gaṅgā and the ocean. On the earth none except you is able to tell it.

Vyāsa said:

3-9. O dear, I cannot thoroughly tell about the fruit of (the bath at) Prayāga or at the place where Gaṅgā joins the ocean. O Brāhmaṇa, listen to it in brief. O sage, do all those crores of holy places in the universe attain similarity with Prayāga? All gods like Brahmā, Viṣṇu, Śiva praise (the bath) at the confluence of Gaṅgā, Yamunā and Sarasvatī. Those who bathe there in (the month of) Māgha, when the Sun is in (the Zodiacal sign) Capricornus, never return (to his world) from the world of Viṣṇu. The fruit, O brāhmaṇa, due to bathing at Prayāga in (the month of) Māgha would be a crorefold more than that obtained by the wise by (offering) thousands of crores of cows, (performing) sacrifices like the horse-sacrifice, (giving) gifts of gold of the measure of Meru mountain and other gifts, offering oblations into fire and giving gifts to brāhmaṇas at Kurukṣetra, Puṣkara, Prabhāsa and Gayā. Therefore, Prayāga is the best of all holy places.

10-13. Undoubtedly that inexhaustible religious merit which, O best brāhmaṇa, as told in Vedas, scriptures and Purāṇas, is had by practising a severe penance for a long time, by bathing, giving gifts and observing vows in (the water of) Godāvarī, when the Sun is in the Zodiacal sign Leo, is had by bathing at Prayāga in the month of Māgha. Hear from me who am telling it, about the fruit which a man obtains by fasting at Kāśī on Caturdaśī in the dark half of the month of Phālguna. He, freed from sins committed during crores of existences, and having every form, and emancipating a crore of men (of his family), delights with Śiva.

14-15. A brāhmaṇa gets the same fruit as he obtains by worshipping Viṣṇu for a hundred crores of kalpas at other places, by bathing just once at Prayāga in the month of Māgha and worshipping (Viṣṇu) even for a day, when the Sun is in (the Zodiacal sign) Capricornus. I am telling the truth (and) truth (only). All (that fruit) would be inexhaustible.

16-17. A man delights with Viṣṇu for as many hundred kalpas as many days a man stays there (i.e. at Prayāga) in the month of Māgha. He who has once bathed in the water of Gaṅgā and Yamunā is instantly freed from all sins by seeing it.

18-19. If men desire to cross this ocean of mundane existence very difficult to cross, they should devoutly see (the idol of) Viṣṇu after bathing in Gaṅgā and Yamunā. O brāhmaṇa sage, if men, by offering their body, worship him there, they instantly get whatever they desire. There is no doubt about it.

20-24. In this matter I shall tell you a historical account. Listen to it, hearing which a man is freed from all sins. There was a very wealthy vaiśya named Praṇidhi. He was solely devoted to worshipping deities and guests, O brāhmaṇa. His wife, Padmāvatī by name, was chaste, loyal wife, of a beautiful body, endowed with good character, born of a good family and speaking in a pleasant manner. O best brāhmaṇa, all those virtues which the highest god has produced as fit to be present in the bodies of women, were present in her. O brāhmaṇa, that vaiśya Praṇidhi, having taken much wealth, went for trade at an auspicious time and on an auspicious day.

25-27. Piety springs from wealth. Great glory springs from wealth. A man secures a (noble) family through wealth. What would take place without wealth? Even a friend runs away by seeing a man without wealth. In autumn a cloud without water would be reduced to big pieces. As long as relatives get to eat, they remain (with him). He who has wealth has (i.e. is born in) a (noble) family. He (alone) is intelligent (and) wise.

28-31. A man, without wealth, though living, is like a dead one. He whose mind turns away from attaining religious merit, material wealth and knowledge should be known to be a fool. Greater is the fruit of more (exertion). Piety should always be practised. Wealth should always be earned. Knowledge should always be learnt (i.e. got) by wise men. Wealth and knowledge increase everyday by giving them (to others). Piety of men does not increase without its being preserved. A man should not abandon even (a piece of) wood or (a blade of) grass after having got them.

32-37a. A man given to storing never sinks. Then that vaiśya Praṇidhi skilled in domestic affairs, put his wife in his house, and went for trade. O brāhmaṇa sage, once his wife taking unguents to rub and cleanse the body with, went along with her friends for bathing. Then (a cāṇḍāla), the resting place of sins, Dhanurdhvaja by name, saw her who had the beauty of an expanding golden lotus, whose face was like a blooming lotus, whose eyes were like those of a young deer, whose breasts were charming, large and raised, bathing as she liked. Seeing the vaiśya-wife that cāṇḍāla, smit with love, and not considering his own figure, laughed and said (these) words:

Dhanurdhvaja said:

37b-40a. O auspicious one, O you having large hips, O you of a charming smile, O you beautiful one, who are you? O dear one, why do you take away my mind with charms of your exuberant youth? O you of large buttocks, O you slender one, you, who are virtuous, should enjoy full happiness with me who am (also) virtuous.

O brāhmaṇa, hearing Dhanurdhvaja's words, her friends, getting angry, and biting their lips, spoke (these) words:

The friends said:

40b-44a. O fool, O wicked one, O you born in the family of the wicked, she will not throw even her foot at (i.e. will not even kick) you. This lady is a loyal wife, highly devoted to religious practices. Those who desire their own happiness do not look at her with an evil eye. Those who are foolish and who are afflicted with the fire of the passion of love, are burnt on seeing the beauty of the face of the wife of another person and the wealth of others. O you of a sinful mind, go away. Do not speak words which are very unbearable. We shall not touch you even with our feet.

Dhanurdhvaja said:

44b-48a. Fie upon this word 'caste', since you have not honoured me knowing all virtues in my cāṇḍālahood (i.e. due to my being a cāṇḍāla)! On reaching gold covered with necklaces and remaining in a pitcher, which man, conversant with the collection of excellences, will not seize it? Therefore, O friends, act in such a way that I shall now secure this young lady. I submit myself to you.

O best brāhmaṇa, to the fool who was repeatedly speaking like this, the friends, with great curiosity produced in them, spoke these words (to him):

The friends said:

48b-53. O you very wicked one, if you indeed long for this young lady then quickly cast your body into the confluence of Gaṅgā and Yamunā.

Looking at one another's face, and laughing, they then took the good man's wife, and entered their houses. Then that cāṇḍāla who had killed thousands of brāhmaṇas, longing for her died in the water of Gaṅgā and Yamunā. Then that cāṇḍāla, remembering his own account, became a strong person, resembling the figure of her husband, and having all his qualities. Then that vaiśya Praṇidhi, having carried out the trade came home on just that auspicious day. The cāṇḍāla also, O brāhmaṇa, entered his house.

54-56. He resembled Praṇidhi in form, age and qualities. Seeing the two, of the same (i.e. similar) figure, who were mines of virtues, she thought (to herself): 'Whose wife am I? Who is my husband?' Then that chaste woman, seeing the pair of husbands, was amazed, and praised god Viṣṇu with words having pleasing letters.

Padmāvatī said:

57-61. I salute Govinda who has endless forms, whose lotus-like feet are worshipped by deities like Indra, who is the lord of deep and abstract meditation, who is desireless among those who know deep and abstract meditation, who is the giver of devotion, and who is fit to be worshipped by the meditating saints. Salutation to you, the destroyer of Kaiṭabha; salutation to you, the destroyer of Madhu; salutation to you who destroyed the demon Kaṁsa; salutation to you who knocked down Cāṇūra. Salutation to you who took out the Vedas; eternal salutation to you who lifted the earth; salutation to you who are capable of bearing the earth; salutation to you who are the destroyer of the demons. Salutation to you whose feet are washed by the water of Gaṅgā; salutation to you who destroy the kṣatriyas; salutation to you who killed Rāvaṇa's family; salutation to you who destroyed the demons. Salutation to you who denounced sacrifices; salutation to you who destroyed the Mleccha-families; salutation to you seated in the heart-lotus; salutation to you who are an ornament among your enemies (ripudhvaja?).

62-65. O lord, O dear to the cowherdesses, be pleased. O bee to the lotus-face of Lakṣmī, be pleased. O Viṣṇu, be pleased. I constantly salute you. O you lotus-eyed one, be pleased; O you who have the disc in your hand, O you who hold the mace called Kaumodakī in your hand, be pleased. O Viṣṇu, who has held (the conch called) Pāñcajanya, be pleased. I constantly, salute you who hold a lotus. I am constantly roaming, being deluded by you—Keśava, in the curious habitation of the mundane existence, having the darkness of ignorance and the lamp of knowledge. O enemy of the demons, Brahmā, Indra and other excellent gods do not understand your Māyā. (Then) how can I, a human being, understand your Māyā? Kindly remove (this) delusion (taking place) before (you).

Vyāsa said:

66-67. Having heard the praise of (i.e. made by) her, lord Viṣṇu, the master of the world, giving the fruits of the four goals (of human life), took notice of it, and he whose lustre was like that of a crore suns, suddenly manifested himself. She, having looked at (i.e. touched) the ground with her head, saluted the pair of his feet.

68. (She said:) O lord of Lakṣmī, O you who give enjoyment and salvation, salutation to you. Remove the confusion about my husband, of me who am without knowledge.

The lord said:

69-71. O beautiful-bodied one, give up your confusion. Both these are your husbands. O you lady of beautiful hips, always serve them devotedly. That who is your young, very intelligent husband Praṇidhi, has himself become two to enjoy the fruit of pleasure, O chaste lady. O you of beautiful buttocks, you too always enjoy pleasure with them, as Lakṣmī of infinite forms sports with me.

Padmāvatī said:

72. O god, men do not approve two husbands of one woman. O you full of pity, save me who am sunk under the billow of the ocean of shame.

The lord said:

73. O chaste lady, as you are certainly afraid of infamy on the earth, the refore, O you of a beautiful face, come to my city with them.

74-75. Then by the order of the lord, an aeroplane immediately came there and taking the two (with her) she got ready to go to Vaikuṇṭha. She too, while going with her husbands along the path, saw a magnanimous person along with a lady seated in a chariot, O Jaimini.

76-79. He was supported by hosts of messengers, having eyes like lotus-petals, resembling atasī flowers, having four hands, and seated on Garuḍa. That chaste, beautiful lady then asked those messengers of Viṣṇu, of the form of Viṣṇu, "Who is this man seated in the chariot? O magnanimous ones, who are you having lotus-like eyes, all resembling Viṣṇu, having in your hands conches, discs etc.?" Then all those messengers of Viṣṇu, very much delighted, resembling Viṣṇu in valour, laughed and said:

Viṣṇu's messengers said:

80. O chaste lady, we are Viṣṇu's messengers. Taking this man, a meritorious soul, we are going to the high, excellent world.

Padmāvatī said:

81-84. Due to the power of which merit has he acquired such a state? O magnanimous messengers of Viṣṇu, tell it to me.

Viṣṇu's messengers said:

This is a demon named Bṛhaddhvaja. He, causing affliction to the world, lived in a forest etc. He is very powerful and valorous. He kidnapped others' wives, snatched others' wealth, and was an active deceiver. He ate cow's flesh, spoke cruel words, and censured deities. He always did acts that were sinful. O you devoted wife, even in a dream he did not do a virtuous deed.

85-88. O you of large buttocks, this one always tormented by love, getting into a chariot, moves in the sky to kidnap the wife of another man. He, smitten by love forcibly embraces whichever very young woman he sees and wherever he sees her. Once he saw the beautiful wife of a king named Bhīmakeśa (engaged) in sport, and in the prime of youth. Then seeing her bright like a golden lotus, he affectionately said these words to her: "Who are you? What are you doing here?"

89-94. Then that wife of king Bhīmakeśa said: "I, adorned by the name Keśinī and knowing the art of sexual enjoyment, am the wife of king Bhīmakeśa. (But) the king does not even for a moment look at (i.e. care for) me who am conversant with all virtues, who am delighted in love, who am born in his own family, and who am blemishless. I, about whom inquiry is abandoned by the husband, who am grieving over my fate, who am tormented by the fire of separation, always stay here only. O best one, being pleased, please tell me everything: Who are you? How have you come to this garden?" Then he said these words: "O you having a face like the full moon, I am a demon using tricks, and have come here to embrace you. Abandon your angry husband who always finds fault with you. O slender one, resort to me. I shall give you excellent pleasure."

95-99. Then that virtuous (?) wife bound the demon with her creeper-like arms and put her mouth into his (i.e. kissed him). O you of fine hips, having embraced her who got perturbed due to discrimination and excitement, he got along with her into a chariot. With great eagerness they became (i.e. acted like a married) couple. Getting into a chariot with the wind's speed, they went along the aerial path. Then he spoke these words to her: "O slender one, see, from your husband's country we have come to the place where Gaṅgā joins the Ocean". Then the lady in the chariot, seeing the union of Gaṅgā and the Ocean suddenly died due to great fear.

100-102. The demon also seeing the good (?) lady dead, lamented much, and died instantly. By the order of the Garuḍa-bannered (Viṣṇu) we are taking these two, of meritorious deeds and free from sins, to Vaikuṇṭha. Even sinners casting their bodies in water, on ground, or in the air at (the place of) the union of Gaṅgā and the Ocean, reach the highest position.

103-107a. The holy place at the union of Gaṅgā and the Ocean is difficult to be found in the three worlds. Even a killer of a brāhmaṇa, who observes a fast there on the Ekādaśī day in the month of Māgha in winter becomes purified. There is no doubt about this. Having bathed at the place of the union of Gaṅgā and the Ocean, and having seen (the idol of) Hari, Mādhava (i.e. Viṣṇu), and having seen Kārtikeya, rebirth does not take place. Kārtikeya is actually Viṣṇu. The identity between the two is always established. All those who see Kārtikeya, go to (i.e. attain) liberation. Hear (i.e. note) that the holy place at the union of Gaṅgā and the Ocean is superior to all (other) holy places. One who dies there in water, on ground or in the air, obtains liberation.

Vyāsa said:

107b-112. O Jaimini, speaking like this, all those messengers of Viṣṇu, taking the two, went, along the aerial path, to Viṣṇu's abode. That (Praṇidhi's) wife, the chaste Padmāvatī, along with the couple of husbands, became assimilated with Viṣṇu, the giver of the four goals of human life, enjoyed all pleasures there, difficult to be obtained; they obtained the highest knowledge and were assimilated with Viṣṇu. Gaṅgā is full of all holy places. Viṣṇu is full of all holy places. Therefore, devotion for Gaṅgā and for Viṣṇu is laid down. Formerly, a king named Mādhava, practised penance for a long time at (the place of) the union of Gaṅgā and the Ocean, and along with his wife, got salvation.

Jaimini said:

113. Who is this Mādhava whom you have mentioned? What acts did he do? How did he practise penance? O best one, tell all that to me.

Vyāsa said:

114. Listen to the story of that magnanimous king Mādhava, O brāhmaṇa sage. O very intelligent one, I shall narrate it in brief.

CHAPTER FIVE

The Story of Mādhava and Sulocanā

Vyāsa said:

1-4. There was a city named Tāladhvaja. It resembled the city of gods. It was well-known in all the worlds and was crowded with the hosts of meritorious (persons). There was a king named Vikrama, born of a pure family. He was religious, truthful and devoted to the protection of his subjects. His wife named Hārāvatī was excellent in the world, who had vanquished the moon's lustre by means of her face. In a host of his wives she alone was dear to him, as Gaṅgā is to the Ocean in the host of rivers.

5-8. O dvija, due to fate a son endowed with all good marks was born to her after sometime. The sovereign emperor who knew all holy texts, named him Mādhava according to the rite told in the holy texts. O brāhmaṇa, then that powerful Mādhava, endowed with virtues, crossed, after sometime, the river of all learning. O brāhmaṇa, the king consecrated his son, the worshipper of the host of all deities, as the heir-apparent.

9-10. O brāhmaṇa, one day he, through curiosity, went along with an army of four divisions to a great forest for hunting. Having killed many animals there, he at mid-day strove to go to the city from the forest.

11-16. Mādhava gladly came to his city with his army. He

saw a young woman engaged in bathing in a lake. Her body was visible due to substances and garments fit for bathing. With the beauty of her face she had vanquished the moon. Her beautiful cheeks were shining by means of two golden ear-rings. Her hips were covered by her very long hair; she laughed charmingly. She was the bud of a golden lotus. Her breasts were charming and raised. Her waist was slender like that of a lion; her voice was sweet like that of a cuckoo in spring. The beautiful, charming one, was placed by Cupid as the banner in the kingdom of youths. Seeing her like that in the lonely forest, which man carrying his life (i.e. which living man) would not be influenced by the passion of love?

17-20. Then that son of Vikrama seeing that beautiful one like that, had his heart wounded by Cupid's arrows, and thought: 'I have not seen anyone else like this on the earth. I desire to make my life fruitful by embracing her here. Of all people I am the best due to my age, handsomeness and virtues. I shall today take her even though she is Indra's woman. Who can (publicly) speak about the fault due to kidnapping someone else's wife, since my father is the king?'

21-23. Having thus firmly thought in his mind, the passionate one kept his army away and went to (the place) where she was bathing. There is no wonder that in the world the three, viz. wealth, arrogance and desire of carnal gratification destroy the power of discrimination. His father is the destroyer of sins and protector of righteousness of people. It is pity that the god of love himself deludes the entire world!

24-27. Seeing him coming with a great speed, she who was sporting (all) alone, became very much anxious. 'I think that seeing me, the young one, alone in the forest, he speedily runs to me. All sages say: Righteousness when protected, protects (the people). What will happen here, cannot be known just now. Enemies run to the place where there is none to help (a person). In that case running away is commended. Staying there destroys life.'

28-29. That beautiful woman, thinking like this, and placing the pitcher on the left (side of her) waist, decided through fear to run away from the lake. Then that Mādhava also came in front of her with a great speed, O brāhmaṇa, and spreading out his hand, stood (before her).

Śrī Mādhava said:

30-35. O excellent lady, O you of a beautiful body, snatching away my heart by means of the power of your excellent youth, you are running away. I who have lost my sense, am tormented. O you of unsteady outer corners of your eyes, O you of a charming body, what is your name? Who is your husband? Have you come from heaven? (For) there is none else like you on the earth. O beautiful lady, O you whose face is like a lotus, you are the best (lady) here (i.e. on the earth). You are endowed with all (auspicious) marks. How do you, like a maid-servant, carry water? On your bosom you always carry golden breasts; and on your waist you carry the water-pitcher. This is wonderful, O you lady of a delicate body. The toes (turned) red on the path very much heated by the sun, at times appear like the buds of the japā (flowers). O you of large buttocks, resort to me with love; O you of a beautiful face, abandon the pitcher. Just on seeing me, your affliction has ended (i.e. would end).

36-38. I am the son, called Mādhava, of king Śrī Vikrama. With full attachment I, of an excellent body, will be yours, O beautiful lady. In the group of my wives you will be my favourite, as the jasmine is to a bee among creepers having good flowers. Or even if, through pride, you transgress my words, I shall not leave you, since I am the son of the king.

Vyāsa said:

39-42. Hearing the words uttered by him, she left the path, and remained with her face hung down. (Then), O brāhmaṇa, she very slowly said: "Even if you will never listen to the words of me, a stranger to you, yet giving up my sense of shame, I will speak to you. O great hero, I am the wife of a kṣatriya Subāhu. I, Candrakalā, am taking water for the worship of deities. The words which you uttered are not becoming to your family. All (men) born in your family are impotent for others' wives.

43-46. I am a lonely woman. You are the majestic dignity of heroes. What glory will be yours by forcibly embracing me here? By embracing the wife of another there would be pleasure for a moment only. There will be infamy here (i.e. in this world); the rest (i.e. afterwards there) will be misery for more than a hundred kalpas. O brave one, this is the land of religious rites. Meritorious deeds should he done here. Do not put your mind into (i.e. do not think of) kidnapping the wife of another (man). Desire of sensual enjoyments results from greed. Sin results from desire of sensual enjoyments. Death comes from sin. And even after death there (results) residence in hell.

47-51. All your virtues are in vain. Your existence also is fruitless, (since) you, being influenced by lust, long for another's wife. My body is produced from flesh, urine, feces, bones. Even seeing this, are you influenced by Cupid, not afraid of your citizens, because you are born in a royal family? Do you not see Yama, the god of death, roaring over your head? The fish seize the fish-hook; (but) all of them are ignorant. How do you, even being a wise one, seize a fish-hook on reaching it? In the three worlds discrimination is the highest abode of riches. Indiscretion is the highest abode of miseries."

52-55. O Jaimini, having heard the words spoken by her, Mādhava who was deluded by passion of love, again stooping humbly, said: "O dear one, protect me whose mind is shattered by the volley of the arrows of your glances. Protect me. I am seeking your refuge. A woman is most dear as long as she is in youth. A golden bee does not go to a lotus-plant whose fibres have become bud-like (i.e. contracted). O you deer-eyed one, be pleased. Protect mc, your own servant. On hearing your insipid words, my heart breaks."

Candrakalā said:

56-57. O great hero, give up your grief. Listen to my good words. I shall tell you about my mental agony which is capable of removing your grief. In the Plakṣa island, beyond the ocean, there is a well-known city named Vikhyātā, resembling Indra's city.

58-59. There lives the king named Guṇākara, who is the best (king), very glorious, endowed with all virtues, and who, the strong one, resembles fire in valour. His wife, Suśīlā by name, was endowed with all (good) marks. By her service she had won over her husband's heart; (and) she was kind to people.

60-65. O hero, her daughter, named Sulocanā, was born from her womb. By her beauty she conquered all hosts of beautiful ladies. Who on the earth is able to describe her beauty and the heap of her virtues? The creator created another (woman) on seeing her beauty. O great hero, O prince, I was her maidservant. I, a beautiful woman, have through (bad) back, come to your land. There is no (other) beautiful lady like her. There is no (other) handsome man like you. If you desire heavenly enjoyments, then accept her in marriage. Does a strong lion not fix (his mind) to secure, with effort, a female elephant, after having discarded a female fox even though she has come near him? In the world an industrious man obtains great wealth. Tell me which work is (accomplished) without effort, in the world.

Vyāsa said:

66. Having heard those words of her, Mādhava, Viṣṇu's worshipper, put away his passion of love and thus spoke to the beautiful woman:

Mādhava said:

67-68. O lotus-eyed one, by what mark shall I know the girl? Tell me that, O you of beautiful hips, if you favour me. How can I, an ignorant man, go to the other side of the ocean? How shall I have a meeting with her?

Candrakalā said:

69-71. On her left hip is a mark resembling a sesamum-seed. By just seeing that you will recognise the beautiful-eyed one. In your stable there is the son of the noble horse (of Indra) named Uccaiḥśravas. He is an excellent horse, going (i.e. able to go) everywhere. By mounting upon that best horse, having wind's speed, you will speedily go to the (other) end of the ocean, since the earth is easy to subdue (i.e. to tread upon).

72-74. Then the king's son, along with his army, came home. That chaste woman Candrakalā also being very pleased, went home. Thinking over her words, Mādhava, with his mind full of anxiety hastily and suddenly went to the stable. He, the son of Vikrama, endowed with valour, joined there the palms of his hands, and said to the very powerful horses endowed with good qualities:

Mādhava said:

75-77. All of you are noble and endowed with all (auspicious) marks. Which horse is able to take me beyond the ocean?

Then all those horses, on hearing his words, with one another turned their faces towards the ground through fear, and were not ready to take him. One horse, endowed with all (auspicious) marks, went in front of Mādhava, and spoke these words:

78-83. "I shall undoubtedly take you beyond the ocean. But, O prince, listen to my agonies: I eat what is left over after others have eaten. I am bound with cords having crores of knots. O hero, even in a dream, I, a strong one, have not seen grains of rice. Then, O prince, what can be said about other pleasures? O hero, the valour of the good would not be possible without respect (i.e. unless they are respected). How can fire be produced without wood (only) with ghee etc.? I am like this. All these are endowed with decorations. But dogs, (though they are) adorned with all ornaments, are not like lions. O king, O lord, in a moment only I can go round the earth with the mountains, islands and oceans."

Mādhava said:

84-88. O horse, forgive all censures inflicted on you by my father. From today you are the chief (horse) in my stable. In (the mind of) the best man torment given by others does not always abide. Water, heated by fire, would be cool in a moment. Sugarcane causes satisfaction even for a moment due to its sweetness.

Having spoken thus, the prince saluted the horse. And then, at an auspicious moment, that brilliant Mādhava, along with his servant called Praceṣṭa, mounted on the back of the horse, and crossing the ocean, went to the city (of Vikhyātā) which was endowed with all excellences, was like the city of Indra, and bright due to the rows of great mansions.

89. Seeing there, a good lady, a female gardener, present nearby Mādhava, with a smiling face, uttered these soft words, O brāhmaṇa:

90-93. "O old lady, O mother, I am a traveller. O unknown one, I, a rich man, named Mādhava, desire to stay in your house for a day." That woman, (a female gardener,) seller of perfumes, who was hospitable, took the guest, and he being delighted, very devoutly entered her house. O brāhmaṇa, she treated him with respect, according to the manner told (in holy texts). O brāhmaṇa, Mādhava, with his mind full of anxiety, passed that night. O brāhmaṇa, when the bright morning dawned, Mādhava told the (female gardener), seller of perfumes, his entire mission.

94-98. On that auspicious day only, the queen arranged for the rite of anointing Sulocanā with fragrant substances etc. (as a preliminary to her marriage). O brāhmaṇa, having heard about that rite of anointing the princess, Mādhava sank in the mass of the billows of the ocean of grief. 'The rite of anointing her with perfumes etc., longing for whom I left my kingdom, I abandoned my relatives and crossed the great ocean, will take place today only. All the efforts I have made up to now are fruitless. But people will not say that he, fascinated by the sweet one, went over the entire (distance). He who well knows what ought to be done, would not have his exertion foiled.'

99-108. Repeatedly thinking like this in his mind, Mādhava wrote (and put) a love-letter into the garland, flowers, etc. (taken to Sulocanā by the female perfumer): "O maiden, I am the son, named Mādhava, of Vikrama, the magnanimous emperor of Tāladhvaja. O maiden, a female servant of you, Candrakalā by name, lives there. Formerly, the host of your virtues was narrated by her to me. With my heart attached to the host of your virtues, I, having mounted upon a horse, crossed the ocean and came to your city. O maiden Sulocanā, now choose me as your husband, since in this ocean of the mundane I seek your refuge, (and) since no other man knows you (to be) virtuous. A bee alone, and not a frog, knows the virtues of a lotus-plant. So also not one white cloud only appears in the sky (i.e. Many white clouds appear in the sky). But the lotus-plant chooses none else but the moon." Then the prince, handed over that letter, along with a golden ring, to the female gardener. Then the perfumer, putting that letter, along with the ring, into a garland of flowers, went quickly to the princess. Having presented that garland of flowers to her, she went a little distance away from her through fear, and stood there with the palms of her hands joined.

109-118a. The very clever princess then saw the letter along with the ring, and read it from the beginning. The princess who was amazed, also wrote, on the backside of the letter, its reply: "O prince, O you of large arms, I have read all the words that you wrote. O best one, read these my words fitting (to your letter). Today will take place the rite of anointing with fragrant substances etc. (preliminary to marriage); and my marriage will certainly take place tomorrow. Nobody in the world will disregard what is approved by one's father. In case of (a piece of) work which is accomplished with difficulty people should not exert themselves too much. If the work succeeds then no exertion is (felt), but if it does not succeed, then there is exertion (i.e it is felt). Yet, listen to (the means) by which you will (be able to) secure me, for which you have even crossed the ocean. I have to go round this Vidyādhara (chosen as the) groom (for me). Adorned with many ornaments and with my left arm raised I shall go before (i.e. to) him. The hero, would stand facing me. He who is able to take me (away) will be my husband. This is the truth, the truth only, that I have written in the letter. Otherwise it is not possible to transgress the well-fixed rite."

118b-119a. Writing this the maiden handed over (the letter) to her only. She too, taking that letter went to Mādhava.

119b-121. Mādhava, having read what she had written in the letter, again wrote (another letter) with great impatience, O brāhmaṇa: "O virtuous maiden born in a lucky family, all that you have said (in your letter) is just what I had (also) thought. There is no doubt about it." Then, O brāhmaṇa, that female gardener again approached her.

122-125a. And she gave Sulocanā that note (i.e. the letter) of beautiful letters. Then perceiving that her letter was accepted by the prince, she was very much delighted, and was repeatedly amazed, O brāhmaṇa. 'He will undoubtedly do it (i.e. accept me) as he has given his assent. Then is that man Mādhava Indra himself? A husband is always a receptacle of love in this world and the next. Even without seeing him he is respected by me as my husband.'

125b-132. Thinking like this, and sighing again and again,

that chaste lady went with her friends to the perfumer's house under the pretext of (taking) a bath. That respectable perfumer, seizing the maiden with her hand, showed her Mādhava sleeping on a bed. The maiden seeing him resembling Cupid horripilated, and observed his entire great body. The pair of her eyes, merged in (i.e. fixed on) whichever part of the body of him, did not move elsewhere, as it found it difficult to glance anywhere else. (She said:) "He is actually god of love or (Kṛṣṇa) Devakī's son, or actually Śarva, the lord of Pārvatī and the controller of all objects of senses. With such form a man is not born in the world. The life of a deer-eyed one with this one as her lord is fruitful. Did the creator, being influenced by my devotion, create him (as a man) with great effort, when I was born as a daughter? From today this one alone is my lord. There is no doubt about it."

133a. Speaking like this, she decided to go home.

133b-135. The perfumer (the female gardener) said: "O maiden, O good one, you should also keep in mind this consideration. A man does not look as handsome during sleep* as he actually is. O you deer-eyed one, (even) in his sleep (i.e. while he is asleep) all the godly signs like joy, (characteristic) bend in the body, gentle eyes and a peculiar smile (are seen). Though addressed, he will not certainly get up (as is clear from) his lips being bitten (i.e. closed)."

136-137. She slowly touched** his hand with her hands (and said:) "Listen, the princess has courageously come (to see you)." Hearing that Mādhava too, with his mind overcome with confusion, got up and politely said these words to her:

Mādhava said:

138-139. O maiden, my existence is fruitful; my effort is fruitful, that I have actually seen your lotus-like face. O maiden, with all your youth, choose me as your husband. O beautiful one, in the world there is no other groom proper for you than me.

Sulocanā said:

140-141a. O fortunate one, due to my great luck you would

**nindayā* is obviously a misprint. It should be *nidrayā*. (Ed.)

***adarśayat* is perhaps a misprint for *amarśayat*. (Ed.)

be my lord. The words that I uttered are very reliable. O glorious one, order me. I shall go home.

Mādhava said:

141b-143a. If I speak 'wait', O maiden, it would be arrogance (on my part). The word 'go' does not come from my mouth. Having thought for yourself, O beautiful-bodied one, do what is proper. Since the words are true, you will be very much devoted.

143b-151. Thus addressed by him, the maiden, being delighted, went home. Mādhava, surrounded by many attendants, stayed there only. The charming Vidyādhara just remained as the groom. All the men there, adorned with garlands and sandal, and wearing divine garments, shone. In that city at places there was singing, at places there was dancing, and at places there was a row of lamps (put) by someone. The ten quarters were filled with the neighing of the groups of horses, the trumpets of elephants and the delightful notes of birds. O Jaimini, the entire atmosphere was full of hosts of various banners and royal mansions. Some blew conches, some sounded large and (small) drums, so also the sweet(-sounding) musical instruments etc. Then all young ladies, with lotus-buds, and with faces resembling the moon, sang good, charming songs. The ground there appeared like a maiden, due to the garlands dropping down on account of mutual friction, and due to sandal flowing on account of perspiration.

152-155. The beautiful Sulocanā, surrounded by relatives, mounted upon a seat made of gambhārī-wood, and went to an excellent place. In the meanwhile Vikrama's son (Mādhava), asleep on the bed, did not, due to (his ill-)luck, know about the marriage of Sulocanā, of beautiful eyes. Those that are deluded by hundreds of tricks of the creator, are not happy in the world. Therefore, this man (Mādhava) forgot his own agreement, and slept happily. A lotus-plant that leaves the forest through fear of fire and enters water, is burnt (i.e. bitten) there by frost-fire. Whatever is one's fate cannot be changed.

156-158. Let people recite the entire holy texts like that of the Veda. Let them serve a king. Let them practise severe penance everyday. Yet prosperity does not go to the luckless. Pains and pleasures remain over (one's) head. O best one, they come at the time of others (i.e. Pains come when pleasures are expected and vice versa). Praceṣṭa, seeing the unhappy Mādhava sleeping, and knowing the agreement between the two, thought:

159-163. 'Fie upon this prince! Deluded by destiny's trickery, he, forgetting his agreement, enjoys sleep. That maiden now near the groom (Vidyādhara) would have been unhappy. What would happen if she is taken (by him)? The agreement with her will be fruitless. O sinful one, keeping sleep over your head, remain (here only). Mounting upon the horse I would carry away that beautiful lady. With a great difficulty does one obtain a gem of a maiden and a jewel. Then what is the use of serving this wicked Mādhava? Kings are served (by men) with full devotion for money. If that itself has gladly come (to me), why should I have the trouble of (rendering) service?'

164-168a. Having thought like this, and having mounted upon the horse, Praceṣṭa went, along the aerial path, to the place where the princess was. Having gone round the bridegroom keeping him to her right, and remembering her agreement, she had stood before the Vidyādhara after raising her left hand (i.e. with her left hand raised). Having seized the maiden's hand, the very powerful Praceṣṭa very quickly put her on the horse's back. Taking the princess to the very beautiful city of Kāñcī, and seeing it, Praceṣṭa, with the fear in his mind gone away, and waving his hand, hurriedly said (to her):

Praceṣṭa said:

168b-174a. See this city named Kāñcī, which is near the sea-shore, which is well-known everywhere, and which gives happiness to all men. O you having a face like the moon, here there is no fear of either that hero Mādhava or the Vidyādhara. O beautiful lady, give extinction, accomplished by your pitcher-like breasts and your hands, to this row of flames of the fire of lust, sticking to the fuel (burning) in my heart. The bee of my mouth would now desire (i.e. now desires) to drink the honey in (i.e. from) the charming lotus of your mouth. O dear one, who waits for one about whom nothing is known? God of love strikes me with his arrows due to the conduct of your charming body. O dear one, protect me, protect me. I have sought your refuge.

The beautiful lady, with her entire body burnt with anger born of grief, seeing the fool, speaking like this thought in her mind:

174b-179a. 'Is this fool, of wicked acts, named Praceṣṭa, written on my forehead (i.e. destined to be my husband)? Oh, I am doomed. Where are my mother, my father, and Vidyādhara—the groom? This one has brought me. Fie upon this doing of the creator! In the world people always fully entertain pride. (But) the creator knows (how) to cut the tree of pride with the axe of exertion. Yet the prudent have recommended four ways out of a calamity: courage, fearlessness coming after that (etc.).' Mentally observing like this, the maiden, expert in all acts, spoke to Praceṣṭa with words of soft letters:

Sulocanā said:

179b-183a. O hero, make your mind steady. I am an unmarried girl. Having embraced me, O wicked-minded one, how will you go? O hero, accept me in marriage (performed) according to the manner laid down in the holy texts. I shall serve you as your maid. What doubt is there? You are my life, my friend, my ornament, and my kinsman. Do you not know that women have no other resort (than their husbands)? Bring objects fit for marriage for (our) marriage. Quickly accept my hand, O you lazy one.

183b-185. Having heard her words, tough within but soft without like a badari-fruit, the fool was very much delighted. The wicked-minded one, putting the maiden at a place on the horse, came to that city to fetch the marriage-string fastened round the wrist. Having thus recommended the rite to him, she thought:

186-194. 'Since the fool, being delighted, and leaving me, has gone what should I do now? Where should I go now? Where should I stay now? How shall I protect myself from this great peril? If I stay here, what then will they (i.e. people) say? Going to a holy place, and with a desire for a birth in the other world, I shall meet death, since it will promote my happiness. Remembering me even for a moment, this fool, so also the Vidyādhara and Mādhava—the three—will not survive. If I live, their life will be preserved. If I die, all the three will die. When these men will cast their life for me, then I shall indeed be responsible for their death. Now at the holy places lord Viṣṇu should be worshipped. When he is pleased, all happiness will come to me. When life perishes, everything will perish. When it remains everything will be accomplished bit by bit. Does not a very beautiful lotus plant that has survived (during) the night, obtain the union with an excellent bee with a mass of fragrant flowers, when the sun with hot rays has put away the moon?'

195-196. O best among the wise, having thus thought in her heart, that beautiful lady mounted upon that very speedy horse, and went to practise penance at the meeting-place of the Ocean and Gaṅgā. In that excellent, auspicious holy place, the meeting place of Gaṅgā and the Ocean, lived a king, named Suṣeṇa, born in the family of Soma (the moon).

197-200. She thought in her mind to go to that king's assembly: (She thought): 'How should I, a young lady, see the king? Around my wrist are (tied) the marriage-threads along with dūrvā grass. I am a young maiden without any company, and mounted upon horse. Indeed my behaviour will cause wonder in one's mind. Concealing myself (i.e. my true nature) I shall go to the king's assembly.' With magical power she became one of (i.e. turned herself into) the figure of a man. O Jaimini, she entered the king's assembly, like that of the assembly of gods.

201. Seeing him (i.e. Sulocanā in a man's garb), an affluent one, having a (missile called) śakti in his hand, seated upon a horse, coming (to him), the king himself asked him: "Who are you? Whence have you come?"

202-204. Having heard these words of him, that maiden in a man's figure, saluted the friendly king, the refuge of the good people. "O lord, I am a king's son, named Vīravara. I have now come to your kingdom for my livelihood. I shall accomplish whatever mission is impossible to be accomplished. When I am there, my lord will be nowhere defeated."

CHAPTER SIX

Happy End of the Story of Mādhava and Sulocanā

Tha king said:

1. O you of large arms, stay here only, in my very auspicious kingdom. I shall undoubtedly look after your livelihood.

2-6. Then, O brāhmaṇa, Vīravara, with his mind set upon serving him, constantly stayed there, in the vicinity of the king. Once in his city, a rhinoceros, named Bhīmanāda, continuously agitated all his subjects, O Jaimini. To kill him, the king angrily sent him. Then Vīravara, with people, went to kill that rhinoceros. That powerful (Vīravara) saw that rhinoceros, of the size of a mountain, with his mouth fearful due to the fangs, sleeping on the ground. Making his horse move in the atmosphere that Vīravara angrily spoke to the rhinoceros with a voice deep like that of a cloud:

7-10. "O wicked one, those trees of sins that you have acquired, have fructified, as trees are when they reach the (proper) season (i.e. in the proper season). In Yama's abode you will see all the beings which you, the sinful one, had devoured in this kingdom. O wicked one, abandon your sleep. Look at me, your killer. What is the use of this sleep to you? You will have 'the great sleep' (i.e. death)." Then that very powerful one also, with eyes red due to anger, with his entire body greyish due to dust, abandoned his sleep and got up.

Bhīmanāda said:

11-13. O wicked one, do not be proud. (Very little) has remained (of the span) of your life. Who is free just on seeing me? As a moth would enter the row of the flames of a burning fire, so you will fall into the heap of (i.e. the large) fire of my anger.

He (i.e. Vīravara), looking at him who was talking like this, uttered a 'hum' sound and burnt him with great anger.

14-15. Then the rhinoceros, shaking the entire earth, and full of (i.e. making) a thunder-like noise, fell dead on the ground.

O brāhmaṇa, seeing the rhinoceros fallen (dead) on the shore (of the place of the union) of Gaṅgā and the Ocean, he proceeded to go in the vicinity of (i.e. to) the king.

16-18. O brāhmaṇa sage, while going he saw on the path a noble (man) blazing with lustre, and as it were another sun. (He was) accompanied by Viṣṇu's messengers, (was) adorned with tulasī-garlands, wore divine garments, was riding in a celestial chariot, and had a smiling face. That Vīravara thus asked him with devotion: "Who are you? Whence have you come? Where are you going? Tell it to us."

The man said:

19-23. O girl who has put on a man's dress, listen to my account. If you desire to hear it, I shall gladly tell it. Formerly I was a king, wild fire of the family of the Caura dynasty. I was known as Dharmabuddhi, devoted to all religious practices. I performed all sacrifices; (gave) all (kinds of) presents. I protected the earth for fourteen thousand years. By (i.e. on listening to) the words of a heretic, I being angry, seized the land of a brāhmaṇa, which was never (before) polluted. Due to that offence of me, Viṣṇu himself angrily took away just at that moment all my royal glory.

24-32. O good lady, I whose wealth was lost, whose mind was burnt by the fire of grief, was subdued by king Yama within a few days. Seeing me, Citragupta brought that action of me to light. He said to the lord, god Yama, Sun's son, of a charming smile and gait: "This is king Dharmabuddhi. He has always done meritorious acts. He has (committed) some sin. Hear it. I shall tell it. Advised by heretics, he took away the royal grant of a brāhmaṇa. Due to that act only, he will have a place in the hell, difficult to be crossed. O Sun's son, he who cuts off the livelihood of a person is guilty of (the sin of committing) his murder. This is decided in the holy texts. Therefore, this king, the killer of a brāhmaṇa, is a sinner. His place is in hell for the period of a hundred crores of kalpas. O king, he who would snatch the land given by himself, or by someone else, goes to (and stays in) hell along with a crore (members) of his family. No atonement for him who would take away the land of a deity or a brāhmaṇa is seen for a period of hundred crores of kalpas. He who protects the land given by others, obtains religious merit which is a crore times more than that of the giver."

33-37. Then by Yama's order I ate pus and earth and always committed harm to beings in (my) existence (as a rhinoceros) in (this) kalpa. I, a wicked one, killed thousands of crores cows, brāhmaṇas and other beings also. O good lady, impelled by Yama, you killed me, born in the stock of the rhinoceros, and having no abode. The holy place of the union of Gaṅgā and the Ocean is difficult to be obtained even by gods; dying on even a dry ground there, will give me liberation. O you of large buttocks, go. You will undoubtedly get happiness. You will soon see your husband.

Vyāsa said:

38-40. Having heard those very wonderful words of him, the maiden saluted his feet. The king Dharmabuddhi then got into a chariot and went to heaven. O brāhmaṇa, that hero Vīravara also went to the king's assembly. And the king having learnt that the fiercely valorous rhinoceros was dead, gave him (i.e. Vīravara) his daughter Jayantī in marriage.

41-43. Having accepted that girl Jayantī, (Vīravara) in a man's form decided to practise penance at (the place of) the union of Gaṅgā and the Ocean. O best brāhmaṇa, having bathed in the morning at (the place of) the union of Gaṅgā and the Ocean, she would worship lord Nārāyaṇa with songs, musical instruments and dances. O best brāhmaṇa, that excellent lady, ate fleshless food fit to be eaten during days of fast or ate fruits, or sometime fasted also.

44-47. (Praceṣṭa thought:) 'Who, seeing her all alone, has seized her on the earth? (Or) has that excellent lady, finding me to be (a) mean (man), mounted upon the horse and gone to her kingdom? Is that princess dead due to the separation of Mādhava or of Vidyādhara, since she would not resort to any other man?' That servant, Praceṣṭa, on her death (i.e. taking her to be dead), went at will. He very much lamented there and grieved very much. Desiring to die he came to (the place of) the union of Gaṅgā and the Ocean.

48. Having bathed at (the place of) the union of Gaṅgā and the Ocean, and having adorned himself with the earth (from the

root) of a tulasī-plant, Praceṣṭa, after having joined the palms of his hands, said these (words) to (Gaṅgā) Bhīṣma's mother:

49. "O mother, I shall now cast my body into your pure water, so that you will make Sulocanā my wife."

50-58. Her servants took him who was repeatedly speaking like this, after binding him with a noose, to the learned assembly. The very fierce servants tormented Praceṣṭa by Vīravara's order and put him who was alarmed, into a prison. O best brāhmaṇa, at this time only on this wonderful deed being seen, there was a very loud wailing in his kingdom. O best brāhmaṇa, having heard about this wonderful deed, that king Guṇākara, who was inflamed, came there and said this (?). O best brāhmaṇa, at that time the king, overcome by grief, put at every place in the city, men with quivers, warriors who fight from a chariot, soldiers armed with shields, with swords, bowmen, lancers in thousands of crores for protection. All the warriors of unlimited valour, ordered by him, quickly and angrily stood in the city to protect their lord. Through fear, all singers abandoned (singing) songs, dancer abandoned dances, musicians abandoned (their) musical instruments. Then, O brāhmaṇa-sage, the king called his ministers, and, with his mind overpowered by grief, asked them: "What is this?"

The ministers said:

59. O lord, this is a wonderful action. It was never seen nor heard of before. Where has he gone when so many men were seeing (him)?

60-61. Someone said: "Having come to the earth due to Lakṣmī's curse, she, of her own accord, has vanished in your palace." "That lovely lady, full of tricks, lived in your house through trickery. Having shown her trick, she has gone," thus said others.

62. Others said: "The lovely lady, endowed with all (auspicious) marks, will come again also from where Indra, of an excellent body (comes, i.e. from heaven)."

63. Some said: "Thinking her face to be like himself, the Moon took her to be himself and took her for observing her well."

64-65. Some said: "That virtuous lady, having long clothes, and with her face resembling the full moon, has been erroneously seized by the Moon. She, with a face like a blooming lotus, with bud-like breasts and lotus-stalk-like open hands with the fingers spread, has been (struck) by quarter-elephants, mistaking her for a lotus-plant."

66. Some said: "Having created her having beauty and excellences, the Creator took her to create, after seeing her, another lady like her, O king."

67. Some said: "O king, you have conquered all the quarters. She has gone to heaven to vanquish divine ladies by her beauty."

68. The ministers having thus looked at one another's face, became silent, inactive, and nervous.

69-71. The king saying, "O Sulocanā, leaving me, where have you gone?" fell unconscious on the ground. O best brāhmaṇa, seeing the king fallen (unconscious), there was a loud wailing due to grief in that city. There was an echo of the wailing, O brāhmaṇa. There was a conjecture among the people there that the quarters were crying.

72. All the ministers took the king whose body was greyish due to dust and whose hair was loose, and quickly went to the palace.

73. Then that Vidyādhara, born of Śrī Vikramadeva, embraced her seat and wept with a piteous sound:

74-77. "O dear one, O you having tremulous eye-corners, O you having the lustre of a golden flower, O you of a charming face, where have you gone after dropping me into the ocean of grief? O dear one, what fault of me, did you, the faultless one, note, that you, O you having a lotus-like face, O you good one, are not appearing before me? O good one, even for a moment I shall not live without you. Therefore, appear before me, and save my life. If I do not obtain you, superior even to my life, (then) O good one, what is the use of wealth, people, friends, riches or home to me?"

78-79. O brāhmaṇa sage, having uttered such and other very piteous words, he, deciding to die due to his grief, went to (the place of) the union of Gaṅgā and the Ocean. There he bathed in the Gaṅgā-water mixed with the water of the Ocean, offered oblation to the Sun and saluted mother (Gaṅgā, and said):

80-82. "O Gaṅgā, O goddess, O mother, I am casting my body in your pure water. You will do that by which I shall again get her." Then, O brāhmaṇa, the angry, excellent servants of Vīravara, took him to the law fit for him. Then Vīravara said (to him): "Who are you? Wherefrom have you come? Why do you cast your body here? Tell it to me."

83-88. Having heard these words of him, that Vidyādhara told the entire story, causing wonder to the listeners. "And there is no doubt that you are the greatest among the foolish people. That maiden was a female gandharva, a demoness, a female serpent or a female kinnara. She had come (to the earth), as it were, through a curse. Therefore, she vanished of her own accord. That maiden of the form of a deity went to the abode of gods. How can you see her again? Can the wicked crows, though powerful, drink the moon's nectar, fit to be drunk by the cakoras (only). What cannot be obtained can never be obtained. Whatever is fit to be obtained is (alone) obtained (by people). Some people know this; (and so) they are not deluded. A daughter is given (in marriage) by someone, and accepted by someone.

89-94. A groom gets that girl (as his wife) who was such a girl in his former life (also). The purpose of (having) a wife is to have sons. The purpose of (having) a son is (to receive) piṇḍas (from him at the śrāddha ceremony). For this purpose only the wise take a wife. A woman gets as is given by her in this world. The humming bee would put up with a lotus-creeper during the night. (But) even a handsome husband would not please women. Even though the sun is there a bee would drink the honey (from the lotuses) of a lotus-creeper. For a man (these) are matters for laughter: always thinking about women, indifferent to devotion for Viṣṇu, and casting the body (i.e. committing suicide) due to certain afflictions. All these, viz. the wife, the sons, the brother, the country (of one's birth), the kinsmen can be obtained again. But life cannot be had again. You did not give up the objects of senses. You did not do pious acts.

95-98a. O fool, when the present (existence) has gone the future existence is difficult to secure. Due to the sense of mineness, viz. (this is) my mother, (this is) my father, this is my wife, my wealth, the life of men becomes fruitless." O Jaimini, thus admonished properly by that Vīravara, he gave up his dejection and remained there only. Then that female perfumer, laughing (herself) went home. And having gone (home), she saw Mādhava, who was asleep.

The female perfumer said:

98b-99. Get up, get up, O wicked-minded one. Your roaming about would be useless. That maiden has disappeared of her own accord at the time of her marriage."

Hearing her words like these, that Mādhava got up.

100-101. Being overcome by great grief, he rolled on the ground. (He said to himself:) "It is not the fault of the girl, nor of Vidyādhara. It is entirely my fault only, since I had the company of the mean. The Creator does not give happiness to men when they have the company of the mean.

102-111. I have realised just this, since this is my fate. Even a great (being) does not at all obtain happiness in the company of the mean: Śiva became naked, and had broken (pieces of objects) as his ornaments, due to his contact with evil spirits. A mean man, entering a hiding place, longs for a woman, riches etc. Having had some attachment Kārtikeya became six-faced. A mean man, having heard about the virtue of the good, instantly sinks down. He goes to listen to a fault which then would become of a hundred forms. A wise man, desiring his good, should not go to the mean. Even for a moment a wise man should not go to the mean. A wise man does not move even a step with the mean. He who takes the words of the mean to be reliable, instantly sinks down. If he gets to listen to a fault, he carefully comes to listen to it. Then getting an opportunity, he, laughing loudly, manifests it. Those whose minds are controlled, have one (i.e. the same) thing in their mind, in their speech and in their action. (But) the wicked have one thing in mind, another in their speech and (still) another in their action. When that girl, that princess will marry, then there will not be the slightest affliction in my mind. (So also I shall not be sorry) if the girl, endowed with all (good) marks, has gone to heaven. (If) she is taken away by the mean (Praceṣṭa), then there would be unbearable grief in my mind. I am seeing her, of an excellent face, as it were, drawn in a picture at every place.

112-118a. I who am alive, cannot forget her. If the good lady has gone to the bosom of the mean one (i.e. is held in his bosom by the mean one), then she will not live (even) for a moment. Due to the intense grief on her account, that Vidyādhara also will not live. To secure her I had left my country as I had left my mother and my father. Undoubtedly I should cast my life like that only. To obtain her again, I shall abandon my life at (the place of) the union of Gaṅgā and the Ocean." Making such a firm decision, he proceeded to go. At this time only, that very intelligent Mādhava, after having obtained the unguent for the feet from the best sage Nārada, went to (i.e. reached) (the place of) the union of Gaṅgā and the Ocean, after a few days. Having bathed in the water at (the union of) the Gaṅgā with the Ocean, he worshipped Viṣṇu. Then Mādhava, adorned with the garlands of tulasī-leaves, and with the palms of his hands joined, said to that best river, Jahnu's daughter:

Mādhava said:

118b-122a. O goddess, I, who am suffering grief, shall abandon my body. You will give that beautiful girl to me (as my wife) in my next birth.

Having spoken like this, and having saluted Gaṅgā, the mother of the three worlds, he proceeded to get into the deep water (of the river). O brāhmaṇa sage, Vīravara seized the prince by his back, and having speedily come, along with his men to the (king's) assembly, and resorting to love (i.e. affectionately) looked at the prince of praiseworthy beauty. Then he, being asked by Vīravara, "Who are you? How (i.e. why) do you cast your body here?" said to Vīravara:

Mādhava said:

122b-127. I am the son of king Vikrama, named Mādhava. Once I, along with my army, went for hunting to a fierce forest. In the vicinity of the city there was a lake beautiful due to lotuses. I who was lustful, saw there a lonely, beautiful woman. That beautiful woman, named Candrakalā, made a reference of

Sulocanā (as living) on the earth to me, overcome by passion of love. Then mounting upon a horse, and crossing the ocean, I, along with my servant called Praceṣṭa, went to that city. On that day only the excellent (rite of the) application of perfumes etc. (as a preliminary to the marriage-rite) to her (was to take place). Hearing that I sent (her) a ring. What she also wrote on the back of the excellent letter, sent along with the ring by me, is told (now):

128-130. "O best one, there is the son of king Śrī Trivikramadeva, called Vidyādhara. My father will give me to him in marriage. (The right of) the application of perfumes etc. will take place today; and my marriage will certainly take place tomorrow. Yet I shall tell you the means by which you (can) obtain me. I (shall) remain with my left hand raised, and facing the bridegroom. He, who can take me is undoubtedly my husband."

131. Having written that letter the maiden gave it into the hand of the female perfumer. That female perfumer also gave that excellent letter to me.

132-133. Praceṣṭa, facing me, heard about the condition, and, mounting on the horse, took her (away). I was overcome by sleep. Listen, due to this affliction, (and) in order to secure her again, I am keeping awake according to the manner (laid down in the scriptures), O good one.

134-139. Thus addressed, that maiden, in a man's form, appointed many foot-soldiers for his protection, and she, laughing, went to the harem. Then, having put on a woman's dress and adorned with various ornaments, she sent her maid-servant to fetch the prince. Having come (to the harem) by her order, the prince saw that chaste lady, as it were, Lakṣmī incarnate. That girl, with her body graced with horripilation, got up from the golden seat, and saluted his feet, O brāhmaṇa. Then that very intelligent prince, securing the marriage-thread there only, married the girl according to the gandharva-type of marriage. That prince sprinkled with the streams of the water of her love and sporting with her, passed the night there only.

140-145. Then when the day broke that chaste lady having eyes like those of a female deer, told Mādhava the whole account from the beginning. Then that chaste Sulocanā, taking that princess Jayantī and Mādhava, went to Suṣeṇa's assembly. Hearing (from) the girl (the account), the king, being delighted, gave to him in marriage Sulocanā and Jayantī. That king, highly devoted to piety and very much pleased, gave him as the dowry half of his kingdom and hundreds (of coins) of gold. Then that prince, having fashioned a beautiful house, lived in that most holy place, O brāhmaṇa. Then, in the meanwhile, Mādhava, having brought Praceṣṭa, kept in the prison, to the assembly, thought:

146-149. 'I shall not protect this evil-minded, cruel man, treacherous to his master, this fool, the greatest enemy. A cruel man, though protected repeatedly with constant favour, wealth and food, acts like an enemy, when he gets an opportunity. (Such) a man, after reaching prosperity, would cut off the head of the master with the same hand with which, in adversity, he would carry the dust of the (master's) feet. The subjugated rows of kings do indeed kill their lord. Even hot water would instantly put out fire.'

150-154. O best brāhmaṇa, thinking like this in his mind, that prince drove out that insensible Praceṣṭa. O brāhmaṇa, with those two ladies, he, free from grief and malady, lived happily there for sometime. On that Sulocanā (the wife) of that magnanimous Mādhava a hundred sons were born; and two hundred sons were born on Jayantī. Those sons of Mādhava also were very proficient in the science of (using) weapons, were highly devoted to piety and became dear to the people. That Mādhava, associated with Viṣṇu's devotion secured in the former existence, once thought in his mind:

155-159. 'Who am I? Whence have I come? To whom do I belong? Who created me? Where shall I go again (after death)? Where shall I stay? The life of me, enjoying objects of senses, has passed without any religious merit. So, who will save me who am plunged in the ocean of perils. That man who, having taken birth in this mundane existence, has not propitiated Viṣṇu, should be known to be the killer of himself and one that is excommunicated. Birth would repeatedly take place, so also death would take place again and again. Therefore, this mundane existence is said to be very fierce and causing affliction. Without devotion for Viṣṇu birth and death would not be kept off. Therefore, today, having abandoned everything, I shall worship Viṣṇu.'

160. Having thought like this in his mind, and having repeatedly trusted (Viṣṇu), he called Viśvakarman, and said these words to him:

Mādhava said:

161-167. O Viśvakarman, O you of big arms, having fashioned a stone-image of Viṣṇu, giving all desired objects, give it to me.

Then, O brāhmaṇa, by his order, the artisan Viśvakarman fashioned a stone-image of the great Viṣṇu. It was dark like a fresh cloud. Its eyes resembled lotuses. It held a conch, a disc, a mace and a lotus. It had four arms. It was united with Lakṣmī and Sarasvatī. It was adorned with a garland of wood-flowers. It possessed all (good) marks. It was adorned with all ornaments. Having installed that image of Viṣṇu, giving desired objects and having a disc in its hand, in a beautiful pavilion, he started worshipping it. O brāhmaṇa, O best brāhmaṇa, in the same abode he would everyday offer a ghee-lamp with continuous flame. He would himself bathe in the morning, and would sweep (the hall) etc. He would decorate the path, and would smear it (with cowdung).

168-171. Having bathed in the water at (the place of the union of) Gaṅgā and the Ocean, and having offered the five great sacrifices, he would worship Viṣṇu thrice (a day) with excellent offerings, with sandal, incense, with offerings of eatables, tāmbūlas, incense and lamps, so also with songs and musical instruments, discourses, and excellent repetitions of hymns, so also by means of going round the image, keeping it to his right, with salutations, and sacrifices in which presents were given, so also with fleshless food fit to be eaten during days of fast, and by eating fruits. He would mutter the great (prayer) formula of eight letters, viz. 'Salutation to Nārāyaṇa' preceded by Oṁ (*Oṃ namo Nārāyaṇāya*), and giving all desired objects.

172-174. In this way for thousands of years he very devoutly performed the worship, giving all desired objects, of the noble Viṣṇu, the highest soul. By means of that devotion, (Viṣṇu) the crest-jewel of all gods was pleased. The lord, resembling a tulasī-sprout, appeared before him. Seeing Viṣṇu who had appeared before him, Mādhava along with his wives embraced (i.e. touched) the ground with his head, and saluted Viṣṇu's feet.

Mādhava said:

175-190. Salutation to the god of gods. Salutation to the highest soul. Salutation to the highest lord, to the lord of gods; salutation to the giver of knowledge. Salutation to you, O highest joy, O Puruṣottama, O Keśava. Salutation to the lotus-eyed one, to the lord of Lakṣmī. Salutation to you of many forms; repeated salutations to the formless one. Salutation to the conceivable one, to the inconceivable one, to the visible one, and the invisible one. Salutation to the lord of the three worlds; repeated salutations to the father of the worlds. Salutation to the one obtainable by knowledge; salutation to you belonging to all Vedas. Salutation to you, the enemy of Kaṁsa. Salutation to you, the enemy of Kaiṭabha. Salutation to you who seized Madhu; repeated salutations to you, the creator, who taking the form of the Fish, extracted the Vedas. Repeated salutations to you. I resort to you who, in the form of the Tortoise, extracted the Earth along with mountains, forests and groves, from inside the water of the deep ocean. Repeated salutations to you who, in the form of the Boar, held up, with your tusk, the Earth, O lord of the Earth. Salutations to you who, in the form of Nṛsiṁha, tore off the angry demon Hiraṇyakaśipu. O god, salutation to you who, in the form of Vāmana, destroyed Bali's sacrifice, and seized (the earth) for Kaśyapa. Salutation to you, that Rāma (i.e. Paraśurāma) who gratified your manes with the blood of the kṣatriyas and who killed Kārtavīrya. Salutation to you, that (Dāśarathi) Rāma, the son of Kauśalyā, who killed Rāvaṇa, so also Mārīca and Kumbhakarṇa. Salutation to you, that (Bala)Rāma, Revatī's husband, who killed Pralamba, and who cleared the Kālindī (i.e. the Yamunā). Salutation to you that Buddha who, seeing the killing of beasts, censured the Vedas with compassion (for the beasts). Salutation to you, of the form of Kalki, who at the end of the yuga killed* the Mlecchas for the

**vihitā* is a misprint for *vihatā*.

good of all people. O Hari, O Viṣṇu, O conqueror of the demons, O Nārāyaṇa full of pity, save me who am fallen into the fierce ocean of the worldly existence.

191-193. Then that Mādhava washed Viṣṇu's feet through joy, and dropping his entire body on the ground, spoke to Viṣṇu:

Mādhava said:

O Govinda, O you highest joy, O Mukunda, O Madhusūdana, O Kṛṣṇa, protect me, a sinner, since you destroy all sins.

Having heard this hymn of praise of him, the lord, affectionate to (his devotees), being very much pleased, himself said these words:

The lord said:

194. O dear, O Mādhava, O best kṣatriya, choose a boon. What do you desire—the state of Brahman, Śiva, or Śakra?

Mādhava said:

195-196. O lord of the world, I have obtained everything. There is no doubt about it. I am seeing you who are invisible even to deities. You are capable of giving enjoyment, salvation, wealth, prosperity—everything. O lord, I am not fit for devotion. Give me devotion only.

The lord said:

197. I am undoubtedly pleased with this devotion of you. Tell me by giving which thing I shall be free from your debt

Sūta said:

198. O brāhmaṇa, saying so, Viṣṇu who was very much pleased, spread his four arms and embraced him as a father embraces his son.

The lord said:

199-200. Due to the power of the embrace I am acquitted of the debt. O good one, everything will undoubtedly be auspicious. O child, by you having a desire my image was worshipped by means of the yoga of action.

Vyāsa said:

201-204. Having thus given him a boon and having embraced him with his four long arms dear as life, he vanished there only. Then Mādhava, along with his wife, devoutly worshipped that image of Viṣṇu by means of the yoga of action. Along with his sons and grandsons he enjoyed all pleasures. And having met his death along with his wife in Gaṅgā, he obtained liberation. He who with full devotion, recites this chapter containing Viṣṇu's account, destroying all heaps of sins, enjoys all pleasures in this world, and ultimately goes to the abode of lord Śrī Vāsudeva.

CHAPTER SEVEN

Kālakalpa is Liberated by the Touch of Gaṅgā-water

Śrī Vyāsa said:

1-4. I shall just again tell you the excellent importance of Gaṅgā; having heard it all men would obtain all their desired objects. On seeing the face of him who has not bathed in Gaṅgā, the mother of the world, a man should instantly look at the Sun. The sins of him who, in the morning, would devoutly remember the couple of letters 'Gaṅ-gā', perish, as darkness perishes at dawn. All the food, water etc. of (i.e. offered by) him who has not seen the best among rivers, are unfit to be accepted.

5-9. The sins of those who bathe in Gaṅgā leave their bodies and go to the bodies of those who do not bathe in Gaṅgā. Oh, very, very strange it is that fools fall into a hell, (though) there is the name of Gaṅgā (to purify them). That brāhmaṇa who would carry even a drop of the Gaṅgā-water on his head is freed from great sins like the murder of a brāhmaṇa. That meritorious man, on whose forehead an|excellent mark made with the Gaṅgā-sand is seen, undoubtedly purifies the entire world. That man who would see (a man) who has come from the bank of Gaṅgā with great respect, obtains the fruit of thousands of horse-sacrifices.

10. Viṣṇu is pleased with him and gives him all his desired objects who says (to another man): "I am going to the bank of Gaṅgā. You (too) come (with me)".

11-13. That man who, remembering the name Gaṅgā, bathes even in the water of a well, would obtain the fruit of a bath in Gaṅgā. He who, at the time of death, gets a drop of the Gaṅgā-water equal (to the size of) a mustard, would go to the highest position. O brāhmaṇa sage, in this context only listen to an ancient account, by merely hearing which goddess Gaṅgā is pleased.

14-17. In the Tretā age there was a brāhmaṇa by name Dharmasva. He was righteous, calm, controlled, full of pity and had mastered the Vedas and the Vedāṅgas. He spoke the truth, was without anger and free from harming (anyone); he had controlled his senses; he desired the good of all beings; he was always engaged in abstract meditation. To cross the ocean of the mundane existence, that devotee of Viṣṇu worshipped Keśava, the lord of gods, by means of the yoga of action (i.e. religious deeds). Sometime, finding an auspicious day, that best brāhmaṇa, desiring liberation, went to the bank of Gaṅgā to bathe, O brāhmaṇa.

18-24. Having bathed there in the Gaṅgā-water, and having presented libations of water etc. to the manes, he, carrying pitchers of the Gaṅgā-water, decided to go home. O brāhmaṇa, at that time a vaiśya called Ratnakara, surrounded by all his servants, came back after finishing trade. He had a brāhmaṇa servant known as Kālakalpa. He who had committed all (kinds of) sins, came (there) with a staff in his hand. O best brāhmaṇa, one ox of that Ratnakara, fatigued due to the journey, slept on the road. That very cruel Kālakalpa, seeing the bull lying on the path, struck him with the staff in various ways. Due to anger produced by the strokes of the staff, the bull got up and tore him with his very sharp horns. His chest was torn out by the couple of horns, and he (also) lost his sight. Dharmasva, full of pity, quickly went near him.

25-26. Then that intelligent one (i.e. Dharmasva) took an excellent tulasī-leaf from his ear, and sprinkled him with the divine drops of the water of Gaṅgā. O best brāhmaṇa, seeing him dead, he, the knower of the most sublime truth, was amazed, and decided to go home.

27-32. Then going along the path while repeating the names of Gaṅgā, he saw before him, thousands of crores of Yama's messengers. Some of them had one of their legs cut off. Some of them had one of their hands cut off. The ears of some were cut off. Some had one ear only. Some had their noses cut off. Some had their tongues cut off. The teeth of some were broken. Some were without teeth. The entire bodies of some were smeared with streams of blood. Some had their hair loose. Some had lost their mouths. Similarly some of them were naked. The chests of some were pierced. The bodies of some were disabled with very sharp arrows. Others had their fingers and hands tied with strong cords. Others wailing due to agony, were intent on running (away).

33-34. That best brāhmaṇa, seeing Yama's servants reduced to such a state, had his heart trembling, and through fear he was a little motionless. Then mustering courage, that brāhmaṇa, a devotee of Viṣṇu, asked thus with sweet (voice) the savage servants of Yama.

Dharma(sva) said:

35-36. Who are you of deformed figures and having nooses and hammers in your hands, with your mouths fierce due to fangs and resembling charcoal? All you have eyes like very powerfully burning fire. Yet, someone has reduced you to this bad plight.

Yama's messengers said:

37. We all are Yama's messengers, always carrying out Yama's order. This very great sin has come to us with great chastisement (as its fruit).

Dharmasva said:

38. You, of great power and valour, have come all of a

sudden. Who has reduced you, and how has he reduced you to such a very bad plight?

Yama's messengers said:

39-46. O best brāhmaṇa, give up your fear. Listen to the whole account, since this agony of us has become extremely unbearable. We, the servants, have been sent forth by Yama to carry this Kālakalpa who has been torn with his horns by a bull. Ordered by him (i.e. Yama), all of us, with all weapons in our hands have come here to take the greatest of sinners after tying him. This wicked-hearted Kālakalpa whose death was imminent, was torn with his horns by the bull who became the cause (of his death). You, being kind, repeating the names of Gaṅgā, sprinkled the greatest of sinners with the drops of the water of Gaṅgā. Though his sins had gone due to his being sprinkled with the drops of water, we, binding him strongly with cords, exerted to take him (to Yama's abode). The lord of gods, the protector of those who have sought his refuge, also sent his very powerful and valorous messengers to take him (to Vaikuṇṭha). O best brāhmaṇa, certain messengers then came by Viṣṇu's order and angrily said these words to us on the path:

Viṣṇu's messengers said:

47-49. O noble ones, who are you? How do you take this noble-minded one after binding him with a cord? Whose servants are you? Leaving this noble one, run (away) as you please. Otherwise we shall cut off your heads with the edge of (our) discs.

O best brāhmaṇa, having heard these proud words of them, the servants of Viṣṇu, we said to them:

50-53. "We all are the servants of Yama, the lord of (every) life. Taking this greatest sinner we are going to Yama's abode. All you noble ones are adorned with the garlands of tulasī-blossoms. Your eyes are like full-blown lotuses. You are strong, and are Garuḍa-bannered. You have put on divine garments. You are handsome like the peacock's neck. You are holding conches, discs, maces and lotuses. You (each) have four arms. Who are all of you, endowed with all (auspicious) marks? How do you desire to take this greatest sinner?"

Viṣṇu's messengers said:

54-55. All of us are Viṣṇu's messengers. To take this meritorious man to Vaikuṇṭha we have come here now. O servants of Yama, if you desire to live, then quickly release this our man, Viṣṇu's devotee, free from sins.

56-63. O brāhmaṇa, listen to the words we angrily uttered on hearing these words of them, addressed to all. I (shall) tell them. "This one is a sinner, of a bad conduct. He has committed thousands of murders of brāhmaṇas. He is ungrateful. He is the killer of cows, (his) friends, and is evil-hearted. This extremely wicked one has snatched very many (pieces of) gold of the size of the Meru (mountain). He has always kidnapped others' wives. O servants of Viṣṇu, he has committed thousands of crores of murders of living beings in various ways, so also murders of women. Everyday he snatched the deposits kept with him; he committed incest with his mother and ate cow's flesh also. He killed others and set fire to others' houses. He censured others in an assembly, and caused abortions of widows. He, resembling a Yavana, killed at night with sharp swords a guest that had come to his house through greed for wealth, O best one. This mean fool has committed innumerable sins (like) these and other great sins. He has not done even a little producing auspiciousness.

64. Therefore, this great sinner is being taken to the house of torture. O best ones, the sinners are known to be punished by Yama.

65. If you are the messengers of the lord, the god of gods, then how do you wish to take this greatest sinner (to Vaikuṇṭha)?"

Viṣṇu's messengers said:

66-72. You have spoken the truth only. There is no doubt about it. All sinners are always to be punished by the lord of beings. (But) this one is free from sins due to his being sprinkled with the drops of the water of Gaṅgā. Therefore, we all shall take him to Viṣṇu's abode. Till the drops of Gaṅgā-water, very difficult to be secured, do not touch the bodies of men, sins remain in their bodies. As by just one digit of the moon entire darkness is removed, in the same way sin is destroyed by a drop of Gaṅgā-water. By (merely) remembering the names of Gaṅgā a sinner is freed from his sins. What wonder is there if he is freed on actually seeing her water? Even the cold Gaṅgā-water is like fire to the forest of sins, as cold water acts like fire in the case of a lotus-pond. Therefore, this one is a meritorious man, as it were, another Viṣṇu. O servants of Yama, if you desire your well-being, (then) go (back).

73-76. Listen to what we again said, after laughing loudly on hearing these words of those messengers of Viṣṇu. "Oh wonder! Oh wonder! that this abode of sins has been freed from all sins just due to the sprinkling of Gaṅgā-water. A mortal is not freed even after hundreds of crores of kalpas, without experiencing (the fruit of) the act, good or bad, done by him. We have come (here) by Yama's order to take him (to Yama). By whose words should we leave this great sinner?"

Viṣṇu's messengers said:

77-80. Since you do not know the merits of the daughter of Jahnu (i.e. Gaṅgā), you are evil-minded and devoid of discrimination. That act which is prohibited in (i.e. by) the Veda is said to be a sin. That act approved by the Veda is alone said to be religious. We hear that god Nārāyaṇa is evidently self-born. As Viṣṇu is, so is Gaṅgā. Gaṅgā alone destroys all sins. A bad or a good act is fixed by Viṣṇu with his own hands. When Viṣṇu is pleased, where do men's sins remain?

81-84. You have been reduced to this state due to your sins earned (i.e. committed) in other (i.e. former) existences. O you of sinful acts, why do you even now desire (to commit) sinful acts? You censure Gaṅgā; so also you censure Viṣṇu. Therefore, we shall kill you, the sinful ones, with the edge of our discs.

Speaking like this, O best one, those messengers of Viṣṇu, with their eyes red due to anger, started fighting with us. They angrily said: "Kill (these) messengers of Yama". Repeatedly speaking like this, they struck us with the edge of their discs.

85-87. Speaking like that, all those messengers of Viṣṇu, very fierce in battle, and being delighted at heart, suddenly blew their conches. Then, O brāhmaṇa, the three worlds were pervaded by our lion-like roars, like thunderings of clouds, and by our bows being expanded (i.e. strung). Then with trees, stones and showers of rocks, we split those messengers of Viṣṇu.

88-91. In that ocean (of the battle) the messengers of Viṣṇu variously struck us with missiles like double-edged swords, small javelins, arrows, so also clubs studded with iron, axes, knives, staffs and darts, swords, (missiles called) śakti, sharp arrows, maces, edges of discs, and very fierce arrows of iron, and with fearful missiles. Then all of us wounded by the missiles ran away through fear. Thousands of us fell dead in the battle.

92-96. Then those mighty servants of Viṣṇu, seeing us intent on fleeing, joyfully blew their conches. Then cutting off the bond of Kālakalpa, and putting him into an aeroplane, they went to the lord's city, O best brāhmaṇa. O best one, due to the efficacy of the sprinkling of the drops (of the water) of Gaṅgā, that very sinful Kālakalpa obtained residence in the same heaven with Viṣṇu. Having lived there for a hundred kalpas, having enjoyed charming pleasures, and having obtained knowledge there only, he obtained liberation. O lord, due to the efficacy of Gaṅgā, this our affliction has gone. O brāhmaṇa, well-being to you. Being very much pleased, go home.

97. O brāhmaṇa, having spoken like this, those messengers of Yama went to Yama's city. That Dharmasva again went to the bank of Gaṅgā.

98. Having bathed in Gaṅgā, the mother of the world, the brāhmaṇa, with the palms of his hands joined, praised that greatest goddess.

Dharmasva said:

99-112. O Gaṅgā, O mother of the entire world, O you of unsteady ripples, O you having the garland of the flowers of the very charming heads of Anaṅga etc., O you who remove the dust on both the lovely feet of the enemy of Kaṁsa, I salute you who destroy sins. O mother, O you who give happiness to all, O you best among the rivers, O you whose merits have been sung by the hosts of brāhmaṇas like Vyāsa, O you rich in virtues, O you, the boat in the fearful, great ocean in the form of the mundane existence, I salute the pair of your feet, which remove sins.

O daughter of Jahnu, with (i.e. by bowing) my head, I salute you, on having whose drop of water the king named Saudāsa, having (committed the sin of) the murder of crores of brāhmaṇas, obtained liberation, difficult to be obtained even by gods. O you giver of boons, be pleased. By your grace let the body of me, repeating the names like Nārāyaṇa, Acyuta, Janārdana, Kṛṣṇa, Rāma, Gaṅgā etc., fall into your water, O goddess, O mother, O you who remove sins in the worldly existence. O goddess of all, what is the use of austerities, muttering (the hymns etc.), (giving) presents, or of sacrifices like the horse-sacrifice? (For) even very sinful men obtain liberation, difficult to be obtained even by gods, on securing a drop of your water. O you highest goddess, O you who are the cause of the creation, maintenance, and destruction of the world, I salute you of the form of the three guṇas, viz. sattva (i.e. goodness), rajas (i.e. passion), and tamas (i.e. darkness or ignorance), who are that Svāhā (i.e. oblation offered indiscriminately to all gods), that Svadhā (i.e. offering of food made to the manes of deceased ancestors) for the great satisfaction of the hosts of gods and manes. May the entire dust from your feet be on the head of me who always wear your sand, and a vertical mark with your clay on my forehead, who would devoutly repeat your name, the abode of all tastes. May my birth remove the tie with the worldly life, after (my) having lived on your bank, O Gaṅgā, after (my) having drunk your water which removes sins, after (my) having recollected your name, and after (my) having seen your water with waves. Looking upon heaven as having a difficult path leading to it, and taking it to be very important, very happy men have a great fear about it. But O giver of nectar, it is indeed in vain, since your water acts as a staircase for going to heaven. O you goddess of all, O you giver of enjoyments, O you Gaṅgā, the chief among rivers, sins, hosts of diseases remain in the bodies (of men) till they do not bathe in your pure water. O you of an uninterrupted flow, that some call you who are the giver of the highest liberation, to reach whose greatness (gods) like Viṣṇu, Brahmā, Śiva and hosts of gods like Indra (try hard), a (simple) river, is their ignorance! O Gaṅgā, O you who give all pleasures, lord Śiva knows a little of your importance, since he, the best of the good-minded, very devoutly holds you, the (only) goddess of the world, on his head. O Gaṅgā, O goddess, O mother of the world, O highest goddess, nourish me; salutation to you; protect me, your servant. O giver of liberation, can I whose mind is confused, praise you, of the nature of the highest Brahman and the only mother of the world?

Vyāsa said:

113-116. Gaṅgā, the mother of the world, thus praised by the intelligent brāhmaṇa, suddenly appeared before him in an embodied form, O brāhmaṇa. Before him he saw Gaṅgā with two arms, seated on a crocodile, white like a kunda (flower), the moon and a conch, and adorned with all ornaments. Then, he, seeing Gaṅgā before him, saying 'O Gaṅgā, O Gaṅgā,' saluted her after touching the ground with his head. O Jaimini, infatuating him with smiling looks, that highest goddess who was very much pleased, said to him: "O brāhmaṇa, choose a boon."

Dharmasva said:

117-119. O mother, by the touch of your water even the murderer of a brāhmaṇa gets liberation. I am actually seeing you. What else have I to gain? Yet, O highest goddess, I ask for one boon: May I, while recollecting your name, die in your water. O goddess, he who praises you with the hymn composed by me, will, after enjoying all desired objects, obtain a good position in the end.

Gaṅgā said:

120-121. O best brāhmaṇa, by this devotion of you I am pleased. Undoubtedly you will soon have full happiness. Being pleased with the man who would recite this hymn composed by you, three times a day, I shall grant him the excellent liberation.

Vyāsa said:

122-128. That goddess, affectionate to her devotees, having thus given a boon to that (brāhmaṇa) named Dharmasva, vanished there only, O best brāhmaṇa. The brāhmaṇa too, having secured that boon, was as it were fortunate. O brāhmaṇa, he lived there only on the beautiful bank of Gaṅgā. Then after a long time having met a happy death in the pure water of

Gaṅgā, he reached the best position. Even that wicked-minded Kālakalpa, sprinkled with the drops of the Gaṅgā-water, obtained excellent liberation. Then what need one say of others, O brāhmaṇa? The Gaṅgā-water, even though touched unintentionally, gives fruit. I do not know what would happen to those who touch it with devotion. I say repeatedly, there is no other holy place like Gaṅgā, touching a drop of water of which one obtains the highest abode. Those, who devoutly touch in this world just a drop of the water of this excellent river, go to the position of Viṣṇu after being freed from all very fierce sins.

CHAPTER EIGHT

The Love Story of Indra and Padmagandhā

Vyāsa said:

1-6. O chief among brāhmaṇas, I shall again narrate the excellent greatness of Gaṅgā. If you desire liberation, drink the nectar in the form of an account of Gaṅgā. He who has devotion for the mother of Bhīṣma, has given all gifts, has performed all sacrifices, and has worshipped Viṣṇu. O Jaimini, whatever religious rites are performed in Gaṅgā, all those become inexhaustible for him. Seeing flowing water he who gets up and goes to the water of Gaṅgā with devotion, is the performer of a thousand horse-sacrifices. He who does not show devotion (i.e. does not become devoted) when Gaṅgā-water has come (to him), will perpetually have beasthood in every existence. The religious merit earned during crores of existences of him who, having come across the Gaṅgā-water, does not devoutly take it, perishes just in a moment.

7-10. He who stops one desiring to go to the bank of Gaṅgā, would, along with a crore (members of) his family, go to Raurava hell. The expiation for him who urinates or excretes on the bank of Gaṅgā is not seen even after hundreds of crores of kalpas. He who would drop phlegm, spittle, rheum, tears or dirt on the bank of Gaṅgā would be a resident of hell. He who would throw leavings of food and phlegm into Gaṅgā goes to a fearful hell, and gets (the sin of) the murder of a brāhmaṇa.

11-12. The sin which a foolish man commits on the bank of Gaṅgā, would indeed be perpetual and is not destroyed at (i.e. by visiting) other holy places. A sin committed at another holy place is destroyed in Gaṅgā; (but) the sin committed in Gaṅgā is destroyed nowhere.

13-14. Therefore, those who are proficient in the holy texts should not commit a sin in Gaṅgā. They should collect religious merit through (bodily) act, (act of) mind, and through words. They are not countries, they are not mountains, and they are also not the forests where the divine river, destroying sins, would not exist.

15-19. O Jaimini, even if one has (to carry out) a hundred (pieces of) work one should not stay at any other place even for a short while after leaving the bank of Gaṅgā. Even by eating begged food one should stay at the bank of Gaṅgā, but not at other place, even for a moment, even after having obtained the status of a king. By casting his body in Gaṅgā even the killer of a brāhmaṇa is liberated. (But even) the performer of a thousand horse-sacrifices at any other place would not get liberation. He who would live on the bank of Gaṅgā and be devoted to Viṣṇu's worship (would obtain liberation). He who has never worshipped Viṣṇu in any former existence, would not have devotion for Gaṅgā, the mother of the world. O men, all of you listen. I am saying this repeatedly.

20-24 Having bathed in Gaṅgā, he would go to the highest position. That man who would worship Gaṅgā by repeating the name 'Gaṅgā, Gaṅgā', (would) freed from all sins, (live) in heaven for a myriad divine ages. O brāhmaṇa, he who would start (narration of) the account of Gaṅgā at the time of his death, would, with all his sins dropped, go to the abode of Viṣṇu. O best brāhmaṇa, with the wise man who at the time of his death remembers the name 'Gaṅgā' giving liberation, Viṣṇu would be pleased. He who would, at the time of death, have a sectarian mark (on his forehead) of the Gaṅgā-clay (*mṛtpuṇḍra*), so also he who would cast his body after seeing him who bathes in Gaṅgā, would get (the fruit of) death in Gaṅgā even (if his death occurs) in a cremation ground, O brāhmaṇa.

25-26. As long as the bones of a man remain in Gaṅgā, he would, for thousands of kalpas, be honoured in Viṣṇu's heaven. That wise man whose ashes, bones, nails and hair lie dipped in Gaṅgā, would live in Viṣṇu's abode.

27-28. O brāhmaṇa, I shall tell (about) the fate a man has when his bones lie in Gaṅgā. I shall tell the entire fruit of it. Listen attentively. Once the lustful lord Indra, adorned with various ornaments, went along with a young woman Padmagandhā to the pleasure-house.

29-31. She who was called Padmagandhā, who had the prime of youth, contributed to great delight by giving him various pleasures. He, the conqueror, deluded by Cupid and being pleased, sat at the feet of that lady having eyes like those of a young deer, and seated on his wife's golden bed. Indra, being very much pleased and with his mind attracted by her virtues, himself prepared a tāmbūla and gave it to her.

32-33. Just at that time, very beautiful Paulomī, adorned with all ornaments, herself came to that (pleasure-)house. Paulomī, seeing lord Indra, the king of all gods, in that condition, was very angry; and she, of good marks, spoke thus:

Śacī said:

34-37a. O lord, O my husband, O king of all gods, what is this that you are doing? Giving a golden tāmbūla to one who is my maid! O lord, all gods touch your feet with their heads. Then how do you remain at the feet of Padmagandhā? A bee is solicited for its fragrance(?). It would not be its success(?). O lord, how do you, who are the lord of a crore of beautiful women, and who know all flavours, do such an extremely condemned act?

37b-38a. O you virtueless Padmagandhā, O you maid, go away. You, (as if you were) a goddess, are (lying) on the bed, and Indra is seated at your feet!

Vyāsa said:

38b-39a. Thus reproached in various ways by that Paulomī, that chaste woman of a beautiful body angrily spoke thus:

Padmagandhā said:

39b-43a. The lord himself knows my virtue and vice. O

you virtueless one, with what authority are you, after coming (here), censuring me? Others see virtues and vices even with two eyes. O you wicked-minded one, would Indra not see with a thousand eyes, since the virtue of people is not propagated as (as quickly as) their fault? Virtuous people first see the spot on the moon. You are talking nonsense, are cruel, of a bad form, void of virtues. If I am not virtuous, then let your husband resort to you.

Vyāsa said:

43b-44a. Speaking like this, that lotus-eyed Padmagandhā, acting very pitiably, angrily got up from the golden bed.

Indra said:

44b-47a. O dear one, O mistress of my life, O greatest one, leaving me where are you going? Tell me, O beautiful lady, what offence have I committed against you. O dear one, I am your servant and will serve you as a servant. The wife of a servant would be a maid-servant. Do you not hear such words?

Then Indra, with his mind overcome by infatuation, got up and again put that exquisitely beautiful woman on his lap.

Śacī said:

47b-51a. O female curlew, your life is good, (and) my life certainly fruitless. You are loved by the lord, and I, an excellent lady, am always disliked by him, till (your) religious merit (lasts). O female curlew, that religious merit will be exhausted. Being born in the family of curlew you will again suffer grief. Till then sport with the lord of gods as you please. O virtueless female curlew, after a few days (the lord) would not be yours.

Having heard her very amazing words, that Padmagandhā, giving up her antagonism, saluted that chaste lady (i.e. Śacī), and said to her:

Padmagandhā said:

51b-53a. O daughter of Puloman, O beautiful woman,

what you have said is wonderful. Tell me how I am a female curlew. I desire to listen to it carefully. Who am I? Where did I stay? How have I, a chaste woman, come here? After how much time will my religious merit be exhausted?

Śacī said:

53b-60a. O Padmagandhā, formerly you were born of a curlew. You lived on the earth, eating impure flesh and insects. On the charming bank of Gaṅgā there was a fig tree. After building a nest on it, you lived there. Once a black serpent entered the hole on the fig tree and bit you. And you, a wicked one, suddenly died. The serpent angrily ate up all your flesh. O beautiful woman, all your fleshless bones remained there only. O good one, once the tree was hurled down by a strong wind. O beautiful one, being broken it fell into the Gaṅgā along with its roots. When that fig tree fell into Gaṅgā, your bones were submerged, O best lady. As long as those bones will remain in Gaṅgā, you will always be loved by the lord.

60b-65a. O Padmagandhā, I have told you everything as to which of your religious merits has placed (even) Indra under your thumb. Blessed is goddess Jāhnavī (i.e. Gaṅgā) due to whose favour, you, a female curlew, not touched even by cāṇḍālas, lie on the lap of Indra.

The daughter of Puloman, the chaste lady, being insulted even by Indra, with her lotus-face faded, went as she had come. That excellent woman Padmagandhā remained on Indra's lap only. Those words of her remained, as it were, wakeful in her heart. O brāhmaṇa, once the lord of gods very much pleased with her virtues, himself said to her: "O beautiful lady, ask for a boon."

Padmagandhā said:

65b-67a. You are the chief of all gods and the lord of crores of women. Yet, O lord, you are under my influence. (Then) what is the use of other boons? Yet, O best god, you who desire to grant (me) a boon (should) take a pledge before me with your (bodily) acts, mind and words.

Indra said:

67b-69a. O you beautiful lady, order me what I shall give you—(my) life, wealth, kingdom, clothes (or attendants). (What I promise) is true, (certainly) true, is repeatedly true. There is no doubt about it. O you fawn-eyed one, I shall certainly give you what you desire.

Padmagandhā said:

69b-70a. O lord of the three worlds, if you are indeed pleased with me, then give me the boon that I shall be born in the stock of elephant.

Indra said:

70b-74a. O beautiful lady, I who have given a promise, give you the boon. But many griefs have come to my heart. O beautiful lady, I do not get happiness if I do not see you even for a moment. Then how can I put up with the unbearable separation from you for a long time? O you of stout breasts, O you beautiful lady, if you have compassion for me, then stay with me for a few days (more).

Then enjoying the large wealth of the lord of the gods that chaste woman lived for a myriad of years in the house of the lord.

Padmagandhā said:

74b-75a. O lord of gods, give me an order to fulfil my desire. I (shall) go to the land of religious rites (i.e. Bhāratavarṣa). I salute the pair of your feet.

Indra said:

75b-76a. O you having a moon-like face, after living with me, having the measure of an ocean of love for you, for a few days, you will go as you please.

76b-78a. Then, that Padmagandhā, day and night sporting with him in the pleasure-house, lived there for three myriads of years. Then, she, full of joy, said to the lord of gods: "Give me an order. I (shall) now go to the earth."

Indra said:

78b-79a. O you beautiful one, give up your apathy. Stay with me here only. I cannot abandon you; (you are) more important than (my own) life.

Padmagandhā said:

79b-82a. O lord of gods, when, on the exhaustion of my religious merit I shall go to the earth, then I shall have separation from you for a long time. On that separation, O lord, I, having gone to the earth, desire (to come back to) heaven. O Indra, having gone to the land of religious rites, I shall employ that means by which I shall never be separated from you.

Indra said:

82b-84. O good one, when you again desire to do this, then O beautiful one, you will again quickly come (here).

Then, with his body sprinkled by tears trickling from his eyes, he embraced her, and addressing her as "O dear one", said: "You (can) go". Then by his order the chaste woman came to the land of religious rites.

85-92a. O brāhmaṇa, she was born in the stock of female elephants and remembered her former birth. She who was well-born in the stock of female elephants and remembered her account went, after a few days, to the bank of Gaṅgā. Bathing in Gaṅgā, and decorated with the mud from Gaṅgā, and uttering (the words) 'Gaṅgā, Gaṅgā', she entered a deep pool of water. That female elephant, of the form of a mountain, remembering her own birth, went into that pool of the Gaṅgā water, and died. Seeing her boldness, all deities gladly showered her with excellent flowers like pārijāta etc. To bring her, of a dark body, Indra, of a good mind, and surrounded by all hosts of gods, speedily went (to Gaṅgā) due to a long separation from her. Telling her, of a divine body, his own agonies (while) in the Puṣpaka (aeroplane) he went to his own abode, after gladly abandoning, for her sake, Śacī, Rambhā and Pramlocā and Urvaśī, that had come (there).

92b-95a. That excellent lady, increasing the happiness in the mind of Śakra, that fortunate one, dear (to Indra), stayed in the city of Indra as long as her bones remained in Gaṅgā, O

Jaimini. A hundred crores (of the members of) her family lived in Indra's abode for that period. That divine beauty became the object of the friendship of those who were kings of kingdoms in heaven due to the power of their austerities.

95b-97a. O Jaimini, such a fruit is had due to a bath in Gaṅgā. The fruit of (i.e. got by) him who casts his body in Gaṅgā cannot be described. O Jaimini, as long as the dead body and the bones remain in Gaṅgā, till that time, i.e. for a hundred crores of kalpas she resided in the abode of the god.

97b-99a. O Jaimini, listen to the fruit obtained by a man whose dead body is tossed in Gaṅgā by her currents: He, lying on a golden bed, and fanned with the breezes of charming chowries by divine ladies, becomes happy.

99b-104. I shall tell you about the abode of him whose dead body is seen on the sandy bank of Gaṅgā heated by the rays of the sun: With his entire body smeared with divine fragrant substances and sandal he always sports with divine damsels in heaven. Listen to the fruit obtained by him whose body is seen torn by crows, vultures, herons, and (other) birds in (Gaṅgā) the mother of Bhīṣma: He, with his chest embraced by the stout, high, charming breasts of divine damsels, always sleeps on a bed in heaven. O brāhmaṇa, listen to the inexhaustible fruit from me who am telling it, which he who (i.e. whose body) is surrounded by ants, insects and flies and whose bones are seen to have fallen in Gaṅgā, obtains.

105-110. He, with the dust-particles on his feet removed by the ornaments on their crowns and being saluted with their heads by the hosts of gods, behaves in heaven like Indra for a long time. That man whose body falls into Gaṅgā even against his desire, is freed from all sins, and would become Viṣṇu. He whose charcoals (burnt parts of the body) are seen to be tossed by the water in Gaṅgā, would remain in heaven proportionately with the number of the charcoals for more than a hundred kalpas. Maybe all (kinds) of religious merit are exhausted. (But) when the body has fallen into Gaṅgā, the religious merit is never exhausted. What is the use of prolixity in this matter? The greatness of him who has cast his body in Gaṅgā is not (i.e. cannot be) known. That blessed man who, on the earth, sometime devoutly touches the water of Gaṅgā, destroying heaps of very strong sins, crosses the fearful ocean of the (mundane) world and goes to the (other) shore in a boat of boundless pleasure.

CHAPTER NINE

The Greatness of Gaṅgā

Jaimini said:

1. O preceptor, tell me again the excellent greatness of Gaṅgā. Due to its sweetness I again desire to drink the nectar of the account of Gaṅgā.

Vyāsa said:

2-9a. That too I shall tell you since you are a devotee of Gaṅgā. Those feet of men (alone) are fruitful (i.e. meritorious) that go to the bank of Gaṅgā. Those (alone) are (fruitful) ears that hear the sound of the waves of Gaṅgā. That (alone) is the (fruitful) tongue which knows the various (kinds of) sweetness of her water. Those (alone) are the (fruitful) eyes that see the charming ripples of Gaṅgā. That is said to be the (fruitful) forehead which bears a vertical mark of the clay of Gaṅgā. Those (alone) are the (fruitful) hands that are intent on worshipping Gaṅgā. That (alone) is the (fruitful) body, giving the fruit of the four goals of human life, which has fallen into the pure water of Gaṅgā. O best brāhmaṇa. All the manes of the dead ancestors, living in heaven, (seeing their son) going to the bank of Gaṅgā, and seeing her water are delighted, and praise it, O Jaimini, saying: "Formerly we have done religious merit for obtaining a good position; and it will be inexhaustible, since we have such a son. He has now gratified us with the water of Gaṅgā. We shall go to the highest abode which is difficult to be had even by gods.

9b-15. Those substances which our son will offer to us and into Gaṅgā, will, all of them, be inexhaustible for us." So also the manes living in hell and full of all miseries, will, on seeing their son going to the bank of Jāhnavī (i.e. Gaṅgā) speak thus: "Even by the grace of (our) son, all sins that we committed and that give the torments in hell, will perish. All of us are freed from all the torments in hell, extremely difficult to bear. Now due to the grace of our son we shall reach the highest position." The manes of that man who having undertaken a pilgrimage returns home through folly, are disappointed, and all of them go (back) as they had come. While on pilgrimage to Gaṅgā, one should avoid (eating) flesh, coitus, a swing, a horse, an elephant, so also (using) shoes, an umbrella. The trouble due to the fatigue of the journey is not regarded as painful.

16-20. At the time of bath in Gaṅgā one should not remember the pleasure from *padma* (= a mode of coitus) (that is had) in the house. One should avoid, while on the pilgrimage to Gaṅgā, false speech and contact with heretics. (One should also avoid) eating twice (a day), a quarrel, censuring others, greed, pride, anger and jealousy. While on the pilgrimage to Gaṅgā one should also avoid laughing too much, and grief. One should look upon oneself, sleeping on the ground, as sleeping on a bed. While going along the path, a man should utter the good names of Gaṅgā. The greatness of goddess Jāhnavī destroys all sins. Uttering (the name of Gaṅgā) giving happiness and liberation he goes along the path. "O Gaṅgā, O goddess, O mother of the world, present yourself to me."

21-27. With these gentle words he should remove his fatigue. "Oh, how I left my house; how I came here after (so much) exertion". He who would speak like this, does not have the complete fruit of it (i.e. the pilgrimage). Those men who, overcome by such sorrowful thoughts as: "Where is my bed? Where is my wife? Where is my friend? Where is my house? I am sleeping on the ground on this desolate road. How have I come here? What is the position of the things like wealth and grains in my house? After how many days shall I go back to my house?," go along the path, do not have the entire fruit of the bath in Gaṅgā, O brāhmaṇa. "O Gaṅgā, this pilgrimage is undertaken to reach your bank. O best river, due to your favour I shall succeed in it without any obstacle." Having uttered this hymn, especially at the time of the pilgrimage, he, with delight, should go from his house along with devotees of Viṣṇu, O Jaimini. He should not go with a great speed, nor very slowly.

28-30. The wise ones should not undertake any other work

during the pilgrimages to Gaṅgā. Half of the religious merit of him who carries on trade, business etc. on the bank of Gaṅgā or at Prayāga, perishes. "All my sins, small or great, committed in existence after existence will perish due to the favour of the goddess Gaṅgā." Saying so, a wise one, being very much delighted, should go to the bank of Gaṅgā.

31-35a. Seeing mother Gaṅgā, he should utter this hymn: "Today my existence is fruitful, today my life is well-lived, (since) with my eyes I am actually seeing you of the nature of Brahman, O goddess; just by seeing you the sin of me, a great sinner, produced during crores of existences, has perished." Speaking like this, he, full of devotion, should salute goddess Jāhnavī, by dropping his body (i.e. by prostrating himself) on the ground. Then, O best brāhmaṇa, he, with the palms of his hands joined, with devotion and being very much delighted, should again utter this hymn:

35b-41. "O Gaṅgā, O goddess, O mother of the world, I am touching your water with my feet. Being pleased, pardon this fault of mine. O auspicious one, your water is a staircase for going up to the heaven. Therefore, I am touching it with my feet. O Gaṅgā, O goddess. I repeatedly salute you." Then the wise one, devoutly carrying the Gaṅgā-water on his head, should, saying 'Gaṅgā', enter the stream (of Gaṅgā). "I smear my body with your mud, very soft and destroying all sins. O mother, remove my sin." With his body smeared with the mud of Gaṅgā, and uttering (the words) 'Gaṅgā, Gaṅgā', he should bathe in Gaṅgā, destroying all sins. Then again taking the clay to the accompaniment of the hymn mentioned before, and again taking the clay to the accompaniment of the hymn that will be told (now) he should devoutly bathe.

42-43. "O Gaṅgā, O you of the nature of Brahman, I am bathing in your pure water. Give me the fruit told (in the holy texts)." Then, O brāhmaṇa, the wise one, remembering Gaṅgā, Nārāyaṇa, should, as he wishes, bathe in Gaṅgā, the mother of the world.

44. Having thus bathed in Gaṅgā, he should clean his body with (a piece of) cloth. He should not drop the water from the clothes to be worn into Gaṅgā.

45-46. A wise man should not brush his teeth in Gaṅgā. If

he does so through folly, he would not obtain the religious merit due to the water of Gaṅgā. Having done that act of brushing the teeth etc. in the morning somewhere else, he should abandon the garment worn during the night, and then should bathe in Gaṅgā.

47-48. He who without going to an external land would bathe in Gaṅgā, would also not obtain the full fruit of the bath in Gaṅgā. Having bathed, the wise one should place sectarian marks of clay at various places (on his body). Then with a steady mind he should present libations of water to the manes etc.

49-50. The manes of him who offers them libations of the water of Gaṅgā, are gratified for a period of a hundred crores of years. The manes of him who offers śrāddha to them on Gaṅgā, live pleased in the abode of gods (i.e. heaven), O best brāhmaṇa.

51-52. Observing a fast, and having performed rites like a bath etc. in Gaṅgā, he should then do acts like giving gifts, worshipping deities, (shouting) 'victory (to Gaṅgā)', which being done in Gaṅgā do not perish. Fasting and finishing the rites like bathing in Gaṅgā, he should perform the five major sacrifices (viz. *brahma-*, *pitṛ-*, *deva-*, *bhūta-*, and *nṛ-yajña*) and should worship Gaṅgā.

53-58. A wise man should bathe the image of goddess Gaṅgā, so also of Śrī Viṣṇu with the divine water of a cocoanut. In the absence of the image of Gaṅgā, he should recollecting Jāhnavī (i.e. Gaṅgā) in his heart, put the cocoanut-water into the Gaṅgā-water. He should (then) devoutly worship (the images of) Gaṅgā and Viṣṇu with divine fragrant substances, bright lamps full of ghee, fragrant incense, many beautiful flowers, many very ripe fruits, excellent offerings of eatables, water for washing the feet, respectful offerings, water for rinsing the mouth with, tāmbūlas with khadira, so also with other special presents, with various eulogies, and with offerings of eatables. Then the wise one should devoutly go three times round the image of the goddess that is worshipped and (that of) Viṣṇu, the highest lord, keeping them to his right.

59-60. Then the wise one making a solemn vow through physical acts, mind and speech as "O sinless one, O daughter of Jahnu, remaining without food (today) I shall eat food the next day (i.e. tomorrow); be my refuge", he being extremely delighted should keep awake at night after having controlled his sleep.

61-62. If the wise one is too weak to eat fruits only, then, O greatest brāhmaṇa, he should eat (very) little food, but should not have a (full) meal. O Jaimini, having worshipped (the images of) Gaṅgā and Viṣṇu in the morning, he should give presents to a brāhmaṇa according to his wealth.

63-65. "O best river, may all that—the worship, the keeping awake before you—be faultless through your favour." Speaking like this, saluting her (i.e. Gaṅgā) and having performed his daily rites, the brāhmaṇa himself should break his fast along with his relatives. O dear, listen to the fruit from me who am telling it, of the religious merit of him who thus observes the holy fast on the bank of Gaṅgā.

66-68. He is freed from sins committed during other (i.e. former) existences. He, having Viṣṇu's form and reaching Viṣṇu's city, rejoices (there) with Viṣṇu. Living in Viṣṇu's city for thousands of crores of kalpas and hundreds of crores of kalpas, he enjoys all prosperity, very difficult to be obtained. Then by Viṣṇu's order he goes to Brahmā's world. In Brahmā's world he enjoys prosperity which is very difficult to be had even by gods.

69-70. Living in Brahmā's world for that much period (i.e. thousands of crores of kalpas and hundreds of crores of kalpas), he, then, getting into a beautiful chariot, goes to Śiva from Brahmā's abode. There he enjoys pleasures of various kinds, which are extremely difficult to be had. He also gets the headship of Śiva's attendants. What is the use of speaking many other words?

71-78a. Then that meritorious [man, after living in Śiva's abode for that much period (i.e. thousands of crores of kalpas and hundreds of crores of kalpas), would, as it were, another Indra, go to Indra's world. Then he would remain on the same seat with that virtuous (god). Having enjoyed there all his desired objects for a period of a hundred crores of kalpas, he would, like another Moon, go to the Sun's world from there. Having enjoyed nectar there, near the Moon, he would become a sovereign emperor after again having come to the earth. Having protected the earth for a long time and having conquered all his enemies, he would, at the end of his life (-span), happily meet death in Gaṅgā. Again he, the very glorious one, himself getting into an aeroplane, goes to the city of the lord, difficult to be reached even by deities. Having enjoyed all pleasures there for four ages of Manus, he securing the highest knowledge, would obtain liberation, difficult to be secured. There is no doubt that even he who would meet death on the path when he is on his pilgrimage to Gaṅgā would go to the highest abode.

78b-84a. On the earth there was a religious and sweet-speaking king named Satyadharma during the junction of Tretā and Dvāpara yugas. The queen of that king was Vijayā by name. She was beautiful, of good character, and highly devoted to the service of her husband. Having enjoyed for seven thousand years this earth, he whose time of death had come sometime died along with his wife. Then the couple, causing fear, tied by Yama's soldiers went to Yama's abode along a painful path. Seeing them Dharmarāja also said to Citragupta: "O Citragupta, consider all acts of these two." O Jaimini, Citragupta, being (thus) ordered by him, considered their acts from the beginning, and with the palms of his hands joined, spoke:

Citragupta said:

84b-85. O king, listen. I am telling all the acts of these two. Listen, I am also telling the remedy against their ill-luck (due to) whatever good or bad act they did on the earth.

86-88. Once, O competent one, a deer frightened by tigers, came from the forest to save its life, to his assembly. Seeing it coming, he, being very curious, got up and quickly struck on its hip with his sword. The king struck the deer even though it had sought his shelter. Therefore, O lord, this king, along with his wife, should be punished by you.

89-96. There is no doubt that he, along with crores and crores of members of his family, would reside in hell for as many thousands of ages and hundreds of ages of Manu as the number of hair on his body. Listen to the religious merit of the wise one who with (i.e. at the cost of) even his life and wealth protects him who has sought his shelter. Freed from all sins, chief among them being a brāhmaṇa's murder, he would at the end (of the span) of his life go to liberation difficult to be attained even by meditating saints.

Then by Yama's order, his messengers put the king with his wife in a very painful hell where the trees have leaves as sharp as swords. Since the leaves of the trees there resemble swords, the wise call it Asipatravana. Then living in that Asipatravipina (hell) for hundreds of crores of Yugas, he, along with his wife resorted to the hell called Vyāghrabhakṣya. (One) who enters that hell full of all troubles, would be a prey of tigers. Therefore, it is known as Vyāghrabhakṣya.

97-99a. The king, along with his wife, stayed there for thousands of crores of yugas, and at the end of his sins was born, after having gone to the earth, in the stock of frogs. The two, the male frog and the female frog, remembering their (former) births, were very much pained. Always eating insects, they lived on a bank (of a river). Once, finding (i.e. on) an auspicious day (some) men were going along the path to the bank of Jāhnavī. O brāhmaṇa, the two (frogs) saw them.

The frog said:

99b-102. Due to all those sinful acts I did due to my ignorance, even now pain does not abandon us. Casting their bodies into Gaṅgā, even the sinners would be freed. Yet, how can we experience such a kind of unhappiness? Now I desire to cast this body (of me) into Gaṅgā. O dear one, tell me, what is the remedy? I desire to cross the ocean of agony.

The female frog, having heard his words, spoke politely:

The female frog said:

103-105a. O lord, it is not possible to bear this agony. Do so quickly.

O brāhmaṇa, the couple, then, remembering Gaṅgā, giver of auspicious things, was delighted and at once undertook the pilgrimage in order to die. A poisonous, fearful deadly serpent saw them, hungry for a long time, going along the path.

The deadly serpent said:

105b-112. O sinful frogs, you, whose time of death has come, have arrived. Therefore, you should be eaten by me who am hungry.

Then the unhappy, very much frightened couple spoke with reverence to the deadly serpent, that was in front of them, these words: "In our heart, O serpent, there is not the slightest fear of death. Formerly, I was a king called Satyadharma on the earth. This was my queen named Vijayā. Through temptation I, a wicked one, resorted to her(?) Due to that act I experienced pain for a long time in the abode of Yama. To undergo the remaining (fruit of) my act I went to (i.e. was born in) the stock of frogs along with my wife. The act done by a sinner does not leave (him). O serpent, we truly desire to go to the highest abode. We are going to the bank of Gaṅgā to cast our bodies (into her). O serpent, give up your indiscrimination, causing torment in the hell. How much pleasure will you have by devouring us?

113-116. Viṣṇu dwells in our heart. (In the same way) Hari (i.e. Viṣṇu) dwells in your heart also. Therefore, what enmity do we have with you, O serpent? The wise should never harm a living being. If it is done, then it is the Destiny that brings it about. Giving harm to men (i.e. causing them to commit harm) the wicked Destiny itself would take away (their) life, sons, wives, riches and glory. What is the use of mutterings (of names of deities), austerities, (giving) gifts, or sacrifices to him in whose heart the two letters 'hiṁ-sā' (i.e. harm) always remain?

117-118. That man who harms a living being just harms Viṣṇu (also). The revered lord of Lakṣmī lives in the bodies of all living beings. Lord Viṣṇu, having created himself in many ways, plays like a child in the pleasure-house of the mundane existence.

119-122. The body of a sentient being is the abode of the highest soul. Viṣṇu himself is the highest soul. Therefore, one should avoid doing harm. By destroying another's life one's own pleasure is had. (But) one's pleasure would be momentary (while) another would lose his life. This is the wonderful behaviour of people on the earth: Killing another person with great effort they bring about their own pleasure. An intelligent one never knows himself.

123-127a. He should think in his mind: 'I am Viṣṇu. He is (also) Viṣṇu.' He, who, in this worldly existence, is pained due to another man's agony and is happy on his happiness, should be known to be actually Viṣṇu himself. Fie upon the happiness of the men deceived by delusion, and the happiness which would be had by causing harm to another (being), O serpent! Men soon get the fruits of those pleasures and pains which are given by them to a living being on the earth. Therefore, O serpent, give up (doing) harm, and be happy. When you are pleased, we shall go to the other shore of the ocean of unhappiness."

The serpent said:

127b-133a. When there would not[1] (?) indeed be a major sin (involved) in killing others, then Oh, how (i.e. why) has the Creator created those that are the preys and those that eat them? You have told the truth that harm should not be done to others. But in the case of all preys harm is not involved. Viṣṇu is of a universal form. It is the truth. There is no doubt about it. He himself has created the union of the prey and the one who eats it. He himself creates himself and himself protects himself. He himself eats himself. Such is the creation of Viṣṇu. Am I able to kill you? The creator of the form of Death, Viṣṇu himself, has sent me for this mission. That god who created you, and who always protects you, and who is of the nature of Death today kills you making me the instrument.

Vyāsa said:

133b-141. Then the serpent ate up (the couple of frogs), which was uttering, through great hunger, (the words) 'Gaṅgā, Gaṅgā', on the path. These two persons at every step obtained the great fruit of horse-sacrifices in their pilgrimage to the bank of the Gaṅgā. Therefore, these two noble ones have (the credit of) many horse-sacrifices. None is like them, since (even) I have

1. The word '*na*' (not) is redundant as it gives a sense not intended in the context.

performed (only) a hundred sacrifices. Indra, in his own authority depending upon another came (there) on foot with materials of worship in his hand and surrounded by gods. The beauties like Rambhā and Urvaśī, proud of their youth, said to one another: "This very handsome man of taste, the best among the meritorious, has come. With my service I shall bring him under my influence." Someone said to someone else: "I know all arts. Therefore, only I shall be the beloved of this king." Someone said to someone else: "Even your Indra is under my influence. Then what wonder is there that this king also will be under my influence?"

142-149. "This one is my husband. This one is my lord. This one is my master. This one is my protector." Thus all the women, appreciating good qualities, said with great delight. O brāhmaṇa, hearing these various (talks) of them, a virtuous, appreciative woman said: "This king has taken that charming one (viz. Vijayā) belonging to Sudāsa as his wife. O ladies, (then) what is the use of quarrelling?" Then, O brāhmaṇa, those beauties, adorned with all ornaments, gave up quarrelling, and came there delighted at heart. They then worshipped that king with his sin vanished, and along with wife with (i.e. by giving him) water for washing his feet etc. Indra then spoke (to him) thus. Indra put him, along with his wife, into the chariot (decorated) with flowers. Heaven was full of noise with the sounds of kettle-drums, tabors, melodious small drums, and large drums, so also with the sounds of bracelets and clappings, and the shouts of victory given by gods. He, fanned with the breezes produced from white chowries in the charming hands of the divine ladies, and seated in a chariot with his wife, went to heaven. Then the god Indra, fearing destruction, gave that king Satyadharma half of his seat.

150-152. Due to Viṣṇu's compassion, that king, sitting on the same seat with Indra, acted as Indra in heaven. Enjoying all pleasures for thousands of crores of yugas he got into a chariot by the lord's order, and went to Vaikuṇṭha. Having enjoyed all charming pleasures there for a Manu period, and having obtained the higest knowledge there, he, with his wife, obtained liberation.

153-159. O brāhmaṇa, I have told you the entire fruit of this kind of (i.e. got by) him who casts his body while going on a pilgrimage along the bank of Gaṅgā. Philosophers, great sages like Nārada, have not declared any restriction as regards time on going to the bank of Gaṅgā. O best brāhmaṇa, whenever a man would bathe in Gaṅgā, he certainly obtains inexhaustible religious merit. It is certain that Gaṅgā destroys all sins. If a man repeatedly commits sins, Gaṅgā does not purify him. O people, if you desire beatitude, then, giving up wicked thoughts, bathe in Gaṅgā, the mother of the world. By means of which very difficult acts do men get that religious merit which they would have by means of a bath in Gaṅgā? It is possible (for a man) to count the number of sharp showers and dust particles on the earth. (But) O brāhmaṇa, he cannot narrate the merits of Gaṅgā.

160-161. Having considered all your holy texts I say: "A man gets liberation after bathing (just) once in the water of Gaṅgā. Even he who, thinking of the lord of gods, and of Gaṅgā, destroying the mass of the affliction of all the afflicted ones, and the fear of sins, bathes in the water of a well, is freed from the masses of all sins like the murder of a cow, and due to the favour of Gaṅgā, O brāhmaṇa, he would go to Viṣṇu's city, giving all pleasures."

CHAPTER TEN

The Efficacy of Campaka Flower

Jaimini said:

1. O preceptor, through your grace I have heard this (description of the) greatness of Gaṅgā. Now, I desire to listen to the fruit of Viṣṇu's worship.

Vyāsa said:

2-3. O dear, listen to the excellent fruit of the worship of the lord of Lakṣmī, hearing which all men obtain excellent knowledge. O brāhmaṇa, listen to the rules according to which the Eternal One should be worshipped in the twelve months like Māgha. I shall (now) tell them.

4-8. When the auspicious month of Māgha, the best of all months, comes, the best devotee of Viṣṇu should give up (eating) flesh and coitus. He should everyday bathe in the morning; he should also avoid (the use of) oils; he should avoid taking food twice (a day) and also the food of others in the month of Māgha. A man, wearing a white garment, should, with a firm mind, begin worshipping Viṣṇu in the morning after having performed the five major sacrifices (viz. *brahmayajña* etc.). With lukewarm, pure water he should give bath to (the image of) the immutable Viṣṇu. He should besmear the parts of the body (of the image) of Viṣṇu with loose (i.e. soft) sandal. He should worship these of the lord of the world, the chief of gods, the Disc-holder. He should dry the vessels that are washed.

9-11. Having bathed (the image of) the lord of the world with lukewarm water, he should carefully dry his body with a divine garment. O best brāhmaṇa, I (shall) tell about the fruit which he who bathes (the image of) Viṣṇu with lukewarm water in the month of Māgha, gets. Freed from all sins committed in former existences, he enjoys all pleasure in this world, and (to enjoy) the remaining pleasure he goes to Viṣṇu's abode.

12-14. Listen to the religious merit of (i.e. obtained by) him who, after having washed the vessels and having purified them with water, would worship the (image of) the lord of the world. Free from all diseases, he, enjoying all desired objects here (i.e. in this world), would finally dwell for thousands of yugas in Viṣṇu's abode. In the morning and in the entire evening a devotee of Viṣṇu should place a smokeless, burning fire in front of (the image of) the Disc-holder (i.e. Viṣṇu).

15-19. Listen to the fruit of, i.e. obtained by, that devotee of Viṣṇu, who would burn fire in the morning and in the evening before (the image of) Viṣṇu in the month of Māgha to keep off cold. He, along with his sons and grandsons, enjoys all desired objects in this world, and in the end goes to Viṣṇu's city, difficult to be reached even by deities. As is his soul (to him) so is Viṣṇu. There is no doubt about this. A man should keep away cold from (the imags of) Viṣṇu sleeping on the bed as he keeps away cold from himself. What does the best god, being pleased, not give to him who would bathe (the image of) Viṣṇu with milk during the month of Māgha? In the same way he should remove the cold (of the image) of the Disc-holder with a divine garment.

20-26. I shall tell the fruit of (i.e. obtained by) him who would worship (the image of) Viṣṇu after bathing him (it) with cocoanut water and milk in the month of Māgha. He, having lifted up a crore of men of his family sinking due to their own acts in the ocean of hell, difficult to cross, goes to the position of the Disc-holder (i.e. Viṣṇu). O best brāhmaṇa, especially during the worship of Viṣṇu on the fifth day of the bright half in the month of Māgha, so also on the Ekādaśī day and the fifth day[1] (in the dark fortnight) rice boiled in milk along with a lamp should be offered to Mura's enemy, the god of gods along with (his spouse) Lakṣmī. O Jaimini, O devotee of Viṣṇu, I shall tell you about the fruit of (i.e. obtained by) him who, everyday in the month of Māgha, offers rice boiled in milk along with incense to the Disc-holder (i.e. Viṣṇu). (Please) listen. Having at the end (of his life) gone to Viṣṇu's city, he enjoys (there) charming pleasures for four periods of Manu due to the grace of the Disc-holder. Again having come to the earth he would be a sovereign emperor. (There) he enjoys pleasures for a very long time and when dead (i.e. after death) goes to Viṣṇu's abode.

27-29. O Jaimini, a devotee of Viṣṇu, who is unable to give (rice boiled in milk) to the enemy of Mura on the fifth day, the seventh day or the eleventh day, should offer him best food. O best brāhmaṇa, the bright half is especially superior to the dark half. On the days (mentioned above) of the bright half one should give food to Viṣṇu. Viṣṇu is not difficult to be attained by him who would give rice boiled in milk along with cakes to Viṣṇu, the conqueror of demons, at least on one day in Māgha.

30-33. There is no doubt that whatever is offered by a man to please a brāhmaṇa in the month of Māgha, would be inexhaustible for him. O brāhmaṇa, there is no destruction of the (fruit of the) act, good or bad, done in the month of Māgha, even after hundreds of ages of Manu. He who would worship Viṣṇu with campaka flowers in the month of Māgha would, after being freed from all sins, go to the highest abode. He stays in

1. The reading should have been '*saptamyām*' in place of '*pañcamyām*', as it rightly occurs in line 27a below.

Viṣṇu's abode for as many thousand yugas as the number of campaka flowers offered to Viṣṇu by him.

34-37. That fruit which is (obtained) by giving gold equal (in weight) to Meru, is obtained by worshipping Viṣṇu with (only) one campaka flower. O best brāhmaṇa, a campaka flower is always dear to Viṣṇu. Especially in the month of Māgha it is pure and dear to Viṣṇu. He who has not worshipped Viṣṇu with divine campaka flowers, would be without gems, without gold etc. in every birth. I am specially telling you the fruit of (the offering of) a campaka flower. O best brāhmaṇa, listen to it, the excellent one, along with its history.

38-44. O brāhmaṇa, a king named Suvarṇa, knowing all holy texts, became powerful in the entire Āryāvarta[1] due to his vigour. O brāhmaṇa sage, he, mad with royal glory, knowledge and youth, was always engaged in sins. By the words of his heretic ministers, he, through his greed for money, punished the good (even) without their fault, O brāhmaṇa. He, without sacrifices and gifts (i.e. who did not perform sacrifices and give gifts), surrounded by music and musical instruments squandered all the wealth obtained unjustly. He, always deluded by sins, did not support his kinsmen, did not feed deities and brāhmaṇas, and did not gratify the suppliants. He, always attached to sins, never honoured a guest. That king, the abode of sins, everyday went (away) from a temple. Was anyone among the indiscriminate ones able to count, even for hundreds of years, the other sins which he had committed?

45-52. Once that wicked-hearted king, deluded by lust, went to a prostitute's house at night. Seeing the king coming, (the prostitute) named Ujjvalā, suddenly getting up from the bed saluted him. Having washed his pair of feet with water from a golden pitcher, she, embracing the king with her arms, seated him on the bed. That king, sprinkled with the streams of the nectar of her love, and being curious remained on that bed. Then that harlot who was quite young, herself gave, with a smile, campaka flowers to the king. A flower from the garland of

1. Āryāvarta: Abode of the noble or the excellent (Āryas). Name of the region extending from the eastern to the western sea, and bounded on the north and south by the Himālaya and the Vindhya respectively.

flowers dropped on the ground from the hand of the king, and pervaded the atmosphere with its fragrance. Seeing the flower that had fallen down, the king, through great confusion said (the words) '*Namo Nārāyaṇāya* (salutation to Nārāyaṇa)' preceded by the syllable '*Oṃ*'. All the sins of the king perished due to (his having uttered) the word 'Nārāyaṇa' and due to the offering of the campaka flower.

53-58. All the villagers also gathered there and killed him that night in the prostitute's invincible house. Yama, who was very angry, sent his servants to take the king, the greatest sinner (to his abode). The messengers ordered by him, with their eyes red due to anger and having nooses and mallets in their hands came there very speedily. Yama's messengers exerted to take him to their abode. Then Nārāyaṇa's (i.e. Viṣṇu's) servants holding conches, discs and maces, and mounted upon Garuḍa came to take the king (to Viṣṇu's abode). Seeing the king bound by a noose, the very powerful servants of Viṣṇu struck Yama's messengers with discs and maces. Putting him into a divine chariot, they blew excellent conches.

59-61. Then the king who had got in the chariot, who was adorned with tulasī (leaves and) flowers, who had put on yellow silken garments, who was adorned with golden ornaments, who was being praised by hosts of sages, masters of the Vedas and the Vedāṅgas, who was surrounded by Viṣṇu's messengers, came to Viṣṇu's world. Then, O best brāhmaṇa, Viṣṇu himself got up, embraced the king with his four long arms and said to him:

The lord said:

62-65. O king, O best among all meritorious souls, tell (me) about (your) welfare. Now let us know what still remains to be attained by you. I always look after him who would even once say: 'Salutation to Nārāyaṇa.' He is my brother; he is my father. I accomplish all the desired objects, like a father to his son, of the man who would sometime remember my name 'Nārāyaṇa'. O best king, you are my devotee. Therefore, disclose your desire. What wonderful object shall I give you now?

The king said:

66-73a. O ocean of pity, you have undoubtedly given (me)

everything. Even a sinner like me has reached your inaccessible place.

By these words of him Lakṣmī's lord was pleased, and he affectionately made him sit. Listen to it (i.e. that account). He, full of pity, himself adorned him with golden ornaments fashioned by Viśvakarman. Viṣṇu, the extremely tolerant one, gratified the king with various kinds of eatables, very difficult to be had even by the divine ones. In this way the king lived in Viṣṇu's abode everyday for thousands of Manu's ages and nine hundred years. The righteous king protected his subjects. With great devotion he always worshipped Viṣṇu with charming campaka flowers and various kinds of offerings of eatables. When the span of his life was over the king died in the water of Gaṅgā and obtained liberation by the grace of Viṣṇu.

Vyāsa said:

73b-78. O brāhmaṇa, I have told you this efficacy of campaka flowers. Sinful persons have been liberated after worshipping Viṣṇu with campaka flowers. O brāhmaṇa sage, revered Viṣṇu, worshipped with a full-blown campaka flower gives the highest position in a short time. Those who worship the highest soul intentionally or even without an intention are freed from all sins, and they also go to the highest position. When Viṣṇu is pleased, nobody is a sinner, since that king, even though he had committed a sin, crossed this deep worldly ocean through Viṣṇu's favour and attained liberation. That man who, abandoning sin, would, with devotion and great respect, worship Nārāyaṇa (i.e. Viṣṇu), having large eyes like lotus-petals, with divine, fragrant campaka flowers would go (to Viṣṇu).

CHAPTER ELEVEN

The Rules of Viṣṇu Worship

Vyāsa said:

1-8. O Jaimini, O brāhmaṇa sage, I (shall) tell you the mode in which Viṣṇu should always be worshipped. Listen to it attentively. A wise man, having got up from his bed in the morning and taking a pot (full) of water, and covering his head with (a piece of) cloth, should go to a place outside (the town). There, the wise man, keeping mum, putting the sacred thread on his ear, should sit in the northern direction and urinate and excrete. He should not urinate or excrete in a temple of a deity, on the way, in cowpens, places where four roads meet, on the main road, in a ploughed soil, at the root of darbhas, in a courtyard, on the sandy bank of a river, at the root of a fig tree standing on a sacred spot, so also in a forest, in lakes and wells. A wise man should urinate and excrete till he does not see the sun, the moon, brāhmaṇas and the ten quarters. To cleanse himself he should not take the clay from inside the holes dug by mice etc. or (from) ploughed soil. A wise man should purify himself with water after bringing it from (a place of) water. A wise man does not purify himself by keeping his foot in water.

9-10. A wise man should answer the nature's call at night by facing the south. Covering his head with (a piece of) cloth he should answer the nature's call. A wise man should apply one (layer of) clay to his organ of generation, three (layers) to his anus, seven to his left hand, and ten to both the hands.

11-21. The wise should apply six (layers of) clay to both the feet. A wise man should brush his teeth after having (thus) purified himself. The cleansing of the teeth along with that of the lips etc. should be done. He should not brush his teeth by facing the south or the west. If he would do so, he would be a resident of hell. O brāhmaṇa, he should brush his teeth with the middle finger or the ring-finger or the thumb but never with the forefinger. A wise man should not brush his teeth with a twig of aśvattha or fig tree or of dhātrī tree; so also with that of devadāru or asura tree (for by doing so) the entire fruit of his daily rites perishes. O Jaimini, the manes of him, so also gods and divine sages, being disappointed with him who brushes his teeth at the time of his bath go (away). The deities do not accept the worship of (i.e. offered by) him, and the manes do not accept the (libations of) water of (i.e. offered by) him who brushes his teeth in the noon or the afternoon. He who brushes his teeth at the time of his bath in a lake, should be known to be a cāṇḍāla till he sees Gaṅgā. The manes of him who brushes his teeth after the revered sun has risen, eat that stick with which he brushes his teeth and being grieved, go (away). A man brushing his teeth on a fast day or a śrāddha day does not get the fruit of it (i.e. of the fast or the śrāddha), O brāhmaṇa. O best brāhmaṇa, he should clean his teeth in the morning and his tongue with (a piece of) cloth. He should have twelve rinsings with water.

22-24. O Jaimini, the man who brushes his teeth in this manner on a fast day or the day of (offering of) śrāddha to the manes, gets the entire fruit. Doing the purification in this manner, the wise one should go into his house and abandon the night-garment. Then the wise, pure one, seated at the door of the chamber of the deity should remember the infinite god, the highest lord, Viṣṇu.

25-30. 'O Rāma, O you of a dark body, O Viṣṇu, O Nārāyaṇa, O you full of pity, O Janārdana, O you abode of the world, O Keśava, remove my sin. O you wearing a yellow garment, O infinite one, O Padmanābha, O you full of the world, O Vāmana, O god, O lord, be the refuge of him who has sought your shelter. O Dāmodara, O greatest of the Yadus, O Śrī Kṛṣṇa, O ocean of pity, O lotus-eyed one, O lord of gods, O Vāsudeva, favour me. O Garuḍa-bannered one, O Govinda, O supporter of all, O holder of the mace, O you having the conch in your hand, O you having the disc in your hand, O you having a lotus in your hand, remove (my) calamities. O you pleasure of Lakṣmī, O Viṣṇu, O Hṛṣīkeśa, O best of gods, O Puruṣottama, O enemy of Kaṁsa, O enemy of Kaiṭabha, remove (my) fear. O Śrīpati (i.e. lord of Lakṣmī), O Śrīdhara, O lord, O Śrīda, O Śrīkara, O Mādhava, O highest Brahman, O highest abode, O immutable one, be my refuge.'

31. O best brāhmaṇa, having thus remembered Viṣṇu, the wise man with the palms of his hands joined, having gone into the house, speaks like this:

32-35. 'O god, O Śrīpati, O Kṛṣṇa, O son of Devakī, O lord, O master of the world, abandon your sleep. It is the morning time.' Then the wise man should think in his mind that Devakī's son along with Lakṣmī is seated on the bed after having given up sleep. Then the devotee of Viṣṇu should give to Kṛṣṇa, a divine, covered pot full of water for washing his face. The intelligent ones serve the highest lord as servants serve their master for their livelihood.

36. O brāhmaṇa sage, the desired object of him who serves the lord of the world as his servant, is soon accomplished.

37-39. As the servants serve their master through fear, so the wise ones always serve Viṣṇu, the lord. O brāhmaṇa, he who, being fearless, serves him with this desire of him, is just a bad servant. He would not be (a devotee). Therefore, O best brāhmaṇa, a man desiring final beatitude, should always render service to the lord of Lakṣmī.

40-44. In the morning a devotee of Viṣṇu should take off from the body of Viṣṇu (i.e. his image) the used flowers, the garment worn during the night, and stale sandal also. Then the wise man should himself sweep the temple. He should slowly clean it with a groom. That man would live in Viṣṇu's house for as many hundred periods of Manu as the number of particles of dust that go out of the temple. Even a murderer of a brāhmaṇa, who sweeps the temple of Viṣṇu, goes to the highest position. What is the use of saying much? He should smear the temple with wool and cowdung. In that temple a wise man should recollect Viṣṇu.

45-51. O Jaimini, I shall tell you in brief about the religious merit of him who smears Viṣṇu's temple. Listen to it. He would happily live in Viṣṇu's house for as many thousands of kalpas as the dust particles that perish (i.e. are removed). One who sweeps and smears Viṣṇu's temple obtains the highest abode. Then what to say about him who knows how to worship the lord? When due to a calamity due to Indra he is not able to do it himself, then he should appoint his wife in Viṣṇu's temple. Or he should appoint his devoted son of good character, or his brother or sister in the god's temple. He should himself very carefully wash the things (needed) for Viṣṇu's worship with pure water seven times or three times. There is no doubt that copper vessels are purified with acid, the vessels of bell-metal are purified with ash, and iron-vessels with fire.

52. Viṣṇu is not pleased with a rich man who bathes Viṣṇu, the lord of the world, with water in an iron pot.

53. If (he does so) through ignorance, he is purified by means of a bath in Gaṅgā. O best brāhmaṇa, in prosperity (i.e. when one is wealthy) one should always follow a rule.

54-62a. It is laid down in the holy texts that there is no rule in adversity. O best brāhmaṇa, when a conch which is carefully washed, touches the ground, it becomes pure after washing it a hundred times. Having in this way carefully washed the materials for worship, he should take materials for his bath and should go to a lake. If he comes home without taking a bath, the hosts of his manes do not accept the libations offered by him on that day. That man who foolishly puts in an obstacle for him who goes for bathing or for taking a meal, would be a resident of hell. There is no doubt that the manes of him who, having gone to a lake for a bath, would urinate or excrete (there) would eat urine and feces. Then having bathed and offered libations according to the rules, a wise man, remembering Viṣṇu, should come home. Then, O brāhmaṇa, the best brāhmaṇa after having washed both his feet in the courtyard should enter the temple of the deity. The religious merit earned during a year, of him who would enter the temple without washing his feet, perishes that moment only.

62b-67. Therefore, a wise man, having come after having bathed, should wash his feet in the courtyard and then enter the temple of the deity. Having sat down, the wise man should wash the pair of his feet with his left hand. Then he should carefully wash both his hands, O brāhmaṇa. O best brānmaṇa, Lakṣmī certainly abandons the fool who washes one of his feet with another or with his right hand. Then the intelligent one, having sat down, and with full concentration should commence the worship of Viṣṇu, giving all desired objects. After sitting upon a pure seat of deer-hide or tiger-hide, or merely on a cloth-seat, or also on the seat of darbhas or of flowers, he should worship Lakṣmī's lord.

68-79. A learned brāhmaṇa should never worship Viṣṇu (after sitting) on a wooden seat. 'O Earth, you are held by Viṣṇu, you sustain all people. Therefore, O you who bear everything, give me an excellent seat to stay.' Speaking like this the worshipper of Viṣṇu should sit on the seat after spreading it out. He should never worship Viṣṇu by facing the South. Having poured water very fragrant and purified with a hymn into a conch, he should bathe the master, Lakṣmī's lord, along with Lakṣmī. O best brāhmaṇa, Jaimini, I shall tell you the fruit of (i.e. obtained by) him who bathes (the image of) the revered Janārdana with (water from) a conch. Listen. Being free from the sins of the murder of a brāhmaṇa, a cow, a woman, or of causing abortion or drinking liquor, he goes to Vaikuṇṭha, and (there) enjoys all pleasures. O brāhmaṇa, if a man on seeing (the image of) Viṣṇu, would worship (it) him, he quickly obtains whatever (he desires) through the grace of Lakṣmī's lord. O best brāhmaṇa, a wise man should, in the absence of a conch, put the fragrant water and tulasī (leaves) in a pot, and should bathe (the image of) Viṣṇu. Then having bathed (the image of the) god and having put (it) him on an excellent seat, he should smear his entire body with fragrant sandal. The man who treats the body of the Disc-holder with the mire of tulasī wood (tulasī-plant), has Viṣṇu always pleased with him. 'O lord of the world, this garland of tulasī leaves, giving pleasure by means of its fragrance is offered to you. Always be very well pleased.' O best brāhmaṇa, what does the great Viṣṇu, adorned with the garland of tulasī leaves to the accompaniment of this hymn, and pleased, not give? Then he should make the solemn observance with the hymns from the Veda.

80-89. The wise ones should then fix the directions with hymns from the Purāṇas: 'May Kṛṣṇa protect in the east. May Devakī's son protect in the south-east. May the enemy of demons protect in the south. May Madhusūdana protect in the south-west. May the Śrīmat (i.e. having Lakṣmī) protect in the intermediate directions. May Śrīdhara protect upwards. May the universal soul, of the form of the tortoise and full of pity protect from below. May all those who cause obstacles at the time of (Viṣṇu's) worship, go away, being struck by the missile of Viṣṇu's name.' Having thus fixed the directions he, bowing and with his palms joined, makes a solemn vow by means of the hymn to be told (hereafter): 'O god of gods, O Janārdana, make this worship commenced by me free from obstacles and successful. Be pleased, O highest god.' Having made a solemn vow (like this) a devotee of Viṣṇu, knowing everything, should assign the various parts of his body to different deities, and should meditate, with his heart on god Viṣṇu, resembling a fresh cloud, having eyes like lotuses, wearing a yellow garment, having a very charming, smiling face, adorned with the garlands of kadamba flowers, having very large arms, having ear-rings with the row of peacock's feathers on his head, deluding the ten directions with the sweet sound of his flute, surrounded by cowherdesses, and living in the charming Vṛndāvana. Having thus meditated upon the lord of gods, Viṣṇu, giving all desired objects, the devotee of Viṣṇu should then devoutly invoke him.

90-92a. The wise one should then offer water for washing his feet, materials of worship and water for sipping to Kṛṣṇa who is invoked and who grants the four goals of human life. The wise one should worship Śrī Kṛṣṇa, Devakī's son and the lord of all gods, with tender tulasī leaves or charming flowers.

92b-101. 'Salutations to Matsya (incarnation), to Kūrma incarnation. Repeated salutations to Varāha (incarnation). Salutation to you, Hari; repeated salutations to Vāmana. Salutation to the powerful Rāma, Rāma, Rāma. Repeated salutations to pure Buddha (the enlightened one), having pity. Salutation to you, Kalki; salutation to you of many forms. Salutation to you, Nārāyaṇa, Kṛṣṇa, Govinda, the holder of the Śārṅga bow, to Dāmodara, to the lord, to the god of gods. Salutation to Hṛṣīkeśa, to Śānta (the tranquil one), to Vyomapāda (whose feet are extended in the heaven). Salutation to the lord of Lakṣmī. Salutation to (you) having lotus-like eyes. Salutation to you Ananta, to you having mace in your hand, to you, Garuḍa-bannered (one), to you having the disc in your hand. Repeated salutations to you having the lotus in your hand, to Acyuta. Salutation to you, the enemy of demons and giving all desired objects. I always salute Mādhava, Sureśa (lord of gods), Viṣṇu, the highest soul, the one having a crown and ear-rings. Salutation to you, the revered one.' The wise one (should invoke Viṣṇu's) vehicle called Garuḍa with the hymn: 'Salutation to Garuḍa. Salutation to (his) conch, to (his) disc. Repeated salutations to (his) mace. Repeated salutations to (his) lotus, to his sword Nandaka.'

102-104. Having thus worshipped the lord of gods along with his consort and vehicle and weapons, the wise one should repeat the eight-syllabled formula. The wise one having then devoutly repeated the eight-syllabled formula, should offer Viṣṇu many excellent eatables. The devotee of Viṣṇu should also offer god Viṣṇu incense, lamp, tāmbūla and other presents.

105. The desired object of him who would offer Viṣṇu excellent incense made fragrant with sandal and agaru, is accomplished quickly, O best brāhmaṇa.

106. O brāhmaṇa, he who offers Viṣṇu incense made fragrant with ghee, would, after being free from crores of sins, go to Viṣṇu's abode.

107. He who would offer Viṣṇu incense made fragrant with resin, goes to the highest abode, inaccessible even to gods.

108. Viṣṇu in a moment removes all the sins of him who offers him a lamp with ghee or sesamum oil.

109. O best brāhmaṇa, O Jaimini, he who would give a tāmbūla made fragrant with camphor to Viṣṇu, gets liberation.

110. He who gives a tāmbūla with khadira, ultimately goes to Viṣṇu's place after having enjoyed all pleasure here (i.e. in this world).

111. A man, after offering a tāmbūla with ṣaṣṭimadhurikā (?) and nutmeg to Viṣṇu, would obtain heaven.

112-113. O Jaimini, the devotee of Viṣṇu, should go round him (i.e. his image) after keeping water in a conch, to the accompaniment of the hymn which will be told (now). 'O Janārdana, friend of the world, O you protector of those who seek your refuge, O lord, give me the status of the servant of the servant of your servant.'

114-119. O Jaimini, I shall tell you in brief the fruit of the religious merit of him who would go round (the image of) Viṣṇu with (i.e. repeating) this hymn. At every step of the going round (the image of) Viṣṇu sins like the murder of a brāhmaṇa, and (other) major sins perish. For as many thousands of kalpas a man rejoices with Viṣṇu as the steps he would devoutly walk while going round Viṣṇu. When a man slowly walks step by step while going round Viṣṇu, he obtains the fruit of a horse-sacrifice at every step. A crore-fold greater fruit would be obtained by going round (the image of) Viṣṇu than the fruit (obtained by) going round all (other images) in the worldly existence. Even he who goes round himself in front of (the image of) Viṣṇu, gets the same fruit. What is the use of many other words?

120-123. An intelligent man, while going round (the Liṅga of) Śiva, should not cross the receptacle for receiving the water with which the Liṅga has been bathed. By crossing it (i.e. if a man crosses it) his worship (of Śiva) would be fruitless. O best brāhmaṇa, he who would even once go round Viṣṇu, would certainly become a sovereign emperor in every birth. O brāhmaṇa, he who would go round Viṣṇu twice, obtains Indra's position within three days. There is no doubt about this. The man who would go round (the image of) Viṣṇu twice, would enter, after being freed from all sins, Viṣṇu's body.

124-125. O Jaimini, he who after entering a temple, would wave a conch over (the image of) Viṣṇu, would be honoured by gods. The sin in the body of him who would salute (the image of) Viṣṇu (by prostrating himself) like a staff on the ground, is reduced to ash that moment only.

126. Lakṣmī's lord Viṣṇu gives him who would salute Janārdana with his palms joined and placed on his head, the highest position.

127-129a. O brāhmaṇa sage, listen to the efficacy which I am telling, of the religious merit of those men who drop their entire body (i.e. prostrate themselves) on the ground and salute Viṣṇu. For as many thousands of kalpas as the dust particles with which their bodies are decorated, these men stay with Viṣṇu. Then the flowers taken off from (the image of) Viṣṇu are offered to the devotees of Viṣṇu.

129b-131. I shall tell you about these devotees of Viṣṇu. O best one, O Jaimini, listen. 'May Śuka, Sūta, so also Vyāsa, Nārada, sage Kapila, Prahlāda, Ambarīṣa, so also Akrūra and Uddhava, Bibhīṣaṇa, Hanūmān, and other devotees of Viṣṇu also accept the flowers taken off from (the image of) Viṣṇu, giving all desired objects.'

132-133. Saying so the devotee should drop on the ground the flowers taken off from (the image of) Viṣṇu. Then he himself devoutly accepts the flowers taken off from (the image of) Viṣṇu. O best brāhmaṇa, he on whose head are seen the excellent flowers taken off from (the image of) Viṣṇu, should be known to be actually Viṣṇu himself.

134-138. All deities take the offerings of eatables to Viṣṇu, and flowers taken off from (the image of) him, which are difficult to be had, and which destroy sins. Then what need one say about human beings? O Jaimini, all the sins remaining in the body of the devotee of Viṣṇu, who smells a tulasī leaf, perish. The diseases in the body of him, into whose nose the fragrance of a tulasī leaf enters, instantly perish. O best brāhmaṇa, joy always exists in the house of him who rejoices after smelling the fragrance of a tulasī leaf. A wise man, with his palms joined, having praised the lord of the world with eulogies, should recite this hymn:

139-140. 'O Nārāyaṇa, O you of the form of the world, O you lord of the world, go home. O god, go to your place. Always be pleased. O lord of the world, O you full of the world, may the worship which I offered according to my capacity be faultless through your grace.'

141. Then the wise one should devoutly take the water (flowing) from the feet of Viṣṇu, the highest soul, and destroying all sins.

142. He who carries (on his body) even a drop of water (flowing) from Viṣṇu's feet, has bathed at all holy places. I have told you the truth.

143. He should touch the water (flowing) from the feet of Viṣṇu. It would give him the fruit of a bath in Gaṅgā, since the water of Gaṅgā is the water (flowing) from the feet of Viṣṇu.

144. For him who would touch the water (flowing) from Viṣṇu's feet there is no untimely death nor any fear from a disease.

145-147. May even sinful men drink everyday the medicine of the water (flowing) from the feet of Viṣṇu for the destruction of their sins and diseases. O brāhmaṇa, the sin in the body of that man who would drink the water (flowing) from Viṣṇu's feet perishes just in a moment. As by a medicine (the disease) in a human body is very much destroyed, in exactly the same way all the sin is destroyed by the water (flowing) from Viṣṇu's feet.

148-149. O brāhmaṇa, I shall tell you about the religious merit of (i.e. obtained by) him who would carry on his head the pure water (flowing) from Viṣṇu's feet along with a tulasī leaf. He, freed from all sins like the murder of a brāhmaṇa, and assuming Viṣṇu's form, ultimately goes to Viṣṇu's city and rejoices with him.

150. A greater fruit would be obtained by touching the water (flowing) from Viṣṇu's feet than by giving gold equal to the measure of Meru (mountain).

151-154. A man who touches the water (flowing) from Viṣṇu's feet obtains that fruit which men get by giving a crore of horses, or which one would get by giving the earth with the seven islands to brāhmaṇas. A greater fruit would be obtained by touching the water (flowing) from the feet of Viṣṇu than the one that would be (obtained) by performing thousands of horse-sacrifices. A man would get a bigger fruit by touching the water (flowing) from the feet of Viṣṇu than the religious merit declared (to be got) by giving a hundred wells. What is the use of speaking much in this matter? I shall tell it in brief.

155-160a. A man becomes free due to the touch of the water (flowing) from Viṣṇu's feet. O best brāhmaṇa, I am repeatedly telling (this) firmly. He who touches the water (flowing) from Viṣṇu's feet, does not get rebirth. He who would devoutly eat the remnants of the eatables offered to Viṣṇu, which destroy all the sins, would go to the highest position. The body of him who, O best brāhmaṇa, eats the eatables offered to Viṣṇu, which are difficult to be had, abandons the sins even like the murder of a brāhmaṇa. The land of liberation, difficult to be obtained even by deities like the greatest god, would be obedient to him like a maid, who eats the articles of food offered to Viṣṇu. Viṣṇu soon takes him to his own body, who worships Viṣṇu without abandoning any of the eatables offered to Viṣṇu.

160b-169. How can I tell you the efficacy of the eatables offered to great Viṣṇu, on the enjoyer of which even Viṣṇu is dependent, O lord of brāhmaṇas? O brāhmaṇa, he who would devoutly offer excellent worship to Śrī Viṣṇu in this manner, even without the proper religious ceremony, every month, also would be dear to Viṣṇu, and would obtain the same fruit which he who knows the religious ceremony would get after performing the worship of Viṣṇu with the proper religious ceremony. O brāhmaṇa, O lord, if there is no devotion, then the lord would not be pleased even if he is worshipped with many offerings of eatables. There is no doubt that one gets as much fruit as is his devotion to the god. That worship of Viṣṇu which men perform without devotion would be a worship at a wrong time, O best brāhmaṇa. Knowledge is the root of devotion. Devotion is the root of Viṣṇu. For the coming up of the liberation due to worship, the root is the propitiation of Viṣṇu. All that, even very little which a man does with faith, would be inexhaustible, O wise one; (for) every act is accompanied by faith. O brāhmaṇa, he who devoutly worships Viṣṇu even (with) little water, obtains the position of Viṣṇu, since Viṣṇu is dependent on his devotees.

170. O brāhmaṇa, this entire world is worthless. Worship of Viṣṇu is the only truth. Therefore, a man desiring his good should worship Kṛṣṇa of infinite forms.

CHAPTER TWELVE

The Greatness of the Holy Fig Tree

Vyāsa said:

1-2. O best brāhmaṇa, a devotee of Viṣṇu should everyday in (the month of) Phālguna devoutly worship Śrī Kṛṣṇa saluted by gods. Listen properly to the fruit which I shall tell, of (i.e. obtained by) him who would bathe Devakī's son with clarified butter in Phālguna.

3-6. He, having received the fruit of all sacrifices and of all gifts, and freed from all sins goes in the end to Viṣṇu's place. Having enjoyed pleasures in Viṣṇu's abode for thousands of crores of yugas, he, having obtained excellent knowledge, obtains liberation there only. He who offers, in winter, sweet-meat made of sesamum-seeds to Kṛṣṇa, of the form of a cowherd, would go to Viṣṇu's abode. He who would offer sweet balls made with ghee to Viṣṇu, the highest soul, would drink nectar in heaven for a period of hundreds of Manu's ages.

7-9. Viṣṇu, with his mind pleased, cuts off the bond of the mundane existence of him who offers pleasing candied sugar to

Viṣṇu, O Jaimini. O brāhmaṇa, a man should offer a beautiful fruit to the god. In the end he goes to Indra's city and would be honoured by gods. What does he who, the devoted one, would offer pure sugar to Kṛṣṇa, not obtain through Vāsudeva's grace, O brāhmaṇa?

10-12. Listen to the fruit of (i.e. obtained by) him who offers a very ripe, sweet, badari-fruit to Kṛṣṇa in the month of Phālguna? Along with his sons and grandsons he enjoys all pleasures here (i.e. in this world), and getting into a beautiful chariot, goes to Viṣṇu's abode in the end. A man should not give a badari-fruit with jaggery to Viṣṇu. O best brāhmaṇa, if, through ignorance, he would give it, he would be a resident of hell.

13-16. O brāhmaṇa, listen from me who am telling it, to the fruit of (i.e. obtained by) him who offers a very ripe pomegranate to Viṣṇu in the month of Phālguna. The lucky one stays for as many ages of Manu as there are seeds in the pomegranate in Viṣṇu's abode. O best brāhmaṇa, he who offers a mixture of flour and molasses ground and boiled together to Viṣṇu in the month of Phālguna, should be known to be the performer of a thousand horse-sacrifices. O best brāhmaṇa, the man who would bathe (the image of) Viṣṇu with honey in the month of Caitra, obtains the highest position of Viṣṇu.

17-18. The Sun's son (i.e. Yama) never makes an inquiry of him who would bathe (the image of) Nārāyaṇa, Anāmaya with honey (in the month of Caitra). The name of him who would bathe (the image of) Lakṣmī's lord with a kiṁśuka flower, is not written by Citragupta in his record.

19-21. When in Caitra Kṛṣṇa, the lord of the worlds, is worshipped with tilaka flowers by a man, then he is not reborn on the earth. A man worshipping Kṛṣṇa, the crest-jewel of all gods, with a black aśoka flower, never meets with a calamity. He who with a pleased mind, worships in the spring, the lord with fragrant vernal (flowers), is honoured even by gods.

22. The lord, seated on the altar, himself gets up and honours him who would worship Viṣṇu with divine, unbroken sprouts.

23-24. A man who would worship Viṣṇu with fresh, tender dhātrī leaves, soon obtains his desired object. He who would worship lord Viṣṇu with bilva leaves, with flower of white thorn-apple and flowers of sun-plant, crosses the ocean of the worldly existence.

25. O brāhmaṇa, all gods like Indra day and night honour him who would offer an excellent plantain fruit to Viṣṇu.

26. O brāhmaṇa, he who would devoutly offer wheat-flour to Viṣṇu of the form of a cowherd, is freed from all sins.

27-32. When the sacred month of Vaiśākha, dear to Viṣṇu, arrives, a devotee of Viṣṇu should abandon flesh, coitus and oil. In the month of Vaiśākha a devotee of Viṣṇu should bathe in the morning, should avoid the food of others, and should not eat twice (a day). In the morning, O brāhmaṇa, he should worship Viṣṇu according to the mode mentioned already. In (the month of) Vaiśākha he should bathe (the image of) Viṣṇu with water made fragrant with flowers. Till twilight he should bathe (the image of Viṣṇu) in cold water. Thrice a day (i.e. at dawn, in the noon and at sunset) he should devoutly worship the lord with various offerings of eatables. O brāhmaṇa sage, what would the lord of Lakṣmī, the highest god, decorated with the garlands of damana in Vaiśākha, and (therefore) pleased, not give (to the devotee)? Which wise man is able to measure the religious merit of him who would offer barley-food to the Disc-holder (i.e. Viṣṇu) in the month of Vaiśākha?

33-34. All that is offered to Viṣṇu only in the month of Vaiśākha to please him, would be inexhaustible. O brāhmaṇa, any other good act done in the month of Vaiśākha to please Viṣṇu, does not perish.

35-38. A man who puts up a place where water is distributed to travellers in the month of Vaiśākha to please Viṣṇu, everyday gets the fruit of a horse-sacrifice. Vaiśākha is a month difficult to be had. It gives the fruits of all acts. Abandoning even hundreds of other acts Viṣṇu should be worshipped during that month. He who worships Viṣṇu even for a day in Vaiśākha, obtains that fruit which is obtained by having worshipped Viṣṇu for six years. A man should worship Viṣṇu of the form of the holy fig tree everyday in Vaiśākha for securing the four goals of human life.

39-42. He who would worship the holy fig tree with a handful of water, would, after being free from crores of sins, go to the highest place. What would the lord in the form of the holy fig tree not give to him who binds the roots (i.e. puts up a platform around the roots) of the holy fig tree with stones etc., O brāhmaṇa sage? He also, who, on seeing the holy fig tree, salutes it, goes to the highest place. (The span of) his life increases. There is no doubt about this. O Jaimini, there is no want or excess in the rite which, O brāhmaṇa, a man performs at the root of the holy fig tree.

43-55. O Jaimini, all holy places like the Three-streamed (Gaṅgā) are present there where even one holy fig tree, the best among the trees, stands. O brāhmaṇa, he who would worship the holy fig tree, worships Viṣṇu, since the lord himself is of the form of the holy fig tree. There is no act in the world doing which he who, a fool, through disrespect, hurts the holy fig tree, is purified, O best brāhmaṇa. This holy fig tree, the lord of trees, is glorified to be Viṣṇu's form. Therefore, there is no savior of those who hurt a holy fig tree. O brāhmaṇa, Viṣṇu would remove the sin remaining in the body of him who seeing a holy fig tree, afterwards touches it and salutes it. Yama himself extracts with fish-hooks the eyes of him who sees him who harms a holy fig tree, and though capable, would not ward him off. Yama himself cuts off with a knife the tongue of him who, a fool, would not say: 'Do not cut off the holy fig tree.' That man who hurts even one small branch of a holy fig tree, obtains the fruit of a crore of murders of brāhmaṇas. That fierce sin which is involved in the murder of a brāhmaṇa, in violating the wife of one's preceptor, in drinking liquor, so also in snatching others' deposits, that sin which is involved in causing an abortion, in killing a cow, in the murder of a woman, in adultery, in killing him who has sought one's refuge, so also in killing one's friend, in not speaking in confidence, in killing one's husband, in censuring others, in eating on a day of (i.e. sacred to) Viṣṇu, is committed by men by cutting off a holy fig tree. No sinner, comparable to him who hurts a holy fig tree, Viṣṇu's form, is heard on the earth.

56. I am telling the importance of the holy fig tree along with its history. O best brāhmaṇa, O dear, listen to it attentively.

57-63. O brāhmaṇa, formerly in Tretāyuga there was a brāhmaṇa devoted to Viṣṇu and engaged in the welfare of all beings. He was always delighted in honouring his relatives; he was always delighted in offering a lamp (to Viṣṇu). He spoke the truth; he had conquered his anger. He was harmless and without religious hypocrisy. O best brāhmaṇa, he, striving after final emancipation, always worshipped lord Viṣṇu, the highest god, with great devotion. The lord, knowing his very firm devotion, took away his entire wealth with some motive. Yet that very intelligent, best brāhmaṇa, everyday worshipped the noble Viṣṇu with great devotion. O brāhmaṇa, all his wealth earned with difficulty, perished. The brāhmaṇa, knowing the highest truth, seeing that also with grief that cannot be conceived by mind, gave up eating (food) after making his mind firm in the worship of the great Viṣṇu.

64-67. Knowing the devotion of that brāhmaṇa Viṣṇu, giving tranquillity, also again brought about the destruction of his relatives. O best brāhmaṇa, the brāhmaṇa's relatives, deluded by Viṣṇu's Māyā, always commenced doing harm (to others). The brāhmaṇa accomplished by means of restrictions and pleased, always worshipped Viṣṇu with great devotion. The brāhmaṇa, having made arrangement to secure money for the worship of Viṣṇu, (worshipped) Mādhava, the lord of the world, and gave up grief for his relatives.

68-69. O Jaimini, great Viṣṇu, though kind to him, being curious, took away even his sons day by day. Yet that best brāhmaṇa everyday worshipped Viṣṇu, the destroyer of distress, with double the former devotion.

70-73. O brāhmaṇa, then his wife, extremely distressed due to grief and affliction, and being deluded by Viṣṇu' s Māyā, went to her father's house. That lonely brāhmaṇa, highly given to Viṣṇu's devotion, never minded any calamity on account of his good heart. O best brāhmaṇa, once he, the best among Viṣṇu's devotees, taking an axe on his shoulder went to a forest. The brāhmaṇa, having no clothes, warded off cold everyday in winter after bringing wood from the forest.

74-77. Once the best brāhmaṇa was unable to go to the forest. (So) he cut off a branch of a holy fig tree standing in the courtyard (of his house). Meantime great Viṣṇu, the best of gods, with his mind distressed by agony came out of the holy fig tree. In front of him the brāhmaṇa happily saw Viṣṇu, the highest god, having four arms, large eyes like lotus-petals, having worn a yellow garment, having ear-rings, good hair, and having his weapons like the lotus etc., resembling a new cloud, very much reddened in the evening, due to large streams of blood flowing (from his body), (resembling) fire, and invisible (even) to the hosts of gods. The brāhmaṇa with his pair of eyes charming due to streams of tears of joy, praised (him) with soft words.

The brāhmaṇa said:

78-85. O Hari, Murāri, the only lord of the world, Govinda, Dāmodara, Mādhava, lord of Lakṣmī, Keśava, enemy of Keśin, Nārāyaṇa, infinite one, lord, be pleased. How can I describe your advent? In this world there is none else except you. O Acyuta, having given one the entire world full of virtues or having given compassion whereby one looks upon one's own (persons) and others as equal, why do you, O Viṣṇu, why do you take away the devotion for you, which resides in one's body? By getting (i.e. if I get) wealth I shall give (i.e. part with) my joy. Devotion given to the great is very blessed. Since I constantly look upon the greatest sinner as a noble one, a sinner (like me) never sees your pair of feet meditated upon by gods. Though I am the greatest among the unhappy, yet I myself, with my eyes, am actually seeing you, like Indra, the soul of the worlds. I do not know even a small worship of you. Nor have I ever given any wealth to you. Yet, O Keśava, in front of me you, the only adorable one, are seen in a bodily form. You have given me this tree of devotion. It is full of piety, material welfare, and desire of sensual enjoyments. O lord, it, sprinkled with the water of your sight, has today borne the fruit of final emancipation. O Keśava, O you of a universal form, of all the heads in the world my head will be the best. O god of gods, my mind now goes to the couple of your lotus-like feet.

Vyāsa said:

86. That brāhmaṇa, having thus praised Jagannātha (i.e. lord of the world), Nārāyaṇa, Anāmaya, again, with the palms of his hands joined, devoutly spoke to him thus:

The brāhmaṇa said:

87-88. O god of gods, O lord of the world, O you who favour the world, with these strokes of the whip your body is wet with blood. In a battle you killed the members of the family of the demons. O lord, on the earth who is able to kill you? This is very wonderful.

The lord said:

89-90. O dear, you have undoubtedly spoken the truth. Neither a demon nor a fiend can kill me. O brāhmaṇa, I am just of the form of the holy fig tree. You cut me off with an axe. Therefore, there was now bleeding from my body.

Vyāsa said:

91-94. Hearing these words of him the brāhmaṇa, distressed with fear, censured himself in many ways. "Fie upon me, the unfortunate one and the greatest among sinners, who caused great grief to the heart of the lord of the three worlds. Viṣṇu removes all sins and he was hurt by me. Who can make me go beyond this sin? He, on whose being pleased sinners are honoured by gods, is distressed due to the trouble given by me. Oh, I am doomed!

95-96. I, a sinner, have caused pain to the heart of him whom gods like Brahmā please with great devotion. What is the use of austerities, mutterings of hymns, or life in the house to me, (since) this only giver of piety, material welfare, of sensual enjoyments and liberation is distressed with pain."

97-98. O best brāhmaṇa, speaking like this he decided to put that axe only at his throat (i.e. to cut off his throat with that axe), to please Viṣṇu. Seeing his great devotion, the kind lord of Lakṣmī, loving his devotees, quickly took it away from his hand.

The lord said:

99-100. O dear, how (i.e. why) do you do such a very dreadful act? I am never pleased with men who commit suicide? I am very much pleased with your devotion. O best one, do not entertain fear. O best brāhmaṇa, choose a boon that is in your mind.

The brāhmaṇa said:

101. O highest god, I caused great pain to you. O lord, may it not remain in your body. This is the boon I choose, O lord.

The lord said:

102-105a. O dear, O brāhmaṇa, you did this act through ignorance. You should not, therefore, even regard it as a great offence. I am always obedient to you, since you are the greatest among devotees. Everyday I know your errors (i.e. you erred). Yet your devotion for me always increased. Therefore, O dear, I now desire to be free from your debt. Giving up all fear, choose a boon in front of (i.e. from) me.

The brāhmaṇa said:

105b-106a. O Viṣṇu, O best god, may I have very strong devotion for you in every birth.

Vyāsa said:

106b-108a. Hearing these words of him spoken due to affection for Viṣṇu, (Viṣṇu) being pleased, then gave him the garland that was (put) around his own neck. Then as a father embraces his son, he embraced the brāhmaṇa, with his four long arms, and spoke (these) soft words (to him):

The lord said:

108b-114. O brāhmaṇa, since you are my devotee, therefore you will soon have all prosperity. O brāhmaṇa, O best one, everyday propitiate me in the form of the Aśvattha tree with the employment of (proper) rites. I shall accomplish all your desired objects.

Speaking like this to the best brāhmaṇa and embracing him again, Viṣṇu, the abode of compassion, disappeared just there. That best devotee of Viṣṇu, that brāhmaṇa, having received the garland from the neck of Viṣṇu, regarded himself as having done his duty and remained in his own house. Then, O brāhmaṇa sage, Kubera himself, by Viṣṇu's order, showered much wealth into his house. The architect (of gods) Viśvakarman fashioned for him, by Viṣṇu's order, an excellent palace like that of Indra.

It was having male and female servants. It was adorned with various things.

115-118. His abode crowded with crores of elephants and horses, shone. Even his relatives who were dead, were (again) united with him. His wife who had disrespected him, came home of her own accord. O brāhmaṇa, his wife whose sons were dead, had stable progeny due to the favour of Viṣṇu, and she was highly devoted to her husband. That best brāhmaṇa, having, for a long time, along with his sons and grandsons, enjoyed all pleasures, attained at the end of his life along with his wife liberation.

Vyāsa said:

119-120. The excellent, holy fig tree is actually Viṣṇu himself. Those men who worship it, never face any calamity. O best man, Viṣṇu, being pleased, gives him who, meditating upon Viṣṇu, worships the holy fig tree, the highest position.

CHAPTER THIRTEEN

Viṣṇu's Worship with Lotuses: The Story of Prajā

Vyāsa said:

1-4. O best brāhmaṇa, in the month of Jyeṣṭha (a man) should devoutly worship lord Viṣṇu after having bathed him (i.e. his image) with cold water. Everyday in summer unguents, fragrant āmalaka, fragrant oil should be offered to Viṣṇu. In a pavilion (having free access) to people he should everyday install (the image of) the lord of Lakṣmī in a temple which is made very fragrant, which is cool and very charming. One should not install (the image of) the lord of Lakṣmī in a hot place, in a place full of smoke or fuel, or in a lying-in chamber.

5-11. O best brāhmaṇa, what does the lord of Kamalā, very much pleased when fanned with very long, white chowries in Jyeṣṭha, not give? O best one, Viṣṇu fanned with fans made of the feathers of peacocks in the summer soon gives everything that is desired. All those who fan Viṣṇu with breezes from a fan or from a pure (piece of) cloth, go to heaven. O best brāhmaṇa, one who in summer, when it arrives, smears the body of Mādhava with fragrant pastes or with sandal, enters his body. There is no doubt that he is liberated. One should install (the image of) Viṣṇu in a garden with blossoming flowers, so also in a tulasī-grove, having gentle breezes at twilight. He who has adorned Viṣṇu with pāṭala flowers in Jyeṣṭha, should be known to be the performer of a thousand horse-sacrifices.

12-16. Viṣṇu would give that man the position of a king in every birth, who would give a necklace of pearls to him in summer. O brāhmaṇa, listen to the fruit of the religious merit of him who decorates Śrī Kṛṣṇa with jewelled necklace, from me who am telling it. He, decorated with a jewelled necklace, would live in Viṣṇu's city till Brahmā creates the entire world, O Jaimini. He also, who decorates Kṛṣṇa with golden or silver ornaments in summer, would get the (same) fruit. He who gives god Viṣṇu a beautiful bed with a pillow, is never unhappy. In summer heavy garments should not be given (to Viṣṇu).

17-21. O best brāhmaṇa, light, pure silken garment should be given to Viṣṇu (in summer). He who would worship Viṣṇu with divine, fragrant fruits of acyuta (Morinda Tinctoria), would in the end go to Indra's city, and would gladly drink nectar (there). He too, who would worship Lakṣmī's lord with the divine fruits of priyāla (Buchanania Latifolia), would get the (same) fruit. What is the use of speaking so many words? That devotee of Viṣṇu, who devoutly offers in summer very cold rice-gruel with sauce (does not again drink the milk from a mother's breasts, i.e. is not reborn). O best brāhmaṇa, that wise man also, who, in the month of Āṣāḍha, would devoutly worship Viṣṇu, after bathing him (i.e. his image) with curd, does not again drink the milk from a mother's breasts (i.e. is not reborn).

22-23. O brāhmaṇa sage, he who at the advent of rainy season worships (Viṣṇu) dark like a cloud with kadamba flowers, would obtain the highest position. That brāhmaṇa whose pavilion looks like fire with garlands of kadamba flowers, would have the fruit of a horse sacrifice, O greatest brāhmaṇa.

24-25. O best brāhmaṇa, the lord of Lakṣmī worshipped

with fragrant ketakī flowers does remove all miseries of human beings. Lord Viṣṇu worshipped with divine, very ripe bread-fruits mixed with ghee, would give excellent affluence.

26-33. O best brāhmaṇa, a devotee of Viṣṇu, desiring liberation, should devoutly offer boiled rice mixed with curd to Viṣṇu everyday in the month of Āṣāḍha. That devotee of Viṣṇu who offers butter to Kṛṣṇa, is purified from all sins, and goes to Brahmā's world. He who would worship the highest soul with the flower of śephālikā (Vitex Negundo) and jasmine flowers, would go to the highest position. He who would worship Viṣṇu with full-blown fragrant, jasmine flowers, would not be (born) due to the religious merit on account of that, O brāhmaṇa. The man, worshipping Viṣṇu, the friend of the world, with kanda (Amorphophallus Campanulatus) flowers, obtains all his desired objects. Viṣṇu is always pleased with him who would worship Viṣṇu with large flowers and full-blown Barleria flowers. He who worships Viṣṇu with sairīyaka (Barleria Cristata) flowers, herb-flowers, and karavīra (Terminalia Arjuna) flowers, goes near Viṣṇu. O brāhmaṇa, all-round prosperity exists in the house of him who would offer parched grain with ghee to Viṣṇu in Śrāvaṇa.

34-35. O greatest brāhmaṇa, a wise man should devoutly worship Nārāyaṇa, Anāmaya, giving the four goals in human life, in the month of Bhādrapada. He should install (the image of) lord Viṣṇu having lotus-like eyes in a house newly constructed and free from every obstacle.

36-37. A man should not install (the image of) Viṣṇu in an old house crowded with gad-flies, mosquitoes and flies etc. A wise man should not install (the image of) the highest lord Viṣṇu in a house with mud, with its doors and walls falling down.

38-39. O best brāhmaṇa, a man who fashions a beautiful candrātapa (a hall with a roof only) in Viṣṇu's temple, goes to the world of the Moon. At night at the time of worship he should drive away, with many kinds of incense in the lord's temple, gad-flies and mosquitoes.

40. In rainy season he should install (the image of) Viṣṇu lying on a bed in a divine temple at night after covering him with emeralds.

41-42. He who desires liberation, should, everyday in the month of Bhādrapada worship the lord of gods with fresh, fragrant lotuses. He should not worship Viṣṇu with ketakī flowers in Bhādrapada, since in the month of Bhādrapada ketakī is like liquor.

43-45. He who worships Yadunandana (i.e. Kṛṣṇa) with ripe, divine palmyra fruits, does not again have the great trouble of remaining in the womb (i.e. being born). That man who devoutly would offer a ripe palmyra fruit mixed with ghee and milk to Viṣṇu would go to Viṣṇu's abode. O best brāhmaṇa, a devotee of Viṣṇu should offer, in the month of Bhādrapada, palmyra powder along with ghee to Viṣṇu in order to obtain the Absolute.

46. O brāhmaṇa, Viṣṇu's devotee, desiring liberation, should not eat any vegetable in the month of Bhādrapada. He should not eat at night.

47-49a. O best brāhmaṇa, Lakṣmī's lord accepts that water as nectar which people offer to him, O brāhmaṇa, and which removes distress, in the forenoon (of a day) in the month of Āśvina.

49b-50. O best brāhmaṇa, that water which is offered at midday to Viṣṇu, should be known as water, and he accepts it (as water). That water which is offered to Govinda in the afternoon, would be like blood. Viṣṇu does not accept it. Therefore, O best brāhmaṇa, one should worship Viṣṇu in the forenoon.

51-54a. Due to Viṣṇu's compassion one gets all desired objects. O best brāhmaṇa, one should not worship Viṣṇu while having (just) one garment on one's body. If one performs (Viṣṇu's) worship like that, Viṣṇu does not accept it. That worship of Viṣṇu which one performs, with the garment on one's body not washed, is fruitless; and Viṣṇu is not pleased. Those who, without tying the tuft of hair on the crowns of their heads, perform the worship of the Disc-holder (i.e. Viṣṇu), do not obtain the fruit of the worship. It would be accepted by hogs.

54b-56a. O best brāhmaṇa, that worship of Viṣṇu which is performed in a house that is not purified, would indeed be accepted by hogs. O brāhmaṇa, a wise man does not bathe, worship deities, give gifts or honour his manes without having (sectarian) marks (on his body).

56b-57a. That entire holy act which is done without having

sectarian marks on his body by a devotee, is reduced to ash. And the doer would be a resident of hell.

57b-60. O best brāhmaṇa, he whose body is marked with (the marks of) a conch, a disc, a mace, a lotus, should be known to be Viṣṇu himself. There is no doubt that he who would draw (the marks) of a conch and a lotus on his right hand, and (the marks of) a disc and a mace on his left hand is Viṣṇu (himself). All sin of him who would draw (the mark) of a lotus upon (the mark of) the conch perishes in a moment.

61. Even gods like Indra salute him who would draw (the mark of) a mace upon (that of) the disc, O brāhmaṇa. A wise man should also draw (the marks of) the couple of the feet of Viṣṇu on his forehead.

62-67. Seeing him, even a sinner becomes free from his sin(s). That best devotee of Viṣṇu who would draw on his chest the eight-syllabled great formula, (the marks of) a fish and a tortoise purifies the three worlds. Kṛṣṇa, the lord of the world, gives him whose body is everyday marked with drawings of Kṛṣṇa's weapons, the highest position. All that act, auspicious or inauspicious, that a man whose body is marked with (the drawings of) the weapons of Kṛṣṇa, would be inexhaustible. Seeing him having marks of the weapons of Kṛṣṇa on his body, all demons and fiends, so also spirits and vampires, goblins, serpents, yakṣas, vidyādharas, kinnaras, guhyakas, evil demons, young evil demons seizing upon children, so also (goblins called) kuṣmāṇḍas, female goblins, so also others that bring about obstacles, run (away) through fear.

68-70a. Elephants, tigers, so also other inhabitants of the forest, run away through fear on seeing him who is marked with (the drawings of) the weapons of Kṛṣṇa. Severe diseases like jaundice causing the fall of the body (also go away). That man, who devoutly sees the body (of a man) marked with (the drawings of) the weapons of Kṛṣṇa, gets the fruit equivalent to that of seeing Kṛṣṇa.

70b-72a. The progeny of him who would worship Viṣṇu in Āśvina with three-bladed dūrvā grass, proceeds without any interruption. O brāhmaṇa, in the heart of him who would offer a karkaṭī (Cucumis Utilissimus) fruit to Viṣṇu in the month of Āśvina, unhappiness is never produced.

72b-73a. A wise man should devoutly worship Dāmodara, god of gods, when the auspicious, the best of all months, viz. Kārtika has arrived.

73b-75a. O best brāhmaṇa, a wise man should bathe in the morning in the proper manner to please Viṣṇu in the month of Kārtika. He who would give up (eating) flesh, copulation in the month of Kārtika, goes to the highest position after being freed from sins committed during existence after existence.

75b-77a. O best brāhmaṇa, when the Sun enters the Libra sign of the Zodiac, a bath in the morning, offering of clarified butter and celibacy destroy great sins. O best brāhmaṇa, he who enjoys flesh, copulation in the month of Kārtika would become a village hog in existence after existence.

77b-79a. When the month of Kārtika has arrived, a devotee of Viṣṇu should, even with effort, avoid eating twice (a day), food of others and oil. O brāhmaṇa, I shall tell (you) in brief the fruit of (i.e. obtained by) him who offers a lamp to Viṣṇu in Śrāvaṇa. (Please) listen.

79b-80a. Being freed from agonising sins like those of the murder of a brāhmaṇa, he goes to the city of Dāmodara and would stay (there) for a period of a crore of yugas.

80b-81a. Seeing a lamp burning (before Viṣṇu's image) in Śrāvaṇa, all gods like Indra, being delighted, say to one another:

81b-82. "This one highly devoted to worshipping Viṣṇu is the best among the righteous souls, since he offers a lamp to the Disc-holder (Viṣṇu) in the month of Kārtika. O best brāhmaṇa, Viṣṇu is always pleased with him in the month of Kārtika.

83. That man who would continuously offer a lamp in Viṣṇu's temple in Kārtika, obtains the fruit of a horse-sacrifice everyday.

84. That man who would worship Viṣṇu with lakhs of tulasī leaves in Kārtika, obtains the fruit of a lakh of horse-sacrifices.

85. He who would worship the immutable Viṣṇu with a lakh of bilva-flowers, obtains liberation due to the favour of the lord of the world.

86. Whatever is given after dedicating it to Viṣṇu in Kārtika, all that would be inexhaustible. This is the truth told by me.

87. O brāhmaṇa, he who would offer the sura leaf smeared

with ghee everyday in the month of Kārtika, remains in front of Viṣṇu, O brāhmaṇa.

88-90. What is difficult on the earth for the best brāhmaṇa who would worship Lakṣmī's lord with a white or black lotus that is full-blown? What has he who has offered a lotus to Viṣṇu in the month of Kārtika, not given to Viṣṇu, the conqueror of the demons? What does the revered lord of Lakṣmī not give to him who just takes a lotus and offers it to the enemy of Kaiṭabha?

91. Lakṣmī (i.e. Prosperity) does not stay during existence after existence in the house of him who has not worshipped Viṣṇu with lotuses in the month of Kārtika.

92-93. He who would offer lotus-seeds to the magnanimous Viṣṇu, is born in a brāhmaṇa family in every existence. He, born in a brāhmaṇa family, would be the friend of the four Vedas, be wealthy, have many sons and maintain the members of his family.

94-95. O Jaimini, I tell you the truth: There is no (other) flower like a lotus with which even a sinner having worshipped Viṣṇu enjoys liberation. O best brāhmaṇa, I shall especially tell the greatness of lotus, along with its history. Listen to it attentively.

96-100. There was a brāhmaṇa named Prajā, who knew all branches of holy literature, and the bee of whose mind always remained in the lotus of Viṣṇu's feet. (Abandoning) hundreds of acts fit and unfit to be done, he always worshipped deities, brāhmaṇas and preceptors (or elderly persons). To him the wealth of others was like poison. Wives of others were to him like his own mother. He did to his enemy what he did to his friend. That brāhmaṇa, knowing the sublime truth, did not have much regard on seeing a best brāhmaṇa as a guest or a suppliant. Desiring to cross the fearful, boundless ocean of the mundane existence, he performed all (kinds of) sacrifices and observed all vows.

101-102. Once that best brāhmaṇa, highly given to devotion for Viṣṇu, thought in his mind about his death and birth: 'Who was I formerly? What act have I done formerly? How have I got this (birth)? Where shall I go again?'

103. Thinking like this and sighing repeatedly, that

brāhmaṇa went to a place sacred to Śiva to know his former account.

104. There, the brāhmaṇa with the palms of his hands joined, praised god Śiva with great devotion and with sweet words.

The brāhmaṇa said:

105-115. O great god, salutation to you. O highest god, salutation to you. O Śaṅkara, O Īśāna, O you giver of boons, O you lord, salutation to you. Salutation to you, of the form of knowledge; salutation to you the giver of knowledge. Salutation to you living in the lotuses of the hearts of all beings. Salutation to you, the creator of the world. Repeated salutations to you, the father of the world. Salutation to you, the destroyer (of the world). Salutation to you, the lord of beings. Salutation to you, Vahninetra (having fire-like eyes). Salutation to you Vahnicakṣus (having fire in your eye). Salutation to you, having the moon and the sun as your eyes. Salutation to you, decorated with ash; salutation to you, wearing a hide; salutation to you, having a string of bones; salutation to you, Nīlakaṇṭha. Salutation to you, Pañcavaktra (having five faces); salutation to you having the trident in your hand; to you who destroyed the pride of Cupid; and to you of a fierce form. Salutation to you, god of gods; salutation to you, Tripura's enemy. Salutation to you, the lord of Pārvatī; salutation to you, of a fierce form. Salutation to you whose mind was very much pleased with Bāṇa's devotion. Salutation to you of many forms and of a universal form. Salutation to you, Gaṅgādhara (who sustains Gaṅgā on his head); to you, the destroyer of Dakṣa's sacrifice. Salutation to you, the lord of the evil spirits; to the holder of (the bow) Pināka. Salutation to you, Īśāna; salutation to you, Manīśa. Salutation to you, the visible and the invisible one. Salutation to you who can and cannot be discovered. You alone are Brahmā; you alone are the lord of gods, Viṣṇu; you alone are the Sun. You alone are the Moon, removing all afflictions. Repeated salutations to you, the highest god.

116-118. Having heard his eulogy, Śaṅkara, the highest lord, who brings about the welfare of the world, was pleased, and suddenly manifested himself (before him). The very devout brāhmaṇa, seeing him, saluted by all gods to have manifested himself, saluted his feet. The best brāhmaṇa, with his mind full of joy and with the palms of his hands folded, also again praised Mahādeva, the lord, who grants boons.

119-122. "I actually see him, the lord of gods, whom even gods including Indra do not (i.e. are unable to) see. This is my great fortune. I actually see that highest god who cannot be seen with the mind set upon meditation. What else have I to accomplish? I see that lord by merely remembering whose name even great sinners go to the highest position. I am blessed, I am blessed, I am blessed, and I am fortunate. O highest god, repeated salutations to you. Be pleased."

Mahādeva said:

123. O best brāhmaṇa, with these words of you I am pleased. O glorious one, ask for a boon. I indeed desire to grant a boon.

The brāhmaṇa said:

124-127. O lord, I am actually seeing you, the highest soul, who cannot be seen even by deities. What is the use of other boons? Yet, O great god, you, full of pity, desire to grant a boon. O highest lord, I ask you something. Tell (i.e. answer) it. O god, who was I formerly? What acts did I do formerly? O lord, how have I fallen into this ocean of worldly existence? A body is obtained through acts. A man is smeared with sin. Again as a result of the sin miserable position is had.

128-130. Due to which acts have I obtained this existence full of many miseries? O Śaṅkara, be pleased, and tell it. This existence is the root of sins. Existence is the cause of misery. Therefore, I desire to know my former account. Due to the maturity of my acts, I, tormented by the digestive fire of the stomach, remained in my mother's womb mixed with urine and feces.

131-134. In the worldly existence no other affliction is said to be equal to that due to remaining in the womb. O lord, O you who remove the misery of your devotees, how did I experience it? O Śiva, O lord of the worlds, how have I fallen into this very fierce, worthless, limitless mundane existence which is full of various miseries, which is deluded by Viṣṇu's Māyā, which has supported sins, which is difficult to cross, which is without kinsmen, which is full of desire for sexual union and anger, which gives affliction and attachment, which also gives birth and death? O lord, if you favour, then tell (i.e. explain) all this to me.

Mahādeva said:

135-136. O best brāhmaṇa, even though this is a great secret among secrets (i.e. the greatest secret), and (therefore) is not to be divulged, yet I shall tell it to you (my) devotee. O best brāhmaṇa, formerly you were born in the family of mountaineers. You were known as Daṇḍapāṇi, and you lived by giving trouble to good people.

137-138. Abandoned by discrimination, and having abandoned the fear of the other world, you took to the livelihood of bandits, which caused great affliction and agony to those who were distressed. Seeing you, the extremely cruel one, to have taken to the livelihood of a robber your other brothers also became robbers.

139-143. O best brāhmaṇa, I (shall) tell you the names of your brothers with whom you formerly committed robbery: These six—Daṇḍin, Daṇḍāyudha, and Dattavān, Dattabhū, Sudaṇḍa, Daṇḍaketu—are said to be your brothers. Along with those very fierce and cruel brothers of yours, you always frightened all people with a club. O brāhmaṇa, due to greed for money, you, along with those wicked brothers of yours, killed hundreds of thousands (of people) in the forest on a desolate road. O brāhmaṇa, you, remaining in the forest, and killing with sharp arrows (cows), always ate the raw flesh of cows along with liquor.

144-145. Then all traders gave up using vehicles. A great calamity always befell (travellers) in that forest. When you took to robbery, the wealth of a man did not remain his wealth, the house of a man did not remain his house, and the wife of a man did not remain his wife.

146. In this way in that very great forest, you, along with those brothers of yours (once) after being fatigued due to the journey went to a lake for bathing.

147-148. O best brāhmaṇa, having bathed there you along with your brothers, being hungry, ate lotus-stalks and (drank) water. O greatest brāhmaṇa, O best one, there you ate, through curiosity, many full-blown lotuses.

149-150. Just at that time, a brāhmaṇa, known as Sarvavedas, roaming in the forest, came there for bathing. The religious-minded one, having bathed there, and desiring to worship Viṣṇu, politely asked you for your lotus.

151-154. Then, O best brāhmaṇa, you gave him, with great devotion, a very clean lotus for the worship of the lord of Lakṣmī. That best brāhmaṇa was pleased with the lotus given by you. And just there he worshipped Viṣṇu, bringing about everything. Seeing that brāhmaṇa absorbed in worshipping Viṣṇu, you too laughed and saluted Viṣṇu, the good giver of desired objects. That brāhmaṇa, having worshipped duly the highest soul, the giver of the fruit of the four goals of human life, went as he had come.

155-156. O best one, due to the present of the lotus and the salutation, and due to seeing Viṣṇu's worship, all your sin perished. O excellent brāhmaṇa, after a few days you, whose death was imminent, died in that great forest only.

157-159. The lord, the abode of compassion, pleased with just that act of yours gave you the highest place, very difficult to be obtained even by gods. Due to the favour of Lakṣmī's lord you enjoyed various pleasures there for thousands and hundreds of Manu-periods. Then at the end of (i.e. after the fruit of your) acts (was enjoyed), you came to this land of religious rites and were born in a brāhmaṇa family due to the fruits of that religious merit.

160-162. O best one, having secured a birth in a pure brāhmaṇa family, you obtained steady devotion for Viṣṇu, which is the abode of all virtues. The lord, the great Viṣṇu propitiated by you with the yoga of (ritual) acts, will give you special knowledge. And you will be liberated by means of (that) knowledge. O brāhmaṇa, being very much pleased, go home. Well-being to you. You have obtained my sight. You are freed from the bond of the worldly existence.

Vyāsa said:

163-164. O brāhmaṇa, having spoken like that, the lord of the world vanished there only. That brāhmaṇa also, being satisfied, went home. To glorify the highest lord Viṣṇu he with effort worshipped him day and night with lovely lotuses.

165-169. Having worshipped Viṣṇu with lotuses, beautiful, good flowers, he slept for a long time. Having obtained knowledge, he attained liberation through the favour of the Garuḍa-bannered (god). If such is the fruit of (i.e. obtained by) him who offers a lotus to Viṣṇu even unintentionally, then what would be the fruit of (i.e. obtained by) him who offers it intentionally? I am telling the truth. I am again telling the truth (only). By worshipping Viṣṇu with lotuses one obtains the highest position. He who offers a lotus (even) once to Mura's enemy, is not reborn in this fearful worldly existence. Those full of major sins, even great sinners who worship Viṣṇu giving desired objects with full-blown lotuses even one day, go to (i.e. obtain) liberation.

CHAPTER FOURTEEN

Prohibition regarding and Fruit of Viṣṇu Worship

Vyāsa said:

1-10. A devotee of Viṣṇu should devoutly worship the immutable Viṣṇu along with the great Lakṣmī in Mārgaśīrṣa, O best brāhmaṇa. So also he should not worship Viṣṇu in a Mleccha region, in the house of a fallen person, or at a place full of bad odour, O best brāhmaṇa. He should not worship Viṣṇu near the heretics or great sinners, so also near those who tell lies. He should not worship Viṣṇu near those who are crying, who are quarrelling or at the place of those who are ridiculing. He should not worship Viṣṇu at the place of those who are engaged in accepting gifts, so also in the house of misers and of those who are greedy of others' wealth. So also he should not worship Viṣṇu in the house of those whose nature is deceitful. O brāhmaṇa, being highly devoted, he should, giving up attention to any other thing, be intent on meditating upon Viṣṇu at the time of worshipping Viṣṇu. He should not worship Viṣṇu, when there is loud wailing, when there are sighs, when there is a doubt, or a talk with the heretics, O best brāhmaṇa. Viṣṇu receives that flower which is offered even into ash by him whose mind is concentrated, to the god of gods, the lord of the world. O brāhmaṇa, the lord does not receive that flower which a man fatigued due to hundreds of thoughts, offers even on the discs of the (śālagrāma) stones. With an undivided mind a wise man should worship Viṣṇu.

11. That act which is done with a confused mind is fruitless. Every act depends upon the mind. The three worlds depend upon the mind.

12-16a. Therefore, after making his mind steady he should worship Lakṣmī's lord. O best brāhmaṇa, he who worships at one place, but whose mind is somewhere else, would not get the fruit of his act even after hundreds of crores of kalpas. He who has become (bodily) pure with effort, and engaged in Viṣṇu's worship, is taken to be like a cāṇḍāla if he is without the purity of mind. O brāhmaṇa, that penance which is duly performed for a long time, but without devotion, would all be fruitless, and would only purify the body. That gold, (even) as much as the measure of Meru (mountain), which is given without devotion to a brāhmaṇa with family for (securing) beatitude leads to the loss of the desired object.

16b-25a. Therefore, a devotee with a concentrated mind and full of faith and devotion, should give in his house vegetables with a dwelling etc. to Viṣṇu. O best brāhmaṇa, he who offers a very ripe, divine, orange to Viṣṇu is honoured by us. A devotee should devoutly and with effort give a new thing dear to Viṣṇu, to him, the enemy of Mura, in the month of Mārgaśīrṣa. The devotee of Viṣṇu should bathe with divine sugarcane juice (the image of) god Viṣṇu, the lord Śrī Kṛṣṇa, who grants boons, when the month of Pauṣa has come. O best brāhmaṇa, he who bathes (the image of) Viṣṇu with sugarcane juice, enjoys all pleasures here (i.e. in this world) and after death goes to the Ikṣu-sāgara. So also he who would offer the sugarcane as an eatable to Viṣṇu, the god of gods, obtains the same fruit. What is the use of uttering many (more) words? A man by giving rice parched and flattened along with milk or with curd to Viṣṇu, would obtain all desired objects. Having removed the old garment (from Viṣṇu's image), he should offer him a new (piece of) cloth for keeping off cold, O brāhmaṇa, when the Sun passes from one Zodiacal sign to another. In Pauṣa (when he is in the Puṣya asterism), a man desiring liberation should give to Viṣṇu with Lakṣmī, a seat of ten colours.

25b-31a. O dear, I (shall) tell (you) the fruit of the religious merit of him who, after worshipping the lord of Lakṣmī, would blow a conch. Listen to it. Being freed from all sins like illicit intercourse, he in the end goes to Viṣṇu's city and rejoices with him. O best brāhmaṇa, I (shall) tell you about the religious merit of him who sounds at the time of (Viṣṇu's) worship a bell marked with Garuḍa. He, being freed from all sins like eating articles that are prohibited, goes after getting into a charming chariot to Viṣṇu's abode. Having enjoyed there all desired objects for a period of hundreds of crores of kalpas, he again comes to (i.e. is born on) the earth as a best brāhmaṇa, well-versed in the four Vedas. Having enjoyed there all desired objects for a period of hundreds of crores of kalpas, he again goes to Viṣṇu's city and obtains excellent liberation.

31b-36a. That man who plays upon the lute at the time of worship of the lord, would become the chief among the learned in every existence. The lord, being pleased with him who beats a tabor at the time of the worship of the enemy of Kaiṭabha, gives him immense fruit. Listen to the religious merit of (i.e. got by) him who beats a small drum shaped like an hourglass, a small drum, or who sounds sweet cymbals, or beats a tabor, a large kettle-drum, a large drum, a sindhuvāraka (?), a gong of bell-metal, or claps, or plays upon a lute, at the time of (Viṣṇu's) worship; being freed from sins like theft, he goes to the abode of the Disc-holder (i.e. Viṣṇu).

36b-37. Getting the highest knowledge (there), he is freed there only. O best brāhmaṇa, I tell (you) about the religious merit of him who would produce sweet sound at the time of the worship of the lord of the world, or would play on the wind-instrument. With crores and crores (members) of his family, he goes to Viṣṇu's abode.

38-42. Having obtained knowledge, he would obtain inexhaustible liberation there only. O best brāhmaṇa, he who devoutly dances in the temple of Viṣṇu, goes to that highest position of Viṣṇu. He who devoutly sings songs in front (of the image) of

Viṣṇu, becomes a king in cities of gandharvas. With that devotee of Viṣṇu, who devoutly praises the lord of the world with hymns of praise, the lord is pleased and gives him all his desired objects. O brāhmaṇa sage, that Viṣṇu soon favours him who would worship Viṣṇu in this manner every month.

43. All those men who desire to cross this mundane ocean which is very deep and which gives all afflictions, should worship the pair of the lotus-like feet of the Supreme Spirit, that is charming and served by the hosts of gods.

CHAPTER FIFTEEN

The Efficacy of Rāma's Name

Vyāsa said:

1-3. O brāhmaṇa, listen. I (shall) again tell you about the greatness of Viṣṇu, having heard which a man becomes free from all sins. O best brāhmaṇa, this entire world is a portion of Viṣṇu. Therefore, those wise men who desire the highest knowledge, look upon it as full of Viṣṇu. All gods like Brahmā, Śaṅkara, Rudra are Viṣṇu's portions. Therefore, worship offered to all gods, goes to Viṣṇu alone.

4-6. By this means or that no inauspicious (things) ever take place in the case of those who remember Viṣṇu's names, removing all sins. O best brāhmaṇa, everything is said to be a sin due to the act (involved in it). (But) the recollection of Viṣṇu is indestructible and destroys sins. A devotee of Viṣṇu, desiring liberation, should, while sleeping, eating, speaking, remaining (at one place), getting up, walking constantly remember Viṣṇu.

7-8. No exalted sages have laid down any restriction about time, destroying all afflictions, on the recollection of Lakṣmī's lord. O brāhmaṇa sage, I (shall) tell (you) in brief about the efficacy of the name of the magnanimous Viṣṇu, along with its history. Listen.

9-10. Formerly, in Kṛta age, there lived a vaiśya named Paraśu, who was the greatest in the family of vaiśyas and who had mastered all virtues. O brāhmaṇa, due to (ill) luck, that vaiśya, suffering from cough and asthma, died in his youth.

11-14. His wife of a beautiful waist and quite young, and named Jīvantī, went to her father's house after her husband was dead. O best brāhmaṇa, since that Jīvantī was proud of the prime of her youth, she went to paramours, though checked by her relatives. She, in the prime of her youth and with her heart attached to the paramours, gave up observing vows and domestic duties. O best brāhmaṇa, she of beautiful buttocks and stout breasts, was blinded by lust, and never followed a religious path.

15-17. Her father, devoted to piety, seeing her of a bad character, was afraid of infamy, and being very angry, spoke to her thus: "O wicked one, O sinner, having secured a birth in my family, without any blemish, why do you commit (this) sin? If you have (set) your mind on (committing) a sin, then there is no (food here for you) to eat. O you inauspicious one, go (away) from my house. Leave my house."

18-19. Thus addressed by her father, she, with her eyes red through anger, left her father's house and went as she pleased. Then that woman moving with a desire for (having) a paramour, and being shameless, lived after resorting to the way of a prostitute.

20-21. A pulinda, a mountaineer or even a cāṇḍāla came to her house, and the unchaste woman, with pleasure sported with him. That prostitute never properly entertained in her mind the fear of the next world, O brāhmaṇa.

22-28. O best brāhmaṇa, sometime a fowler, carrying the young one of a parrot, came to her house to sell it. That prostitute too took (i.e. bought) that excellent young one of a parrot with great delight after honouring the fowler with much wealth. Out of curiosity the prostitute everyday nourished the parrot by (giving) proper food. The prostitute who was childless, nourished that young one of a parrot, looking upon it as her own son. O best brāhmaṇa, that bird too by her order always behaved affectionately with her like her relative. Then that prostitute always taught the parrot that had developed devotion for her the name of Rāma with beautiful letters. That parrot always repeated the name of Rāma, the highest Brahman, great and superior to all (other) gods, and destroying all sins.

29-30. Due to just uttering the name of Rāma the entire, very fierce sin of the parrot and the prostitute perished. O best brāhmaṇa, that prominent prostitute, so also the parrot, both died at the same time.

31-32. Then king Dharma (i.e. Yama) sent his servants like Caṇḍa to bring the two who had committed all sins (to him). Then all those very speedy servants with nooses and mallets in their hands came (there) by Yama's order.

33-34. All the servants of Viṣṇu, as valourous as Viṣṇu (himself), (also) came (there). Seeing the two bound by nooses and lying on the ground, the angry servants of Viṣṇu said to the unconquerable messengers of Yama these words:

Viṣṇu's messengers said:

35-37. Oh, strange are the words heard by us (coming) from your mouths, O messengers of Yama, that these two though devoted to Viṣṇu, are being punished by (Yama) the Sun's son. Oh, the behaviour of the wicked is never excellent, since even with efforts they always harm the good. Wonderful is this behaviour of the wicked who have committed sins.

38-41. The religious-minded ones always look upon the entire world as sinless. The sinners do not look upon it like that. They look upon the entire world as having committed sins. The religious ones rejoice on hearing about the religious merit of the righteous; (but) the sinful persons are delighted on hearing about the sin(s) of the sinful ones. The sinful ones are not so much gratified after getting hundreds of bhāras of gold, as they are after hearing the discussion about sins. Oh, powerful is the Māyā (Illusive Power) of the noble, great Viṣṇu, (since, due to it) sinners commit a sin (in spite of its being) painful to their selves, O brāhmaṇa.

Vyāsa said:

42-43. Speaking like this, Viṣṇu's messengers, highly engaged in devotion for Viṣṇu, cut off their bonds with the edge of their discs, O brāhmaṇa. Then Yama's servants got angry. They, resembling fire, all of a sudden showered heaps of burning charcoals there.

Daṇḍa (Caṇḍa?) said:

44-45. To take the parrot and the sinful prostitute I have arranged like this; and you have (also) come. It is simply wonderful. O best ones, if you desire to take these two, then now fight with us.

46-47. Speaking like this, all the strong, haughty messengers of Yama, who had held weapons, filled the quarters with lion-like roars. So also the magnanimous messengers of Viṣṇu like Supratīka, made the world full of sound with very charming sounds of conches.

48-53. In that very fierce battle, the great messengers of Yama then covered those messengers of Viṣṇu with arrows discharged from (their) bows. In that great ocean (of battle) some angrily discharged spears, some discharged (the missiles called) śakti, some discharged thousands of arrows and some discharged discs. The messengers of Viṣṇu, the great deities, pounded with weapons like maces the great missiles discharged by them. Then the followers of Viṣṇu cut off the feet of certain messengers of Yama and the hands of some with the edge of their discs. Some with their heads out off, some with their chests pierced, some with very amazing wounds, some with their mouths wide open, dropped dead (on the ground). The followers of Yama, with one foot of some cut off, with one hand of some cut off, suddenly left the battle, and fled away from it.

54-55. Seeing those messengers intent on fleeing, Caṇḍa holding a mallet, angrily entered the battle. Caṇḍa, the greatest among the host of Yama's messengers, and very brave, struck with mallets Viṣṇu's servants in hundreds.

56-57. Then Viṣṇu's messengers quickly showered Caṇḍa of a fearful valour with showers of sharp weapons. Then Caṇḍa with his body wetted with flowing blood, struck separately Viṣṇu's messengers.

58-68. The lord's messengers, struck by that Caṇḍa in the battle, gave up their spirit and went behind Suprakāśa. Then that angry and very strong Suprakāśa, having eyes (red) like the japā-flowers, taking a mace in his hand, entered the battle (going on) on the battlefield. He who was angry, and who resembled Viṣṇu in valour, struck (him). From the mallet in Caṇḍa's hand, which frightened the onlookers, a (column of) smoke having the smell of pus, rose. From him who was struck by the quick Caṇḍa, very fearful shower of sparks of fire was discharged. Then the angry Caṇḍa, struck, with that mallet only the very powerful Suprakāśa, O brāhmaṇa sage. Then, O brāhmaṇa, that Suprakāśa who was angry, forgot his pain and struck Caṇḍa, Yama's servant, with a mace. O Jaimini, Caṇḍa, struck by him, was wetted with blood, and he, resembling the young sun, fell unconscious on the ground. Then those messengers of Yama took Caṇḍa, who was in a swoon, and making a loud wailing, and being afraid of the battle, fled away. O brāhmaṇa, O Jaimini, O best brāhmaṇa, all the messengers of Viṣṇu, being very much delighted, blew (their) conches. Then those servants of Yama, wetted with streams of blood, overcome by fear and crying, approached Yama.

Yama's messengers said:

69-72. O Sun's son, O you of large arms, we are obedient to you. Yet the messengers of Viṣṇu have reduced us to such a miserable plight. O lord, though the two (i.e. the prostitute and the parrot) were greatest among sinners, they went to Viṣṇu's abode due to the efficacy of Rāma's name. Even those wicked sinners who are fit to be punished by you, go to Viṣṇu's city! What is your authority then? Oh, the messengers have not done this insult to us. It is, O lord, your insult only, since we are (just your) servants.

Yama said:

73-74. O messengers, they recollect the pair of letters—Rāma's name. So they are not to be punished by me. Viṣṇu is the lord of the two. Listen, O servants, there is no sin in the worldly existence, which does not instantly and thoroughly perish by recollection of Rāma.

75-80. O soldiers, those men who everyday devoutly remember the names which destroy heaps of sins, of Viṣṇu, worshipped by the best among the wise, are not at all fit to be punished by me, even though they are sinners. Those men who, on the earth, utter constantly and devoutly (the names) Govinda, Keśava, Hari, Jagadīśa, Viṣṇu, Nārāyaṇa, affectionate to those who are humble, and Mādhava are not fit to be punished by me, even though they are great sinners, O soldiers. O soldiers, those men who, on the earth, constantly utter (words like) 'O destroyer of the affliction of (your) devotees', 'O lord of gods', 'O friend of the distressed', 'O lord of Lakṣmī', 'O you destroyer of all sins', are not fit to be punished by me even though they are great sinners. O messengers, everyday I salute even those in (i.e. by) whose mouths words like 'Dāmodara', 'Chief of gods', 'One who is fit to be served by the hosts of gods', 'Śrī Vāsudeva', 'Puruṣottama' (and) 'Mādhava' are uttered. O best soldiers, I am always subservient to those men whose very kind heart is always engaged in the reflections on Viṣṇu, Mura's enemy, and the only lord of the world, and who resort to the form of the lotus-eyed (Viṣṇu). O soldiers, even though those who are engaged in Viṣṇu's worship, who are devoted to Viṣṇu's devotees, who are engrossed in the Ekādaśī vow, who are free from fraud, who carry on their heads the water (flowing) from Viṣṇu's feet, are great sinners, they are not fit to be punished by me.

81-82. O soldiers, I salute them who enjoy the remains of the offerings of eatable made to Viṣṇu, which destroy the entire heap (of sins), and who always carry on their ears and head, a tulasī-leaf. O soldiers, I am always dependent on them who are eagerly engaged in worshipping Kṛṣṇa's feet, who are engaged in honouring brāhmaṇas, who resort to virtues, who give great joy to the hearts of the distressed people.

83-85. O soldiers, those men who are always given to speaking the truth, who are dear to people, who are like regents of the quarters to those who have resorted to them, who always look upon others' wealth as poison, are not fit to be punished by me. O messengers, they who are engaged in offering food, who offer water (to the thirsty), who give land, who desire the good of all people, who gratify those people who have no livelihood, who have curbed their senses, who are tranquil, are never to be punished by me. I never make any inquiry of them who speak pleasing word, whose minds are free from hypocrisy, anger, pride and jealousy, who do not have a sinful attitude, and who have controlled their senses.

Vyāsa said:

86-89. When the servants of Yama were thus informed by

Yama, they knew the incomparable glory of Viṣṇu, the lord of the world. O best brāhmaṇa, names of Viṣṇu are superior to (the names of) all (other) gods. The knowers of Brahman have declared Rāma's name to be the best among them. O brāhmaṇa, the couple of letters, viz. Rā-ma, is superior to all magical formulas, by just uttering which a sinner goes to the highest position. Śiva alone and none else knows the efficacy of Rāma's name (which is) the worship of all deities.

90-92. A man gets the same fruit even by recollecting Rāma's name as he gets by reciting the thousand names of Viṣṇu. Oh, wonderful is said to be the behaviour of men, that the wicked-hearted ones do not recollect the name 'Rāma' which gives liberation. To utter it there is not the least effort. It is very charming to hear. Yet the wicked-hearted ones do not utter (the name) 'Rāma, Rāma'.

93-94. In the world, liberation which is attained with great difficulty, is attained by Rāma's name only. What other (better) act can be there? So long as men do not recollect Rāma's name giving pleasure, sins remain in their bodies.

95-97. A wise man desiring the fruit of that act should devoutly remember (the name) 'Rāma, Rāma' at a śrāddha, at the time of offering oblations to the manes, at the time of offering a portion of the daily meal to all creatures, so also at a festival, at a sacrifice, at the time of (making) a present, at the time of a vow, so also at the time of the worship of a deity, so also at other Vedic rites. O best brāhmaṇa, he who would mutter the formula '*Namo Rāmāya*' (salutation to Rāma) preceded by Oṁkāra, obtains absorption into Viṣṇu.

98. A man worshipping Viṣṇu with (this) formula of six letters, obtains all his desired objects through the grace of the Disc-holder (i.e. Viṣṇu).

99-103. O greatest brāhmaṇa, that man who at the time of death would remember (the name) 'Rāma, Rāma' obtains liberation, even though he is the most sinful. There is no doubt that the wise ones who remember the name Rāma while on a pilgrimage, would get success in everything. O brāhmaṇa, he who would remember Rāma's name in a forest, on a desolate road, or even at a frightful cremation ground would not face calamities. A man remembering Rāma's name at the royal gate, at a difficult place, in a foreign country, in front of bandits, on seeing a bad dream, so also at the time of trouble caused by Planets, at the time of fear due to portents, so also at the time of fear due to the disease of gout, meets with nothing unfortunate, O Jaimini.

104-105. The wise should always remember Rāma's name which removes all calamities, which gives desired objects and liberation. O brāhmaṇa sage, that moment at which Rāma's name is not remembered, would be only useless. I am telling the truth.

106. Men, remembering Viṣṇu's names, do not sink down; and a man desiring the destruction of sins (committed) during crores of existences obtains affluence on the earth, and constantly remembers with devotion the very sweet name of Viṣṇu, giving liberation.

CHAPTER SIXTEEN

Cakrika's Story

Vyāsa said:

1. O greatest brāhmaṇa, I am again describing the greatness of Viṣṇu, the highest soul, which destroys all unhappiness. (Please) listen.

2-3. Those brāhmaṇas, kṣatriyas, vaiśyas, śūdras and others belonging to the lowest castes, who resort to Viṣṇu's devotion, are fortunate. There is no doubt about this. A brāhmaṇa who is not a devotee of Viṣṇu, should be known to be inferior to a cāṇḍāla, while a cāṇḍāla who is devoted to Viṣṇu, should be known to be superior to a brāhmaṇa.

4. How can he who is without devotion for Viṣṇu, be a brāhmaṇa? And how can he, in whose mind there is devotion for Viṣṇu, be a cāṇḍāla?

5. One should look upon that cāṇḍāla when he honestly worships Viṣṇu, to be superior to a brāhmaṇa knowing (all) the four Vedas.

6-16. Formerly in the yuga called Dvāpara, there was a mountaineer named Cakrika, who tilled (others') land and who did not have a good birth (i.e. birth in a good family) but was without a good livelihood. He talked like brāhmaṇas, had curbed his anger, was free from harming others, kind, without hypocrisy, and highly devoted to his father and mother. He had not talked about Viṣṇu; he had not learnt the holy texts about liberation. Yet there arose in his mind steady devotion for Viṣṇu. Everyday he remembered names of the Disc-holder (Viṣṇu) like Hari, Keśava, Govinda, Vāsudeva, Janārdana. He, born in a mountaineer's family, first put into his own mouth whatever wild fruit he had obtained. He then knowing its sweetness and taking it out of his mouth again and being very much pleased, everyday offered it to Viṣṇu. He did not discriminate between what is defiled (by being tasted by the mouth) and what is not. The habit of one's own class always remains at the top (i.e. prevails). O greatest brāhmaṇa, once he, while roaming in a forest, found a ripe fruit of priyāla tree. He, not finding (such) a fruit (before), was delighted, and to know (its taste) he hastily put it into his mouth. O Jaimini, just when he put the fruit into his mouth, it got into his throat, O brāhmaṇa. O brāhmaṇa, holding (his throat) carefully with his left hand, he arrested (the downward movement of the fruit through) the entire cavity of his throat with his right hand.

17-20. Then Cakrika, solely absorbed in devotion for Viṣṇu, thought: 'If I do not offer this fruit to that enemy of Mura, then no sinner like me is born in the worldly existence.' Meditating on Viṣṇu in various ways he then decided. Yet that fruit did not come out of his throat, O brāhmaṇa. That exclusive devotee of Viṣṇu cut his throat with an axe. He brought (out) that fruit (from his throat) and offered it to Viṣṇu. He, thinking about him only in his heart, approached him.

21-22. And with his entire body wetted with blood, he fell on the ground. Seeing him dead, lord Viṣṇu was distressed. "There is no (other) devotee like him, since, he having cut his throat, pleased me.

23-25. Since this devoted one has done a good act, what object can there be, by giving which I can be free from his debt? He is blessed, he is very blessed. He is undoubtedly blessed.

Even sacrificing his life, he has pleased me. I do not know whether I (should) give him the position of Brahmā, or of Śiva or an emperor and be free from his debt."

26-27. Saying so, and being very much pleased, the Garuḍa-bannered god touched his head with the lotus in his own hand. Due to the touch of the lotus in his hand, that mountaineer, freed from the anguish, solely devoted to Viṣṇu, got up with great vigour.

Vyāsa said:

28-29. Then Viṣṇu cleaned the dust on the body of that greatest devotee with his own garment as a father (cleans the dust on the body of his son), O brāhmaṇa. Cakrika, seeing Viṣṇu in an embodied form, humbly bent down his head, and with the palms of his hands joined, praised him with sweet words.

Cakrika said:

30-32. O Govinda, Keśava, Hari, Jagadīśa, Viṣṇu, though I do not know (i.e. find) words proper for your praise, yet my tongue desires to praise you. O lord, be pleased; remove this enhanced blemish. O lord of everything, O you having the disc in your hand, those men who, leaving you, worship another god in the world are just fools, since you are favouring even me who am the abode of the heap of sins only. Though I who am extremely sinful and who have been born in a mountaineer's family, know you (only) through devotion for you which removes the bond of the mundane existence of men, yet the lord is very much pleased with me, O you, the only lord of the world.

33-37. O lord, I have today gained the touch of your charming, lotus-like hands which even hosts of gods led by Brahmā do not obtain. There is no one (more) kind than you to his servants. Salutation to you, the most auspicious (god), who, the lord, for the good of the group of gods like Indra, formerly (killed) the demon Kaṁsa, the first enemy of gods, and Nimi's son who had committed all sins. Salutation to you resembling a fresh cloud, who, the very powerful son of Vasudeva and the best god killed the twin Arjuna trees, so also the wicked Kālayavana in a battle, so also Dhenuka. O Śrī Kṛṣṇa, O Dāmodara, O Ananta, salutation to you, the best in Yadu family, who, the lord, the highest god, formerly gave steady prosperity to the lord of gods (i.e. Indra). Repeated salutations to you who took away the pārijāta tree, who vanquished Indra and easily conquered Maheśa.

38-40a. Making Bhīma the instrument you knocked down Jarāsandha. The arms of Bāṇāsura struck by you, perished. I always salute him who killed Śiśupāla. Constant and repeated salutations to him who, the noble one, having killed the kṣatriyas through his Māyā, removed the burden of the earth.

Vyāsa said:

40b-41a. O Jaimini, Viṣṇu, thus praised by the magnanimous Cakrika, being very much pleased, said to him: "Choose a boon."

Cakrika said:

41b-47. O highest Brahman, O highest abode, O highest soul, O you full of pity, I am actually seeing you. What is the use of other boons, O twice-born? I did not meditate upon your form. I did not worship you with offerings of eatables, divine flowers, divine incenses or lamps. I never recollected your names. O lord, I never held on my head the water (flowing) from your feet. I did not eat the offerings of eatables made to you, nor did I observe any vow (in honour) of you. Yet I (am able to) see you. What shall I do with other boons? I am born in a mountaineer's family and am excluded from all religious rites. Yet I have today secured your lotus-like feet difficult to be secured even by deities. What (then) is the use of other boons to me? Yet, O lord of Lakṣmī, when you desire to grant a boon, (then) let my heart remain on you; let it not sink from (want of) your favour.

The lord said:

48-49. I, a sinful servant, have got great satisfaction by this shower of nectar that you have offered, O large-hearted one. O dear, I am very much pleased with this excellent lotus that you offered me. Being delighted (i.e. gladly) I accept your devotion.

Vyāsa said:

50. Speaking like this, Viṣṇu who accepted devotion and who was full of pity, embraced the devotee with his four long arms.

The lord said:

51-52. O dear, O Cakrika, O best one, I am pleased with your devotion. O dear, whatever I have given will certainly come off.

The universal soul, the protector of the universe, the highest lord, having again embraced that great devotee, vanished there only.

53-54. That Cakrika, highly intent upon devotion for Viṣṇu was very much pleased, and abandoning his sons, wife etc. went to the city of Dvārakā. Having, due to the favour of Lakṣmī's lord, thus gone there, he, at the end of his life, attained liberation, difficult to be had even by gods.

55-56. Therefore, god is dependent upon his devotees. He is pleased merely by means of devotion, and not by means of hymns of praise, wealth, austerities or muttering (a deity's names). O best brāhmaṇa, though he gave (Viṣṇu) the fruit that had been defiled by him (by tasting), yet Viṣṇu, knowing his steady devotion, was pleased with him.

57-58. Therefore, in this world those who desire liberation, (should worship) god Viṣṇu. Those men, who worship with a firm devotion the pair of Viṣṇu's lotus-like feet, fit to be worshipped by great deities like Indra, go to (i.e. obtain) liberation.

CHAPTER SEVENTEEN

Bhadratanu's Story

Jaimini said:

1. O preceptor, again tell me the greatness of Lakṣmī's lord. Who is satisfied after drinking the nectar of Viṣṇu's account?

Vyāsa said:

2-3. There is no one pious like you in the mundane existence, since you desire to listen to Viṣṇu's greatness with devotion. O best brāhmaṇa, the charming tale of Viṣṇu does purify the three worlds—(it purifies) the listener, the questioner and the speaker.

4-6. O dear, listen to the greatness of Lakṣmī's lord, which destroys sins. I shall narrate it, giving the four goals of human life, in brief. Viṣṇu would instantly remove the sin, committed during crores of births, of him who would worship Viṣṇu very devoutly even one day. How can he be (called) pious who has not worshipped Viṣṇu? How can he be (called) a sinner who has devotion for lord Viṣṇu?

7-8. There is the best city called Puruṣottama, a city endowed with all qualities and resorted to by hosts of all gods. It is said to be the greatest of all holy places, since in that charming city Viṣṇu actually lives.

9-14. Formerly there lived a brāhmaṇa named Bhadratanu. He was handsome; he spoke pleasing words; and was born in a pure family. The handsome brāhmaṇa, on attaining youth, was deluded by passion of love; and giving up the fear of (not attaining) the other world, he was attached to a prostitute. He did not study the Vedas, nor did he at all study the Purāṇas. Due to the company of heretics he abandoned the excellent Gāyatrī hymn. That brāhmaṇa, highly attached to sins, accepted gifts not fit for sacrificial purposes, snatched others' wealth, and censured religion. He, the mean brāhmaṇa, abandoned the conduct of brāhmaṇas, so also devotion to truth, and also the worship of elderly persons (or preceptors) and guests. He did every act that was more and more sinful. O Jaimini, he never did the most meritorious act.

15. Once that brāhmaṇa who had committed sins and who was not ashamed and afraid of people, performed a śrāddha without faith in it.

16-25. Having gone to the prostitute's house at night he said to her:

The brāhmaṇa said:

O you of large buttocks, this is the day of the śrāddha to be offered to my manes. Yet, bound by your virtues I have come to your house. O dear one, see this night fearful to all people. The sky, (right) from the ground, has multitudes of clouds dropping water, and is covered. Even at this night, at which the way is lost due to fresh clouds, I, with my mind attracted towards your qualities, have come (to you), with the lamp of lightning in the clouds and my longing directing me to the object. O dear one, I, with anxiety about and relying upon your qualities have come (to you) at night. Not seeing you even for a moment, I am not happy. O slender one, I have come to see you with difficulty. O dear, what have I to do with a bath with the water of a holy place? Sprinkled with the holy water of your love I have reached heaven. What fruit would I get by exerting for pleasure in the other world (i.e. heaven)? Due to your favour, O dear one, I get heaven even while alive. O dear one, I performed the śrāddha-rite at home for fear of bad name. I do not have the slightest faith in this śrāddha. O beautiful lady, you are my muttering of prayers, my penance, and my prudence. O beautiful lady, I have resorted to you only in this mundane existence with full devotion. I always belong to you. Order (me) what I (should) do.

Sumadhyamā said:

26-34. With you as his son, your father has become like one who is sonless. You desire to have coitus even on the day of the śrāddha (offered) to the manes. O wicked one, the manes of him who has coitus on the day of (the śrāddha offered to) his manes, and he also eat semen. If a fool, through folly, has coitus on the day of (the śrāddha offered to his) manes, the śrāddha is fit to be received by demons. There is no doubt about this. I have clearly told you. What would one not get if one's mind in accordance with that (i.e. what I have said) would be (set) on Viṣṇu? The life of living beings remains within (the control of) Yama's staff. Yet, O fool, you, being fearless are always commiting sin(s). O fool, life perishes in a moment like a water-bubble. Then thinking that it is eternal, why do you always commit (sinful acts) secretly? How does he, on whose head the couple of letters 'mṛ-tyu' (i.e. death) is written, commit a sin, giving pain to all? Oh! wonderful is great Viṣṇu's Māyā on the earth, since, O brāhmaṇa, a sinner is always delighted. The sacrifice performed in the stage of a householder, burning like fire (says:) "Give place to (your) sin in my body, difficult to be resorted to."

Vyāsa said:

35-40. Due to the sin impelled by destiny that good prostitute spoke like this. The brāhmaṇa who had committed sins, thought in his mind. 'Fie upon me a great sinner, a fool, the greatest among sinners! I, a wicked one, do not have that knowledge which the prostitute has. I, having got birth in a pure brāhmaṇa family, have everyday committed great sin(s), destroying myself. How do I still commit sin(s) through indiscrimination, when death is certain, and Yama is my master after my death! When I have not muttered (the names of Viṣṇu), when I have not observed penance, so also when I have not performed a sacrifice, when I have not studied the Vedas, when I have not practised the conduct of a brāhmaṇa, when I have not honoured guests, when I have not been devoted to my preceptor, when I have not honoured brāhmaṇas, so also when I have not offered a śrāddha to my dead ancestors, so also when I have not offered worship to Lakṣmī's lord, how can I have an excellent position (after death)?'

41-43. That brāhmaṇa, having saluted like (i.e. prostrating himself like) a staff on the ground, the illustrious Mārkaṇḍeya, the best among the knowers of religious rules, praised him with (proper) words. "Salutation to you, O greatest brāhmaṇa. Salutation to you, O long-lived one. Salutation to you the illustrious one, of the form of Viṣṇu. Salutation to Mṛkaṇḍu's son, desiring the good of all people. Salutation to you, the ocean of knowledge. Salutation to you, the immutable one."

44. Thus praised by the brāhmaṇa, the great ascetic Mārkaṇḍeya, master of the significance of all holy texts, being very much delighted, spoke (thus):

Mārkaṇḍeya said:

45. O very blessed one, I am very much pleased by your devotion. Choose a boon. I shall instantly accomplish your desired object. (This will) not (be) otherwise.

The brāhmaṇa said:

46-48. I am the greatest of sinners. I am without (i.e. I do not follow) the practices of a brāhmaṇa. I am always connected with doing harm to others. I am always interested in others' wives. O best brāhmaṇa, I, a fool, always committed great sin(s). I have never done any pious act with regard to the other world.

How can I, a great sinner, cross the fearful ocean of the worldly existence which causes pain and which is very fierce?

Mārkaṇḍeya said:

49-51. O best brāhmaṇa, even if you have committed sins, you are the best among the pious, since (in you) has arisen this knowledge difficult to be found in the world. The liking for religious merit of the pious ones increases everyday. The liking for sins of the sinful ones (also) increases everyday. Though you are a sinner, you (can) keep off your thought for sins. Therefore, the lord indeed appears to be pleased with you.

52-53. They call the man to be the best, who having first committed a sin, turns away from it (afterwards), and who has worshipped Viṣṇu in his former existence(s). Lord Viṣṇu, the great one, seeing his devotee attached to sins, gives him broad understanding, so that he gets felicity.

54-55. Therefore, O best brāhmaṇa, you who have worshipped Viṣṇu in every existence, will soon have good fortune. There is no doubt. (But) O brāhmaṇa, since now it is time for me to perform my religious rites, you will not hear from me (the answers to) whatever you have asked me.

56-62. There is a brāhmaṇa named Dānta, who knows the truth of every object. He will tell you all that. Go to his hermitage.

Advised by that intelligent Mārkaṇḍeya, the brāhmaṇa quickly went to the pure and very beautiful hermitage of Dānta. It was adorned with trees like aśvattha, campaka, bakula and priyaka, so also other flowered trees and was very charming. The atmosphere was filled with the fragrance of full-blown flowers. It had swarms of humming bees. It was very much resounding with the sounds of (i.e. produced by) fruits. Breezes gently blew there. The water there was cold. It was crowded with hundreds of wild beasts, and with pupils and their pupils. That brāhmaṇa, having entered that very charming hermitage, saw Dānta who knew the true nature of Brahman and who was surrounded by the hosts of his pupils. That best brāhmaṇa, having praised that best brāhmaṇa, Dānta, of the nature of Viṣṇu, saluted his feet with (i.e. by bowing) his head.

Dānta said:

63. O good one, who are you that have come (here)? What is your intention (in coming over) here? Tell the truth. With what motive are you praising me now?

Bhadratanu said:

64-65. O distinguished one, I am a brāhmaṇa without (i.e. not following) the practices of a brāhmaṇa. I am known by the name Bhadratanu, and have committed all sins. O brāhmaṇa, since you know the true nature of Brahman, tell me this: How can I, a sinner, destroy the sins (I have committed) in the world?

Dānta said:

66-72. O brāhmaṇa, listen to a great secret. Through affection for you I tell it, by which the fetter of the worldly existence of men is cut off. Give up the company of heretics. Always resort to the company of the good. Give up lust, anger, delusion, greed, pride and jealousy. So also, O brāhmaṇa, carefully avoid falsehood and doing harm to others, while always recollecting the names of the magnanimous, great Viṣṇu. O best brāhmaṇa, in the same way clean and also besmear Viṣṇu's temple. Adorn the path leading to it, and put lamps in it. Always giving water (to the thirsty) and performing the five great sacrifices, serve the brāhmaṇas and your relatives. Listen to the tale of Viṣṇu. Mutter the formula of twelve syllables. O best one, you who will be doing all these acts, will have excellent knowledge, and due to knowledge you will obtain liberation.

The brāhmaṇa said:

73-76. O brāhmaṇa, explain these good (qualities) which you talked about. (Tell me:) What is *moha*, what are religious hypocrisy and jealousy? What is falsehood? What is (doing) harm (to others)? What is pity? What is tranquillity? And what is control? What is said to be impartiality? What is (said to be) the worship of Lakṣmī's lord? What is said to be the day and the night? What is recollection of Viṣṇu? What are the five great sacrifices? What is twelve-lettered formula? O best brāhmaṇa, give me the full explanation of these, so that through your favour I shall reach the highest place.

Dānta said:

77-86. Those who, giving up acts approved by the Vedas, do other acts, and who are without their own practices (i.e. who do not follow practices laid down for their own caste) are declared to be heretics. Those who follow their practices (i.e. practices laid down for their caste) approved by the Vedas, and who are without sins and greed are declared to be good people. O best brāhmaṇa, that constant longing for women and for obtaining wealth is said to be *kāma*, desire of sensual enjoyments. That torment which is produced in one's heart after hearing one's censure should be known as anger. It destroys all virtue. That desire which is produced in one's mind to take others' wealth on seeing it, is said to be greed, O best brāhmaṇa. The feeling of mineness as 'This is my mother, this is my father, this is my wife, this is my house', is said to be *moha* (attachment). The (feeling viz.) 'I am noble, I am rich, nobody is comparable to me on the earth,' which is produced in one's mind is called pride. 'People always censure me. Fie upon my life!' He who says like this to himself (has) contempt for himself. Such contempt is (called) *matsara*, self-condemnation. That which is the statement of facts and which delights all people should be known to be truth. The opposite of it is falsehood. Such a thought—when will his affluence, wife, sons perish?—which is produced in a man's heart is called *himsā*, harm.

87-95. That desire which is produced in the heart to remove the affliction of others even with an effort is said to be pity, O best brāhmaṇa. The satisfaction that is produced in the heart is called tranquillity. Taking away the heart from a censured act is declared by the wise to be self-control and is approved by those who see the truth. O best brāhmaṇa, that contentment which always prevails in misery or happiness, so also viewing an enemy or a friend as equal is called impartiality. O brāhmaṇa, that is said to be the worship of Viṣṇu, when reverence is paid to Viṣṇu with faith by means of offering of eatables, sandal, flowers etc. Abstinence from taking food observed during the day and at night on the first and the subsequent day is known as fast. O best one, the unification of oneself and of Viṣṇu is said to be the recollection of Viṣṇu. Teaching and reciting the Vedas (*brahmayajña*), reception of guests (*nṛyajña*), sacrifice to the superior gods made by oblations to fire (*devayajña*), obsequial offerings (*pitṛyajña*), an oblation to all created beings (*bhūtayajña*), are said to be the five sacrifices. The wise call this—*namo bhagavate Vāsudevāya* (Salutation to the revered Vāsudeva) preceded by (the syllable) *Oṁ* to be a great formula of twelve syllables. O best brāhmaṇa, I have thus told you what was asked by you.

96-97a. Hearing it all men get excellent knowledge. O brāhmaṇa, therefore, having everyday recited the one hundred and eight names of the lord of Lakṣmī, you will obtain liberation which is difficult to be obtained.

Bhadratanu said:

97b. (Please) tell (me) the hundred and eight names of Viṣṇu, the lord of Lakṣmī.

Dānta said:

98-102. O brāhmaṇa, listen. Having drawn the essence of the thousand names of Viṣṇu, the highest soul, I shall tell you the mode of meditation, having meditated in which way the hundred and eight names destroy great sins. Having meditated upon the excellent face of Kṛṣṇa, which has the form of a hemp-flower, of Kṛṣṇa whose eyes are like full-blown lotuses, the entire body of whom (i.e. of the lord) is adorned with the dust from cows' feet, whose excellent head is adorned with the beautiful hair of a cow's tail, the lord who has put on his charming lips the beautiful sound of the flute (i.e. the sweet-sounding flute), who is surrounded by children living in cowpens, who has put on a yellow garment, whose face is like that of Cupid, one should repeat the hundred and eight names of Viṣṇu.

103-117. (He should repeat it in the following way:) 'Oṁ, salutation to him. Of the hundred and eight names of Kṛṣṇa, the seer is Veda Vyāsa. The metre is anuṣṭup. The deity is Śrī Kṛṣṇa. Application is to the muttering: Salutation. Kṛṣṇa, Keśava, Keśi's enemy, Sanātana (ancient), Kaṁsāri (Kaṁsa's enemy), Dhenukāri (Dhenuka's enemy), Śiśupāla-ripu (Śiśupāla's enemy) Prabhu (the lord), Devakīnandana (Devakī's son), Śauri, Puṇḍarīkanibhekṣaṇa (having lotus-like eyes), Dāmodara, Jagannātha, Jagatkartā (creator of the world), Jaganmaya (full of the world), Nārāyaṇa, Balidhvaṁsī (destroyer of Bali), Vāmana, Ditinandana

(Diti's son), Viṣṇu, Yadukulaśreṣṭha (the best in Yadu's family), Vāsudeva (son of Vasudeva), Vasuprada (giver of wealth), Ananta, Kaiṭabhāri (enemy of Kaiṭabha), Mallajit (conqueror of Malla), Narakāntaka (destroyer of Naraka), Acyuta, Śrīdhara, Śrīmat (possessing abundance), Śrīpati (Lakṣmī's lord), Puruṣottama (the highest Brahman). Govinda, Vanamālin (who wore a garland of wood-flowers), Hṛṣīkeśa, Akhilārtihā (who removes all afflictions), Nṛsiṁha, Daityaśatru (enemy of demons), Matsyadeva (the Fish-god), Jaganmaya (full of the world), Bhūmidhārin (sustainer of the earth), Mahākūrma (the great tortoise), Varāha, Pṛthivīpati (lord of the earth), Vaikuṇṭha, Pītavāsas (who wears a yellow garment), Cakrapāṇi (who has a disc in his hand), Gadādhara (who holds a mace), Śaṁkhabhṛt (who holds a conch), Padmapāṇi (who has a lotus in his hand), Nandakin (who holds the Nandaka sword), Garuḍadhvaja (the eagle-bannered god), Caturbhuja (having four arms), Mahāsattva (very powerful), Mahābuddhi (very intelligent), Mahābhuja (having large arms), Mahotsava (very joyful), Mahātejas (very lustrous), Mahābāhupriya (liking the large-armed i.e. mighty ones), Prabhu (the lord), Viṣvaksena (Aniruddha), Śārṅgin (having the Śārṅga bow), Padmanābha, Janārdana, Tulasī-vallabha (lover of Tulasī), Apara (unlimited), Pareśa (the highest lord), Parameśvara (the highest god), Paramakleśahārin (remover of great affliction), Paratrasukhada (giving happiness in the next world), Para (the highest one), Hṛdayastha (remaining in the heart), Ambarastha (remaining in the sky), Mohada (causing delusion), Mohanāśana (destroying delusion), Samastapātaka-dhvaṁsin (destroying all sins), Mahābalabalāntaka (destroyer of the power of the very mighty ones), Rukmiṇīramaṇa (Rukmiṇī's husband), Rukmipratijñākhaṇḍana (who broke Rukmi's pledge), Mahat (the great one), Dāmabaddha (who was tied with a rope), Kleśahārin (who removes affliction), Govaradhanadhara (who held up the Govardhana mountain), Hari, Pūtanāri (Putanā's enemy), Muṣṭikāri (Muṣṭika's enemy) Yamalārjunabhañjana (who broke the twin Arjuna trees), Upendra, Viśvamūrti (of a universal form), Vyomapāda (having his foot in the sky), Sanātana (the eternal one), Paramātman (the highest soul), Parabrahman (the highest brahman), Praṇatārtivināśana (destroying the affliction of those that bow to him), Trivikrama (having three strides), Mahāmāya (having great divine power), Yogavid (knowing the Yoga), Vistaraśravas (far-famed), Śrīnidhi (treasure of wealth), Śrīnivāsa (abode of glory), Yajñabhoktṛ (enjoyer of sacrifices), Sukhaprada (giving happiness), Yajñeśvara (lord of sacrifices), Rāvaṇāri (Rāvaṇa's enemy), Pralambaghna (killer of Pralamba), Akṣaya (inexhaustible), Avyaya (immutable).

118-120. O best brāhmaṇa, I have told you these one hundred and eight names (of Viṣṇu) (selected) from his thousand names, for pleasing Viṣṇu. All of them destroy sins. They destroy (the effect of) bad dreams. They destroy the trouble due to Planets. They destroy all diseases. They give great affluence also. They destroy all harms. They give the fruits of all acts.

121-125. With him who, three times everyday, would repeat these hundred and eight names before Viṣṇu, Viṣṇu is always pleased. The dead ancestors of him, the devotee of Viṣṇu, who would devoutly recite these hundred and eight names at the time of a srāddha, are pleased, and go to the highest position. He who would recite them at the time of a sacrifice, at the worship of a deity, at the time of giving (gifts), during a pilgrimage, would (also) obtain that fruit. By repeating this hymn, one who has no son gets a son, one longing for wealth gets wealth, one desiring knowledge gets it. Never any evil befalls them on the earth who devoutly recite these hundred and eight names of Viṣṇu.

Dānta said:

126-131. O brāhmaṇa, go. Well-being to you. Having very devoutly propitiated Viṣṇu in the manner as told by me, you will obtain the highest happiness.

Thus advised by Dānta, the knower of Brahman, he was engaged in worshipping Viṣṇu in that excellent holy place. O Jaimini, that brāhmaṇa devoutly worshipped Viṣṇu in the manner as told by Dānta everyday for five days. Knowing his very firm devotion, Viṣṇu, full of compassion, and lustrous like a crore of suns, appeared before him. Seeing that lord of the worlds, Acyuta, dear to Lakṣmī, the brāhmaṇa saluted his pair of feet by (bowing) his head. Then the greatest brāhmaṇa, with his mind full of joy, praised Lakṣmī's lord by joining the palms of his hands.

132-134. "O Viṣṇu, you have taken my intellect disposed to sins to your kind devotion giving auspicious objects. Therefore, I, a rustic, who has done abundant sins, have been today made a (gentle) man. O highest lord, I have known this much only: When you whose pair of feet is saluted by the three worlds, are angry, then man's intellect goes towards a sin. And when you are pleased, the same goes to good acts. O lord, I tell you about the efficacy of remembering you, due to which I who have committed all sins, went, after getting into an aeroplane covered with pure gold, to the highest place.

135-136. The hunter Kanika, who was rich in virtues, (but) who had committed sins, knows (the efficacy) of the water (flowing) from your lotus-like feet. O you, the only lord of the world, king Yajñadhvaja, honoured by gods, knows the fruit of smearing the abode of you, the lord, O Mura's enemy, O you the cause of the creation, the maintenance and the destruction of the world. Yajñamālin, his brother Sumālin who is afraid of sins (also) know it, O you having on your banner (Garuḍa) the enemy of serpents.

137-140. Dharma alone, and none else in the three worlds, knows that fruit which would be (obtained) by going round you, Viṣṇu. O lord, on the earth who is able to describe your heart and your kindness? A hunter, having pierced you with arrows, went to the highest place. O lord of the world, even after censuring you Śiśupāla obtained liberation. (Then) what to say about your devotee? May my mind delight in you who, in the form of Brahmā, created this world, O great Viṣṇu.

141-153. O Viṣṇu, the entire destruction of the world is done by you in the form of Rudra in this mundane existence. Salutation to you who are that. Salutation to you, than whom the world is neither smaller nor larger, and who has occupied the entire world. Salutation to you, from the eyes of which god the Sun that causes the day is produced; and from whose mouth fire is produced. O best god, O Keśava, I always salute you, from whose ear airs and vital airs also have sprung up. Salutation to you, (embracing) the chest of whom, of a dark body, Lakṣmī was very happy as the lightning is (after resorting to the body) of a cloud. Salutation to you, the limit of whose greatness even gods like Brahmā have not been able to reach. Salutation to you who would be born in every yuga for establishing righteousness and destroying sinners. Salutation to you who, the noble one, has deluded this world, and due to whose delusion Śiva destroys it. Salutation to you who are pleased by means of devotion alone, and not by means of wealth, eulogies, gifts and austerities. Salutation to you who bring about the welfare of and who favour cows, brāhmaṇas and the good. Salutation to you, the god, who remove the affliction of the helpless, the kinsmen, and the meditating saints. Salutation to you who behave equally with all men, gods and elephants. Salutation to you, on whose being pleased even a mountain suddenly becomes (soft) like grass, and on whose being angry grass becomes (hard) like a mountain.

154-156. May I have my (mind) on you (i.e. may I think of you), as the meritorious ones have theirs on religious merit, as the father has his (mind) on his son, or as the chaste ladies have theirs on their husband. May I have my (mind) on you (i.e. may I think of you) as that of the hungry on food. May I have my (mind) on you (i.e. may I think of you) as those that are tormented by heat have theirs on the moon, as those that are afflicted by cold have theirs on the sun, or as those oppressed by thirst have theirs on water.

157-186. May the sin of cohabiting with my preceptor's wife, which I, who am seeing you, committed, perish. May the sin of the murder of those who did not merit it, who was deluded by (your) Māyā and who am seeing you, committed by me perish. O highest lord, I drank (liquor etc.) that is prohibited. May that sin of me who am seeing you (perish). May the sin which I who am seeing you, committed (when) I emitted my semen in water or in a vulva (perish). May the sin which I who am seeing you, committed, when I, sprinkling (i.e. dropping) my semen on the earth, caused an abortion, perish. May the sin which I who am seeing you, committed, by unintentionally deceiving (others), perish. May the sin which I who am seeing you, committed when I told lies every moment (perish). May the sin which I who am seeing you, committed when I censured the good and always harmed others (perish). May the sin which I who am seeing you, committed (when) I kept phlegm in my mouth (perish). May the sin which I who am seeing you, committed, (when) I cut off a tree which had some life in it, perish. May the sin which I who am seeing you, committed, (when) I urinated or evacuated feces on a path, in a temple of a deity or in a cowpen, perish. May the sin which I who am seeing you, committed, (when) I had no devotion to my father and mother, perish. May the sin which I who am seeing you, committed (when) I stopped (a person) going for a bath or for a meal, perish. O best god, may the sin which I who am seeing you, committed, (when) I took a meal on the Ekādaśī-day (perish). O lord, I did not honour a guest coming to my house. May that sin of me who am seeing you, perish. May that sin which I who am seeing you, committed, (when) I twice took meals on Dvādaśī (the twelfth day) and Daśamī (the tenth day of a month), perish. May the sin which I who am seeing you, committed, (when) I stopped cows running to drink (water), perish. May the sin which I who am seeing you, committed, (when) I gave up a vow without completing it, perish. May the sin which I who am seeing you, committed, (when) I gave a false testimony due to my love for my friends, perish. May the sin which I who am seeing you, committed, (when) I did not approach my wife during the time favourable for conception, perish. May the sin which I who am seeing you committed, (when) I took meals in an unhallowed house, perish. May the sin which I who am seeing you committed, (when) I followed the livelihood of a beggar, perish, O Nṛhari. May the sin which I who am seeing you committed, (when) O lord, I showed ascendancy when I was being punished by the king, perish. May the sin which I who am seeing you committed, (when) I put up an obstacle in the (narration of) the tales from the Purāṇas, perish. May that sin which I who am seeing you committed, (when) I listened to the account of the consequences of acts done by others, perish. May that sin which I who am seeing you committed, (when) I cut off the holy fig tree and the dhātrī tree, perish. May that sin which I committed, (when) I sold curd, milk and ghee, perish. May that sin which I committed, (when) I gave hope to others, and made it fruitless (i.e. disappointed them), perish. May that sin which I committed, when I cast an angry glance at brāhmaṇas and mendicants, perish. May that sin which I committed, (when) through anger I reproached those who gave me means of livelihood, perish.

187-189. What is the use of speaking much in this regard?

The sins of me who am seeing you, have perished. There is no doubt that I am fortunate, I am fortunate, I am fortunate. O Lord of the world, salutation to you, salutation to you, salutation to you." O Jaimini, having spoken like this, that brāhmaṇa, with his body horripilated due to devotion, fell at the charming pair of the feet of Viṣṇu.

The lord said:

190. Rise, get up, O brāhmaṇa, I am pleased with you by your devotion. Tell me what is desired by you. I shall certainly give it to you.

Bhadratanu said:

191-193. O highest lord, O Govinda, O kind one, O greatest one, O Acyuta, who will get on the earth what I have received now? Yet, O enemy of Mura, I ask for one boon from you. O lord, may I have firm devotion to you in every existence. You, being pleased, will give everything desired by that man who would devoutly recite this hymn composed by me.

The lord said:

194-195. O brāhmaṇa, the boon is given to you. There is no doubt about it. Yet, O wise one, I desire to form friendship with you. I do not deserve to have a servant (like you), since you are just like (i.e. equal to) me. Therefore, I have now displayed this friendship with you.

Vyāsa said:

196-201. O Jaimini, then that kind god Viṣṇu, loving his devotees, formed friendship with the pious one. Viṣṇu gladly gave him the garland put round his own neck. The brāhmaṇa also devoutly gave Viṣṇu a garland of tulasī (-leaves). Having spread out his four hands, Viṣṇu embraced him. The brāhmaṇa also joyfully embraced lord Viṣṇu. Having thus formed friendship with that brāhmaṇa, kind Viṣṇu, accepting devotion, vanished there only. Then Viṣṇu everyday played with the brāhmaṇa with a ball in that holy place (called) Puruṣottama. O brāhmaṇa sage, once, seeing the brāhmaṇa (to be) weak, Viṣṇu, full of pity, said (these) words to the brāhmaṇa with affection:

The lord said:

202. O friend, how have you become weak? Who snatched away your wealth? What is the anxiety in your mind? Friend, please tell it.

Bhadratanu said:

203. O lord of the world, to please you I practise penance everyday. Due to that, O lord, my body has become weak.

The lord said:

204-209. I am not so much pleased with anyone else as I am pleased with you. (Then) O best brāhmaṇa, why do you trouble your body again? Seeing you weak, anxiety is produced in my heart. Therefore, O best brāhmaṇa, give up this trouble to your body.

The brāhmaṇa was adorned by the lord of gods with his own upper garments, with his own garments and ornaments, with very charming golden rings, and with bracelets shining round his own hands. Lord Kṛṣṇa took the crown from his own forehead, the pair of anklets from his own feet, a golden necklace from his own neck, and gave them to the best brāhmaṇa. The pious brāhmaṇa, adorned with those ornaments given by Śrī Hari, and knowing the game with a ball would always play with Kṛṣṇa charming like a black lotus. Once Dānta saw him who had adorned his body with ornaments, whose pair of lips was bright due to the redness of tāmbūla, who had put on a divine garment and a very beautiful upper garment and who had a smiling face.

Dānta said:

210-219. O good Bhadratanu, you still do not give up sinful notions. All people, even after seeing your act, condemn it. Since I made you my disciple, all the ornaments are mine. An egotist, one of a bad character, a cruel one, one addicted to sins, one who destroys the teacher's fame, are five defiled disciples. So also, one having no faith, one who is garrulous, one of a fickle mind, one who censures the preceptor behind his back—these are said to be mean disciples. The wise ones should make a disciple after ascertaining his excellent character, since knowledge going to the wicked always causes pain to the preceptor also. Those sciences which are declared by the philosophers to bring fame, instantly destroy the tree of the teacher's fame, when they are taught to the wicked. The sinful ones never like pious deeds, as the flies do not like fragrant sandal. As donkeys are not gratified by eating sweet meats, in the same way the wicked are not gratified by pious thoughts. Lakṣmī and piety, giving all desired objects, would never resort to a wicked one for fear of infamy. Or if they resort to him, they perish. And by chance he obtains, through (good) luck, highest knowledge; (if) he obtains it, (good) fortune leaves him.

Bhadratanu said:

220-221. O brāhmaṇa sage, you are speaking the truth. I am not proficient in the holy texts. You will never have infamy due to me (as) your disciple. O best brāhmaṇa, since, through your favour, I accomplished all my desired objects, you alone are difficult to be secured on the earth.

Dānta said:

222. O brāhmaṇa, tell (me) which desired object you accomplished. How did you terminate your penance just in a short time?

Bhadratanu said:

223-227. O preceptor, I gave up my daily rites etc. by the order of Viṣṇu whom I was able to see with little trouble. O best brāhmaṇa, Viṣṇu was so much pleased with me that he gave me his upper garment, (another) garment, two golden pitchers, the bracelet(s) (worn) round his hand(s), the crown on his forehead, the anklet(s) from his feet, and his own necklace. He who removes the affliction of his servants, has formed friendship with me. O preceptor, I constantly play with him the game with a ball. Though I do not go after (your) having heard these words of me, yet I have told with conviction in your presence.

Dānta said:

228-231. Lord Viṣṇu did not appear before me though I have propitiated him for seven thousand years with great devotion. Oh, having worshipped Viṣṇu only for five days, O best one you had his audience, difficult to be obtained even by gods. You are blessed; you are fortunate. You are (i.e. should be) called actually a god, since the lord affectionately formed friendship with you. O best brāhmaṇa, when you have affection for me, (then) tell me, O brāhmaṇa, how seeing Viṣṇu is difficult for me.

Vyāsa said:

232-233. Thus addressed by his preceptor, the wise, amazed brāhmaṇa, highly devoted to Viṣṇu, went to his own hermitage. Then the next day he went (to Viṣṇu) and played (with him) with a ball. And full of politeness, he said these words to the kind lord of the world:

Bhadratanu said:

234-235. O lord of gods, O kind one, O lord of Lakṣmī, my preceptor desires to see you. Tell me who am here, what your order is. O you having lotus-like eyes, the brāhmaṇa is extremely devoted to you. Therefore, O best god, please appear before him.

The lord said:

236-238. O best brāhmaṇa, you worshipped me with great devotion during many births. Therefore, now I appeared before you. That wise brāhmaṇa, having worshipped me, (should) desire to see me, invisible even to deities, after a few days. He too is my great devotee. He is very much interested in worshipping me. Therefore, O brāhmaṇa, he will sometime have my audience.

Vyāsa said:

239. Having heard these words the brāhmaṇa again devoutly spoke to Viṣṇu, the destroyer of afflictions:

Bhadratanu said:

240-241. O lord of the world, O you who love your devotees, if you favour me, then appear before him in my presence. O god, my preceptor has asked for your audience as his fee. (Therefore,) O lord, having granted him audience, protect me.

The lord said:

242-245. When you laid out as his fee my audience, then bring your preceptor and make him see me.

Thus ordered by him, Bhadratanu went to the excellent hermitage of his preceptor. The preceptor came joyfully. When that brāhmaṇa Dānta, the best among donors, came (there) Viṣṇu showed himself endowed with all (good) marks to him. Then that brāhmaṇa, Viṣṇu's devotee, with his eyes full of tears of joy, joined the palms of his hands, and praised him.

Dānta said:

246-249. O kind one, O lord of Kamalā, O you who protect those who seek your shelter, salutation to you, salutation to you, salutation to you. Today my existence is fruitful; today my penance is fruitful; today everything of me is fruitful, (since) I saw you. O lord of Lakṣmī, O master, I have put before you, deep like crores of oceans, those words which I have thought out before. There is no eulogy of the lord of speech, the master of the world, which will produce love for you in my mind. O lord, protect me, protect me; be pleased, O lord of the world. Choose me even as the servant of the servant of the servant of you.

Vyāsa said:

250. O Jaimini, then that lord of gods, who accepted devotion and who was full of pity, laughed, put his lotus-like hand on his head, and spoke thus:

The lord said:

251. O best brāhmaṇa, you are my devotee. You have seen me. You will have all welfare due to my favour.

Vyāsa said:

252-257. O brāhmaṇa, having affectionately embraced Dānta and Bhadratanu, the greatest god suddenly disappeared just there. In that excellent holy place Puruṣottama, difficult to reach, Dānta, having seen Viṣṇu by means of *kriyāyoga* (employment of rituals), went to the highest place. That brāhmaṇa Bhadratanu very much interested in devotion to Viṣṇu also obtained at the end of his life liberation, difficult to be obtained even by gods. The sin committed during many existences by him who would devoutly worship the highest lord even for a day, (perishes. His) love for Viṣṇu increases. Even today all gods like Brahmā do not know the power of Viṣṇu's devotee on the earth, O Jaimini. O brāhmaṇa, this land of religious rites (i.e. Bhāratavarṣa), where having worshipped Viṣṇu men would be honoured by gods, is more difficult than heaven to be secured.

258-263. O best brāhmaṇa, all gods like Indra, afraid of losing their great religious merit, constantly say to one another: "When shall we just again go to the land of religious rites? When shall we worship there the lord of Lakṣmī? These people are very fortunate and are greater even than we, (since) they worship lord Viṣṇu in Bhāratavarṣa, difficult to be reached. Oh, who can describe the merits of Bhāratavarṣa where having formerly worshipped Viṣṇu we have attained godhead?" O best brāhmaṇa, in this way all hosts of gods like Indra always praise the Bhārata region, giving happiness. In this mundane existence no one like him who, after getting a birth there, has not worshipped Viṣṇu, is either seen or heard of.

264-265. I am telling the truth. I am again telling the truth only. Those men who, without being tired, and with firm devotion, even once worship the lord of the universe in this land of religious rites, are freed from sins easily committed, and quickly reach beatitude.

CHAPTER EIGHTEEN

The Greatness of Puruṣottama

Jaimini said:

1. O preceptor, if you favour me, then tell me about the greatness of Puruṣottama which you said to be the greatest holy place.

Vyāsa said:

2-6. O brāhmaṇa, listen to the greatness of Puruṣottama (told by me) in brief. Who else but Viṣṇu is able to tell it in the world? O best brāhmaṇa, the city called Puruṣottama is (situated) on the shore of the Lavaṇa sea (the Salt-sea), and it is more difficult to be reached than even heaven. Since Śrī Puruṣottama (i.e. Viṣṇu) lives in that city, therefore those who are conversant with the name have called it Puruṣottama. O brāhmaṇa, that rare holy place is ten yojanas (in area) on all sides. The men living there are seen to have four arms by gods. While entering the holy place, all would have the form of Viṣṇu. Therefore, the wise should raise no doubt about it.

7-9. O best brāhmaṇa, since Viṣṇu is a cāṇḍāla there, the food of (i.e. offered by) cāṇḍālas should be accepted by brāhmaṇas (at that holy place). There Lakṣmī cooks the food, and Viṣṇu himself eats (it). Therefore, O brāhmaṇa, the boiled rice there is difficult to be had even by deities. For those men who eat the pure food left over after it is eaten by Viṣṇu, salvation is not difficult to be had.

10-11. All gods like Brahmā everyday come (there) and eat that food which is very difficult to be had. Then what can be said about human beings? All great sages call him the hater of Viṣṇu, whose mind does not take delight in that food which is very difficult to be had.

12-19. O brāhmaṇa, as the water of Gaṅgā is pure everywhere, in the same way that food, destroying sins, is pure everywhere. O best brāhmaṇa, though that food is delicate, divine, and of the size of a partridge's belly, it is capable of removing sins. The sins committed formerly of (i.e. by) him whose devotion proceeds to that food, very difficult to obtain, perish. O best brāhmaṇa, he whose religious merit earned in many existences perishes, does not develop devotion for that food. Those mortals, full of devotion, who bathe in the lake of Indradyumna, in the large and deep pool of Mārkaṇḍeya, in Rohiṇī, in the sea, so also in the water of Śvetagaṅgā, are not reborn on this earth. O brāhmaṇa, the dead ancestors gratified with the water of the Salt-sea, are free from all afflictions, and go to Viṣṇu's abode. The wise ones have declared this sea to be the king of holy places. Therefore, every act done there would be inexhaustible.

20-25. There is no doubt that whatever act—honouring dead ancestors, giving gifts, worshipping the feet of the lord, muttering prayers, or any other act which a man performs in that charming holy place Viṣṇu would be fully inexhaustible. Those men who see (the idols of) Balabhadra, Subhadrā, and lotus-eyed Kṛṣṇa, have nothing that is difficult to be got. A man, even performing hundreds of acts of religious merit, does not get liberation without seeing (the idols of) Śrī Jagannātha, Subhadrā and Bala(rāma). O best brāhmaṇa, all gods like Indra salute him whose body has become red due to stroke(s) of cane there. O brāhmaṇa, all hosts of gods like Indra, remaining in the atmosphere and moving in aeroplanes, and being very delighted speak like this to one another:

26-28. 'When will Lakṣmī's lord give us the existence of a man? Then like a man we shall go to see lord Viṣṇu. When will our bodies be red due to the stroke(s) of cane in that holy place Śrī Puruṣottama?' O best brāhmaṇa, all gods like Indra always long for the stroke(s) of cane in that holy place, granting boons.

29-32. Those men who see there the Akṣaya Vaṭa (the inexhaustible fig-tree) with devotion, are freed from sins committed during crores of existences, and go to the highest position. The liberation of those who see (the idols of) Subhadrā, Balabhadra, Jagannātha, Anāmaya (i.e. Kṛṣṇa), the white Mādhava —the lord of gods, so also the deep and large pool of Mārkaṇḍeya, Jyāmeśvara, Hanūmat, the Akṣaya Vaṭa with devotion, is eternal. Listen to the religious merit of those men who there see Govinda rocked to and fro in a swing in the month of Phālguna.

33-38. Freed from all sins they go to Viṣṇu's abode in the end. Having obtained knowledge there only, they attain beatitude, very difficult to be secured. O Jaimini, he who sees Jagannātha in the west in the month of Caitra, would enter Viṣṇu's body after he is dead. That man who would see the lord of the world on the Ekādaśī of the bright half of Caitra, so also on the Tṛtīyā, is surely liberated. O brāhmaṇa sage, all the desires of that man who would enter (the place of) the great bath of the lord of the world, are fulfilled, in the sky. All gods like Brahmā, remain in the sky, and full of devotion, observe the great bath of the lord of the world. O brāhmaṇa sage, a mortal on seeing (the idol of) Viṣṇu, the lord of the world, on the great full-moon day, obtains that highest position of Viṣṇu.

39-41. There is no doubt that he who would see (the idols of) Lakṣmī's lord and Balabhadra going to the Guṇḍikā-maṇḍapa (the pavilion called Guṇḍikā) in Āṣāḍha, is liberated. He who sees (the idol of) the lotus-eyed lord of the world seated in a chariot, does not get rebirth in the mundane existence, giving every (kind of) affliction. The lord cuts off the painful bond of the worldly existence of those men who devoutly see (the idol of) Subhadrā mounted on a chariot.

42. O brāhmaṇa, that woman who is sonless, or whose son is dead and who sees (the idol of) Subhadrā, has many children, and her children live (long).

43-55. An unfortunate lady (deserted by her husband) that has but one child would indeed become fortunate in the matter of her lord and would have many children. That man who sees (the idol of) Kṛṣṇa that is in the Guṇḍikā-maṇḍapa, so also (those of) Balabhadra and Subhadrā, goes to the highest position. O Jaimini, a sick person or an unhappy person who would see (the idol of) Viṣṇu in the Guṇḍikā-maṇḍapa, is instantly free from the disease or the affliction. O best brāhmaṇa, he who, being sonless, would see (the idol of) Viṣṇu that is in the Guṇḍikā-maṇḍapa, would obtain a son who is Viṣṇu's devotee. One desiring knowledge gets it. One longing for wealth obtains it. One wanting a wife gets her. One desiring liberation would get it. O brāhmaṇa, that king who is deprived of his kingdom and who sees with devotion (the idol of) Viṣṇu in the Guṇḍikā-maṇḍapa gets it (back). The enemies of him who, troubled by his enemies, devoutly sees (the idol of) Viṣṇu in the Guṇḍikā-maṇḍapa, perish, O brāhmaṇa sage. He who, very much harrassed by the king, sees (the idol of) Viṣṇu in the Guṇḍikā-maṇḍapa, would instantly bring the king under his control. Of all pilgrimages the one to Guṇḍikā is said to be the best. Therefore, even by abandoning hundreds of other activities, men should undertake it. That man who in that charming holy city sees Viṣṇu at the time of going to bed or getting up, is honoured even by gods. On the earth who can describe the importance of Puruṣottama, by entering which (holy place) a man would become Viṣṇu? What is the use of prolixity? I tell in brief: Of all holy places Puruṣottama is the best. He who desires to cross this ocean of worldly existence, which is very deep, which causes pain, which is the resort of dangerous hosts of sins, should see Viṣṇu, the best of gods, in the holy place called Puruṣottama, giving all pleasure.

CHAPTER NINETEEN

What Pleases Viṣṇu; What Makes Him Angry?

Vyāsa said:

1-2. O best brāhmaṇa, those men who, full of devotion, resort to Viṣṇu, never face a disaster. I will once more narrate the greatness of Lakṣmī's lord, hearing which all men obtain the highest position.

3-4. Devotees of Viṣṇu are satisfied with listening to the greatness of Kṛṣṇa. Heretics, suffering from trouble in a hell, are not satisfied. O best brāhmaṇa, the excellent greatness of Viṣṇu should not be narrated in the presence of heretics. It should be told in the presence of Viṣṇu's devotees.

5-9. O Jaimini, formerly in Tretā yuga there lived a brāhmaṇa, Urviśu by name. He was always engaged in sinful acts, and was highly given to the censure of religion. He snatched brāhmaṇas' wealth. O best brāhmaṇa, he was always bent upon cohabitation with another's wife. He ate cow's flesh. He drank liquor. He had an ardent longing for the amorous gestures of prostitutes. He harmed him who sought his shelter. He always censured others. He was a traitor. He harmed his friends. He harassed his kinsmen also. He told lies. He was cruel. He used to have the company of heretics. He cut off the livehood of brāhmaṇas. He took away deposits. Seeing him cruel and highly attached to sins like that all his kinsmen who were angry came to his house.

The kinsmen said:

10-14. O fool, the eminence which our ancestors had earned in our pure family is (now) being destroyed by you. Giving up the righteous path, you are always committing sin(s). You are born as the destroyer of the fame of our family and as one giving pain to your kinsmen. In you (i.e. with regard to you) the Creator's creation is thought to be causing wonder. Poison came up from that sea from which the moon had come up. Oh, it is not possible to measure the power of bad sons. In a moment they destroy the fame gathered by many men (i.e. their ancestors). Even a low family becomes the greatest when the best son is born (in it). But even the best family is degraded when a mean son is born in it.

Vyāsa said:

15-20. O brāhmaṇa, speaking like this all the kinsmen, getting angry due to the fear of infamy, deserted that greatest sinner. He, deserted by all his kinsmen and reproached by all people, was sorry, and deprived of all his affluence, became a bandit. All (the members of) the community seized him who did that act of a robber, cruel and harmful to others, and reported him to the king. O best brāhmaṇa, the king, due to affection for his father, did not kill him, (but) expelled him from his country. Then the cruel one, resorting to a forest along with many (other) haughty bandits, remained (there) for snatching the wealth of travellers. O Jaimini, he, fatigued while roaming in the forest, sometime went, along with (other) bandits, for a bath to a river-bank.

21-22. This wicked one saw in that river many blessed brāhmaṇas highly devoted to the lord's worship. Then all the brāhmaṇas, having worshipped Viṣṇu, spoke to one another with great curiosity:

23-29a. "I have today dropped those campaka-flowers (in honour of Viṣṇu)." Someone (else) said: "I have offered tāmbūla to Viṣṇu. In my life I shall never eat a tāmbūla. Today I have offered the best banana to Viṣṇu. Birth after birth I would eat a banana." Someone said: "I have offered a pomegranate to Viṣṇu." Someone said: "I have offered an excellent mango (to Viṣṇu)." Having heard these words of them talking to one another, Urviśu thought, 'What shall I offer to Viṣṇu? I cannot give all those things that are eatables in the worldly existence to Viṣṇu. (Then) What shall I offer to him? I, a thief, overcome by the fear of the king, always stay in the forest. I am never entitled to getting into a cart.'

Vyāsa said:

29b-33. O best brāhmaṇa, the thief, repeatedly speaking like this, gave a cart to Viṣṇu, the giver of the four goals (of human life). Then all the brāhmaṇas went as they had come. That thief also went to his abode along with (other) thieves. Once a traveller carrying a basket of jaggery came to that region of the impudent (thieves) along the same path. Then this fearless bandit, harming others, snatched that basket of jaggery of the traveller. Then the robbers broke the basket of jaggery.

34-36. As his share Urvīśu obtained a cart fashioned from jaggery. O best brāhmaṇa, Urvīśu, having obtained that jaggery-cart thought in his mind recollecting the words (of those brāhmaṇas): 'Formerly I myself have presented a cart to Viṣṇu. Therefore, in this existence, I should not take a cart.' Thinking like this in his mind he intended to give the cart (to a brāhmaṇa).

37-42. To please Viṣṇu he gave it to some brāhmaṇa. O brāhmaṇa, knowing that devotion of that great sinner, Viṣṇu who was pleased, instantly removed all his sin. O brāhmaṇa, on the same day all the angry citizens entered that great forest and killed that Urvīśu. To take him (to his own abode) the lord sent an aeroplane made of gold, so also messengers adorned with various ornaments. Then those messengers of the lord, having put that Urvīśu who was dead, into the aeroplane, instantly went to Viṣṇu's city. Then the best one among the pious obtained Viṣṇu's proximity. After living near Viṣṇu for a hundred periods of Manu, and after securing the highest knowledge, he entered Viṣṇu's body.

Vyāsa said:

43-44. A man who, somehow or the other, is devoted to Viṣṇu, goes, like a royal swan beyond the ocean of the worldly existence. He in whose heart there is devotion for Viṣṇu even for a moment, goes to the highest position. Even though he is a sinner, he goes (to the highest position).

45. One should, after offering even the best thing to Viṣṇu, afterwards enjoy it for the appeasement of the sin.

46. The thing that is offered to Viṣṇu should be given to a brāhmaṇa. The wise should not enjoy any remnant of it themselves.

47. O best brāhmaṇa, a devotee of Viṣṇu should not enjoy whatever things and sweets without offering them to Viṣṇu.

48-51. I shall again tell, along with its history, the greatness of eatables offered to Viṣṇu, which destroy all sins. O brāhmaṇa, being attentive, listen to it. There was a brāhmaṇa, Sarvajani by name, who was born in a pure family. He was calm, controlled, kind and honoured his preceptors (or elderly persons) and brāhmaṇas. He was absorbed in Viṣṇu's worship, and was exclusively devoted to remembering Viṣṇu. He removed the affliction of those who sought his shelter; he was truthful, and had curbed his senses. He (everyday) bathed in the morning. He followed the practices of his own (caste); he abandodned harm (to others); he was absorbed in (observing) the Ekādaśī vow; he was intent upon honouring his kinsmen.

52-54. Once that best brāhmaṇa saw in his dream lord Viṣṇu who was dark, whose eyes were like dustless lotuses, who had a smiling face, who had put on a yellow garment, whose body was bright due to golden ear-rings and anklets and a crown, whose chest shone with the Kaustubha (gem), who was adorned with a garland of wood-flowers. He had four arms, had held a conch, a disc, a mace and a lotus, was endowed with all (auspicious) marks, and had worn a golden sacred thread.

55. Having seen the lord of the world in the dream, the brāhmaṇa joined the palms of his hands, and with his body horripilated, gladly praised him.

56-64. "I salute you, (i.e.) Viṣṇu, who are the lord of the entire world, who destroy the grief, fear and diseases of good people, who are dear to Lakṣmī's heart, who give the nectar of piety, material welfare, and sensual enjoyment. O Murāri, I, being arrogant through folly committed all sins. I am, therefore, frightened. Giving the boat of your devotion, take me out of this deep ocean of (the existence in) the world. O Viṣṇu, though I know that a man quickly obtains sin and delusion on the earth, yet I am always gladly committing sins. Therefore, there is no man here (i.e. on the earth) who is foolish like me. O Viṣṇu, do I who have committed sins, not know that the tree of religious merit suddenly gives the fruit of happiness, O Nṛhari? O lord, I have no wealth to (undertake) the act of offering you a tree having flowers. Be pleased. O lord, what shall I do ? O god, this bee of my heart, leaving the pair of your lotus-like feet, the place of the best nectar, constantly moves to a woman's face—misunderstanding it for a lotus which causes death and which is full of the phlegm of deceit. (My) hand is bereft of (giving) gifts. (My) mouth tells lies. (My) ears are always intent upon listening to sinful things. O Viṣṇu, remove these faults of me, your servant, since, O lord, you always destroy the blemishes of him who has sought your shelter. O Nṛhari, at one time, I have, in this world, obtained the very strong boat of your devotion in (order to cross) this fearful ocean of the worldly existence. Even in that case, I, under the sway of Destiny, remain a wicked-hearted person. I am constantly having an unhappy time. Is there a bright path, kind, pleasant and free from all afflictions, for crossing the mundane existence? O Viṣṇu, my eyes blinded by a great darkness in the form of delusion never go to you in this world. O destroyer of Keśin, O you whose lotus-like feet are saluted by all gods, since I see you today, this mind of me, even of a wicked nature, destroying the trouble of people that are tormented, has perished."

Vyāsa said:

65. Thus praised by him, the revered god, the lord of Lakṣmī, knower of words and saviour from the ocean of the worldly existence, said (these) words:

The lord said:

66-67. O best brāhmaṇa, I am constantly pleased with your devotion. Therefore, you will have full happiness soon. O brāhmaṇa, I have formerly emancipated you, though a sinner. Now you are my devotee. You will not face a calamity.

The brāhmaṇa said:

68-69. O Viṣṇu, who was I formerly? What sin did I commit? How did you formerly emancipate me, though a sinner? Since you are always kind, O lord, tell me all this—How was I born, and how was I created by you in this mundane existence?

The lord said:

70-73. O best brāhmaṇa, though this secret is not to be

divulged, I am telling it through affection for you. Listen. O best brāhmaṇa, formerly due to the ripening of your acts you were born in a region on the earth in the stock of a bird. You, always oppressed by hunger and thirst, wandered, eating insects and (drinking) the hot water of springs. You, born in the stock of a bird, always experiencing various afflictions formerly lived for four thousand years on the earth.

74-77. Once, a brāhmaṇa named Kulabhadra, knowing the full truth, devoutly worshipped me with offerings of eatables etc. on the bank of a river. The best brāhmaṇa, having offered me rice as the offering of eatables, again went home after leaving it just there. Then you, a hungry bird, having come down from the tree, ate all that rice offered as an offering of eatables to me. On just eating it you were instantly freed from very fearful sins. Once, on the completion of your life, you died, O brāhmaṇa.

78-80. Then by all means I sent my messengers to bring you (to me). Then putting you whose sins had perished, into a chariot, the hosts of messengers instantly came to the highest place. Enjoying all pleasures, difficult to be had even by gods, you stayed with me for thousands of crores of yugas. Then, O best brāhmaṇa, you went to (i.e. were born in) a pure brāhmaṇa-family.

81-84a. There (i.e. in that existence) also, very firm devotion for me was again produced in you. O excellent brāhmaṇa, having everyday worshipped me with employment of rituals, you will obtain my position at the end of your life. O brāhmaṇa, when I am pleased, you, though a sinner, will enjoy liberation. When sometime I am angry with a man, he is a sinner, even though he is pious; (but) O brāhmaṇa, when I am pleased, a man, though he is a sinner, obtains liberation. Therefore, O brāhmaṇa, O you of a good vow, may you have welfare. You are my devotee. I shall give you that place which cannot be obtained even by gods.

The brāhmaṇa said:

84b-86a. O lord, due to your grace, I have heard my former account. Now I desire to hear something. O lord, tell it. O lord, with whom are you pleased? O best of gods, with whom are you angry? With great favour please tell me all this.

The lord said:

86b-94. O best brāhmaṇa, I shall tell (you) all that in brief, due to which act pleasure is produced in my heart and due to which anger is produced. O best brāhmaṇa, with him who acts for my sake and who is without egotism, I am always pleased. With him who, full of piety and devotion, speaks calmly for me, I am always pleased. With that man who having secured sweetmeat gives it to me and who is equanimous in honour and insult, I am always pleased. With the man who knows me to be present in the bodies of all beings and who avoids harm to others, I am always pleased. With him who repeatedly thinking well, does his acts and who desires the good of cows and brāhmaṇas, I am always pleased. With him who would, with great effort, keep the word uttered by him, and who goes to him carefully who has sought his shelter, I am always pleased. O best brāhmaṇa, with him who always gives gifts to those who do not oblige him, and whose heart is always in me, I am always delighted. I have told (you) in brief with which act I am pleased.

95-111a. O brāhmaṇa, I (now) tell the act due to which I am angry. Listen to it. He who is engaged in harming others, who is cruel to all living beings, who is egoistic, who is always angry, makes me his enemy. He who tells lies, who is cruel, who is given to censuring others, who destroys the mode of the living of the wise, makes me his enemy. The fool who, through delusion, abandons his parents whose faults are not noticed, so also his wife, brother, sister, makes me his enemy. A dull-witted man who reproaches his parents, who insults his preceptor, makes me his enemy, O brāhmaṇa. Those who destroy groves, who destroy lakes, who destroy villages, make me their enemy. With those people who, on seeing another's wife are dejected, who listen to sinful discussion, I am always angry. With those who hate the lord, who snatch the wealth of the unprotected, who are traitors, I am always angry. With those who take away the price of cow's milk, who are the husbands of Śūdra women, who harm the holy fig-tree, I am always angry. With those who make a distinction among Brahmā, Viṣṇu and Śiva, and who are very much attached to other's wives, I am always angry. With those men of sinful minds, who eat on the Ekādaśī day through greed and who censure the Vedas, I am always angry. With those who are attached to sinful thoughts and to plotting against their friends, and who destroy the dhātrī-tree I am always angry. With those who, deluded by lust, cohabit by day and who cohabit with a woman in her menses, I am always angry. O best one, those who, through folly, approach a woman who has not attained puberty, so also the rogues who approach a woman observing a vow, make me their enemy. I am always angry with them who take a meal at night on the new-moon day, so also with them who take two meals on Sundays. O brāhmaṇa, with those who do not avoid cohabitation, flesh, oil on new-moon day, I am always angry. What is the use of talking much in this matter? I (shall) tell you in brief. So also I am always angry with them who censure Viṣṇu's devotees.

Vyāsa said:

111b-117. Speaking like this lord Viṣṇu suddenly vanished. And that brāhmaṇa, having abandoned his sleep, got up from his bed. Due to the words uttered by Viṣṇu the brāhmaṇa, the devotee of Viṣṇu, gave up all (other) activities and was engaged in the employment of rituals. This is the fruit of (i.e. obtained by) them who even eat the articles of food (after they are) offered to Viṣṇu. I do not know how much fruit would be theirs who have worshipped Viṣṇu. O best one, O Jaimini, I (shall) tell you in brief. Listen. A man, having performed Viṣṇu's worship (but) once, obtains the highest position. In the world manhood is difficult to be obtained. Even in it worship of Viṣṇu is (difficult to be had). O best brāhmaṇa, there also devotion is declared to be difficult. That respectable man in whose mind there is a desire to cross the ocean of the mundane existence, should everyday devoutly worship Viṣṇu with all rites.

CHAPTER TWENTY

The Great Efficacy of Giving (*Charity*)

Vyāsa said:

1. O brāhmaṇa, I have told you in brief the fruit of Viṣṇu's worship. Now I shall tell (you about) the presents. Listen attentively.

2-3. Of giving presents and penance, giving presents is said to be superior. Due to penance, it is said, there is sin. In the act of giving presents there is no sin. Penance is (said to be) the best in Kṛtayuga. And meditation is (said to be) the best in Tretā (yuga). Worship is (said to be) the best in Dvāpara (yuga). Giving presents is (said to be) the best in Kali (yuga).

4-6. Therefore, the wise desiring the highest position, should always make presents for pleasing Lakṣmī's lord in Kaliyuga. As the moon waxes digit by digit, similar is said to be the condition of giving gifts and of penance by the wise. O best brāhmaṇa, wealth should be stored (beginning) with even a straw. A wise man should use his stored wealth in giving gifts.

7-8. A man who, though having wealth, does not enjoy or give it, should be known to be a poor man, deprived of giving gifts or of enjoyment. O brāhmaṇa, with whom does wealth come? Who goes with it? When death comes, that which is given before in this world comes (to a man's help).

9-11. Those men who become poor due to repeatedly giving gifts should not be known to be poor. They are the great lords in the next world. Those who save wealth due to miserliness should be known to be very unhappy. O Jaimini, at the end, giving it up all, they, being disappointed, go (i.e. die). O best brāhmaṇa, a man bereft of a good, strong power (lives) in the other world devoid of wealth and relatives. Whatever is not given by a man, does not stand by him there.

12. O best brāhmaṇa, the devotees of Viṣṇu, having devotion and faith, should everyday devoutly give small gifts.

13-19a. O best brāhmaṇa, the wise have declared the gift of food as the best of all gifts. So also the gift of water. Vital airs cannot stay in the body without food. (Therefore) one who gives food should be known to be the giver of life. (And) the giver of life is the giver of everything. Therefore, the giver of food obtains the fruit of all (kinds of) gifts. O Jaimini, giving water is similar to giving food. Food would not exist without water. Therefore, water is given. O best brāhmaṇa, hunger and thirst are said to be equal. Therefore, the wise have said the gift of water to be the best. Water is the life of men. Life is not their life. Therefore, for the protection of life, a wise man should give water. O best brāhmaṇa, he who has given food and water on the earth, has given all gifts. There is no doubt about it.

19b. Listen to the greatness of the gift of food and the gift of water:

20-26a. In the city of Hastināpura itself there lived a prostitute beautiful like a divine damsel, rich like Kubera. She was known as Ratividagdhā, and had all the marks (of a beautiful lady). There (also) lived a brāhmaṇa lady, named Kṣemaṅkarī, born in a great family. That daughter of a brāhmaṇa, who possessed all virtues, was a widow. O best brāhmaṇa, that brāhmaṇa lady had her mind attached to paramours. She, doing prohibited act (s) became thoughtless. O brāhmaṇa, the brāhmaṇa lady, being near the prostitute, formed friendship with her, and took to the life of a prostitute, O Jaimini, the prostitute and the brāhmaṇa lady together, joyfully, everyday committed innumerable sins. Then that Ratividagdhā attained old age. The brāhmaṇa lady of a bad character also (became old). Sometime that chief prostitute who was aging, who was very much amazed, and who was full of modesty, said these words to her friend, O brāhmaṇa:

Ratividagdhā said:

26b-32a. O friend, along with you, I committed many fearful sins. Even now I have a great thought (i.e. a strong desire) for (committing) sins. All my beauty and strength has been taken away by old age. (The condition) like this causing ill-health, does not make (me) give up hope. I, who have committed sins, have secured very great real estate. Seeing this my death, as it were, has approached. Who will protect my wealth obtained through sins which I committed, when I die issuless? Therefore, O friend, if you consent, I desire to give to brāhmaṇas all my wealth obtained unjustly.

The brāhmaṇa lady said:

32b-34. See, I have always given to unworthy recipients all the wealth which I had collected. Therefore, I am without wealth. What shall I give to a brāhmaṇa? If you have wealth, then make a present of it quickly.

Hearing these words of her, the prostitute was very much glad.

35-43. With all her wealth she made a present of food. There was an excellent brāhmaṇa named Hariśarman, who very devoutly always worshipped lord Viṣṇu. He who had curbed his senses and his anger, who was free from harming (others) and hypocrisy, practised a great (i.e. severe) penance to please Lakṣmī's lord. With sandal, flowers, offerings, incense, ghee and lamps he everyday worshipped Viṣṇu, the lord of gods. Even though the brāhmaṇa was rich he was always afraid of spending money. O best brāhmaṇa, in the house of the miser, ants, rats and other living beings, were always hungry. O best brāhmaṇa, he, without (i.e. not doing) the act of giving gifts, himself enjoyed everyday all the wealth that he had earned. For fear of being requested (to give) money, he never conversed with his friends and his brāhmaṇa relatives. O best brāhmaṇa, counting his very large wealth in his own house, he, regarding himself as the greatest, delighted himself. O brāhmaṇa, at the time destined for death, that very rich brāhmaṇa, that prostitute and that brāhmaṇa lady died at the same time.

44-45. Then, very fierce messengers, with nooses and mallets in their hands, of god Dharmarāja (i.e. Yama) came to take them (to him). Then, O Jaimini, those messengers like Caṇḍa, took them and instantly went to Yama's city along a difficult path.

Caṇḍa said (*to Yama*):

46. O lord of life, by your order Hariśarman is brought here. So also the prostitute, the brāhmaṇa lady (are brought here). Look at them standing before you.

47. Seeing them, the lord of life laughed, O best brāhmaṇa, and spoke thus to Citragupta skilled in all jobs:

Yama said:

48. O wise, very intelligent Citragupta, think over, from the beginning all the good and evil acts of these.

49. Then by Yama's order, the wise Citragupta considered all their good as well as evil acts.

Citragupta said:

50-56. O god, listen I shall tell (you) their religious merit and sins, which this prostitute, this brāhmaṇa lady and Hariśarman did. It is not possible to narrate the sins which this prostitute called Ratividagdhā, of a very wicked heart, committed. O Sun's son, this one, when she became old, gave food with all her wealth that was unjustly earned. Due to the efficacy of the gift of food, she was abandoned by all her sins committed during crores of existences, which would have resulted in her residence in houses of torments (i.e. where torments are inflicted). O great king, those who, even though they are sinners, give gift of food on the earth, go to the highest position of Viṣṇu. As many sins of (i.e. due to) brahminicide perish as the number of foods given by men on the earth. There is no doubt about it. Sin, leaving the bodies of the givers of food, goes to the vessels of those receiving it, O Sun's son.

57-58. Therefore, the wise ones do not accept the food of sinners. Those fools who accept it through delusion are sinners only. O lord, I have told the good and evil acts of the prostitute. Listen to the good and evil acts of the brāhmaṇa lady.

59-67a. O lord, this brāhmaṇa lady named Kṣemaṅkarī, born in a pure family, and the wife of Bhadrakīrti, committed evil acts. Abandoning the acts of (i.e. suited to) the stage of life, she, proud of her youth, ardently longing for union with paramours, became most sinful. O king, once in her childhood, while playing with (other) children, she dug a ditch having four corners on the road. On the same day clouds showered water. O lord, that ditch made by her was filled with water. O king, at noon, a thirsty bull scorched by the sun's heat drank water there. Due to the efficacy of the act of giving water only, all her great sins perished, O wise son of the Sun. Freed from all sins, she went to Viṣṇu's abode. O lord of gods, this wicked brāhmaṇa lady who had committed sins, became freed from all sins due to the effcacy of the gift of water. This brāhmaṇa is a great devotee of the Disc-holder, the god of gods. Therefore, O lord of life, Viṣṇu alone is said to be superior to him.

Vyāsa said:

67b-69. Having heard those words of Citragupta, Yama saluted the prostitute, the brāhmaṇa lady and the brāhmaṇa. Having heard about the worship of them and the members of their family, Yama, very much pleased, laughed and spoke words containing soft letters (i.e. spoke soft words), O Jaimini.

Yama said:

70-71. All you noble ones have all your sins perished. Go to the place of Viṣṇu, lord of Lakṣmī, which gives all pleasures.

Then Yama, having put them into a divine (chariot) which was made of gold and to which royal swans were yoked, sent them to the place of the Disc-holder (i.e. Viṣṇu).

72. Then all of them, freed from sins, mounted upon a divine chariot, and adorned by all ornaments, went to the lord's city.

73-75. That prostitute, with all her sins perished, obtained the proximity of the god, and lived happily for a long time, O brāhmaṇa. So also the brāhmaṇa lady. Seeing that Hariśarman in the assembly Viṣṇu, through affection, gave him an excellent seat made of gold. Having gladly honoured the best brāhmaṇa by offering him water for washing his feet, a respectful offering, water for sipping, Viṣṇu asked him seated on an excellent seat (there):

The lord said:

76. O brāhmaṇa, tell me about your happiness (i.e. How do you do?). Since you are my excellent devotee, stay for a long time in my abode, free from all troubles.

The brāhmaṇa said:

77. O god, O lord, on remembering you, you are seen. (And

the devotee) gets happiness. I have obtained your proximity. What greater happiness is there than this?

Vyāsa said:

78-80. Hearing his words spoken through affection, the lord gave the brāhmaṇa his similarity (i.e. assimilated the brāhmaṇa into himself). The lord of Lakṣmī, gave him all happiness difficult to be obtained; but remembering his miserliness, did not give him his measure of food. After a couple of days, the brāhmaṇa, being without food (and therefore) overcome by hunger, and being humble through modesty, said to Viṣṇu, the lord of gods:

The brāhmaṇa said:

81-90. O lord, as the fruits of many austerities I have secured your position. O lord, even here how am I everyday suffering from hunger? Even on beds I am fanned with breezes from white chowries by celestial hosts of divine maidens who have attained the prime of youth? O lord, like the best king, I am adorned with large garlands of fragrant flowers and my entire body is smeared with sandal. O Viṣṇu, by your order, everyday ladies with beautiful bodies dance to the accompaniment of songs before me. Everyday, gods like Indra always carry the dust-particles from my feet (on their heads), which beautify the crowns on their heads. And, O lord of the world, gods, divine sages, (other) sages, always praise me with eulogies like (my) servants. I have become Viṣṇu, having four arms, dark, holding a conch, a disc, a mace, and a lotus, having eyes like full-blown lotuses, wearing a yellow garment, and fine ear-rings. I am having a golden sacred thread, a crown and also ear-rings. By gods I am seen to be another Garuḍa-bannered (god) like you. O lord, you have given me all these pleasures difficult to be obtained. (Then) O highest lord, how (i.e. why) do you not give me food? As a tree is burnt by the fire in its hollow, my body is being very much scorched by the fire of hunger.

91-93. O Viṣṇu, with the digestive fire of the stomach blazing, I, whose body is afflicted, do not like this happiness given by you. None else worshipped by hosts of gods, except you, the lord of the world, has ever been worshipped by me through (physical) acts, mentally, or through speech. I have not been devoted to him (i.e. any other god than you) even in a dream. (Then) due to which fault (of mine), O lord, you are not giving me food?

Vyāsa said:

94-95. Then lord Viṣṇu, full of joy, said to him: "Well-being to you, O brāhmaṇa. Go quickly to Brahmā."

Hearing these words, the brāhmaṇa quickly went to Brahmā. Pointing out to him his miserliness, Brahmā said to him:

Brahmā said:

96-97. There is no doubt that (the fruit of) an action, obtained with difficulty, which is not given to a brāhmaṇa nor enjoyed by oneself, perishes. I have told you the entire cause of your affliction. O brāhmaṇa, well-being to you; you who have come from Yama, (now) go without any doubt.

The brāhmaṇa said

98. Through your grace I have heard fully (about) this maturity of my acts. Now tell (me) which gifts should be given by men.

Brhamā said:

99-101. There are many (kinds) of gifts. (All) cannot be described. O brāhmaṇa, I (shall) tell (about them) in brief. Listen attentively. O best brāhmaṇa, the pious one who has made the gift of land, the best of all gifts, should be known to be the giver of all (kinds of) gifts. O best brāhmaṇa, he who gives (a piece of) land measuring a gocarman,[1] would, being freed from all sins, go to the highest place.

102-107. Listen to the religious merit of (i.e. earned by) him who gives land along with the crop to a poor brāhmaṇa, O best brāhmaṇa. Freed from all sins, he would go to Viṣṇu's city. There he enjoys all happiness as long as fourteen Indras (rule).

---

1. Gocarman—A particular measure of surface thus defined by Vasiṣṭha:
daśahastena vaṁśena daśavaṁśān samantataḥ/
pañca cābhyādhikān dadyādetadgocarma cocyate//

Again obtaining land, he would be a sovereign emperor. That man, enjoying the entire earth for a long time, would become Viṣṇu. Since, brāhmaṇas should accept the land, even after abandoning (i.e. not accepting) hundreds of (other) gifts, the giver of the land and its receiver both go to heaven. O best brāhmaṇa, that dull brāhmaṇa who would reject the gift of land, would be very much afflicted in every existence. Even with him Viṣṇu is pleased and gives the highest position to him who would give a gift of land, even after obtaining it from others.

108-110. O brāhmaṇa, listen to the religious merit of (i.e. obtained by) him who gives or causes (someone else) to give a village to a poor brāhmaṇa. The wise one would live in Viṣṇu's world for as many periods of Manu as there are dust-particles on the earth or as there are drops in showers. O brāhmaṇa, I am telling you about the religious merit of the noble one who gives a milch-cow along with her calf (to a brāhmaṇa). Listen.

111-121. A man who gives a cow to a brāhmaṇa would obtain that fruit which one would get by giving the earth with the seven islands along with the crop (on it). He who gives a bull to a brāhmaṇa with a family, is freed from sins and goes to Rudra's world. For as many thousands of kalpas as the number of small hair on the body of the bull, he rejoices with Rudra. He who gives a cow to one proficient in the Vedas, never returns (to this world) from Rudra's world. O best brāhmaṇa, he who gives a bull with sesamum seeds (to a brāhmaṇa) would live in Rudra's abode in accordance with the number of the sesamum seeds. He who gives gold even of the measure of a sesamum seed to a brāhmaṇa, goes, along with crores (of the members) of his family to Viṣṇu's abode. He who would devoutly give silver to a poor brāhmaṇa, reaches the world of the Moon and drinks nectar (there). O best brāhmaṇa, he who gives a diamond or a pearl or a coral or any (other) gem, goes to Indra's world. O best brāhmaṇa, he, the generous-minded one, who gives the gift of a horse (to a brāhmaṇa) obtains the kingship of kings of gandharvas. There is no doubt about it. He who gives a young elephant without blemishes, would become a partner in the kingdom of gods like Indra, O brāhmaṇa. He too, who would give a palanquin carried by men, along with presents, to a brāhmaṇa, would also, having secured Indra's position, live there for four kalpas.

122-126. O brāhmaṇa, I shall tell, in brief, (about) the religious merit of (i.e. got by) him who gives the gift of śālagrāma stone to a brāhmaṇa; (please) listen. The giver of a śālagrāma stone obtains the same fruit as one obtains by giving the earth with the seven islands and with mountains and forests. The giver of a śālagrāma stone would get a crores times greater fruit than the one which men obtain by giving gold, jewels or other valuable things equal to their own weight.[1] O best brāhmaṇa, he who has given a śālagrāma stone has indeed given the fourteen worlds. O best man, that man who gives gold etc. equal to his weight, (lives) in heaven wearing divine garments, and (becomes) a king.

127-130. He is not born again in (i.e. from) the mother's womb. That best man who gives his daughter adorned (with ornaments, in marriage, to a worthy groom), would go to Viṣṇu's abode without (being required) to be born again. That foolish man who through delusion, sells his daughter, would go to the fearful hell called Purīṣahrada. O brāhmaṇa, that son that is born from the daughter (thus) sold, should be known like a cāṇḍāla, expelled from all religious rites. A man knowing the holy texts, should never see the face of him who sells his daughter.

131-136. If through ignorance he sees it, he should look at the Sun. O brāhmaṇa, all that auspicious act that is done in the presence of him who sells his daughter, would become fruitless, O brāhmaṇa. For the seller of his daughter there is no escape from hell. The one who gives his daughter (in marriage) does not again return from heaven. What is the use of talking much in this regard? I shall tell (it to you) in brief. The fruit of (the gift of) a diamond, (a piece) of land, and a daughter is hundred times more. Listen to the religious merit of (i.e. obtained by) him who gives a pair of shoes, an umbrella on the earth. I shall tell it to you in brief. Endowed with all affluence he would live here (i.e. in this world) for a hundred years. Reaching Indra's city after death (he would live there) for four hundred kalpas. He who gives a new garment goes to the best position.

1. Tulāpuruṣa—Gold, jewels or other valuable things equal to a man's weight (given to a brāhmaṇa as a gift).

137-147. He who would give an old garment, or an aging[1] cow or a girl in her menses, would always go to hell. O brāhmaṇa, a man who gives (the gift of) a fruit, goes to the abode of gods (i.e. heaven). There he enjoys the fruit like nectar for thousands of kalpas. O brāhmaṇa, the giver of vegetables goes to the position of lord Śiva. There he enjoys, along with gods, rice boiled in milk for two kalpas. A giver of milk, of curd, of ghee and of butter-milk obtains the drink of nectar in front of lord Viṣṇu. O brāhmaṇa, a man who gives flowers, sandal, (would go) to the abode of gods (i.e. heaven and), decorated with flowers and sandal would stay there for thousands of yugas. O best brāhmaṇa, he who offers a bed, comes to Brahmā's world, and lies for a long time on a bed there. O best brāhmaṇa, he who offers a lamp or a seat, being free from all sins, is seated, surrounded by rows of burning lamps, on divine throne. O king(?), the giver of a tāmbūla enjoys all auspicious things. Lying on the bosom of divine ladies in heaven, he eats tāmbūla. O best brāhmaṇa, O best man, he who gives knowledge, would, after securing Viṣṇu's proximity, stay (near him) for a couple of hundred yugas. Then, O best brāhmaṇa, having secured knowledge there, he obtains, through the grace of Lakṣmī's lord, liberation, difficult to obtain. He who teaches a helpless, much afflicted brāhmaṇa, goes to Viṣṇu's abode, from which return (to this earth) is difficult to be had.

148-153. Even the best brāhmaṇa belonging to a noble family, does not shine without knowledge. Therefore, those who teach a brāhmaṇa, go to the highest position. A brāhmaṇa, to whom deities resort, is actually a god. The preceptor of all castes does not at all shine without knowledge. He who has taught a brāhmaṇa, has given (all) the gifts like gold, that are there in the world. O best brāhmaṇa, I (shall) tell you in brief the religious merit of that man who devoutly gives the gift of a book. For every letter that is there on every leaf of the book, he would get the fruit of giving a crore of tawny cows. The giver of the book would live in Vaikuṇṭha for as many periods of Manu as the days twice-borns read that book.

1. Rajatī—*Jaratī* seems to be the correct reading and not *rajatī* which means 'whitish'.

154-160. O brāhmaṇa, there are many such gifts. Even in two hundred (months) who is in this world able to describe them correctly? All those sins like brāhmaṇicide which are committed by men are destroyed (by gifts). Therefore, one should give gifts. The fruit of that gift is obtained as long as the material of the gift given by the three castes through their religious merit, exists. There is no doubt that a man obtains the religious merit, crore times more than the gift given to please Lakṣmī's lord. O brāhmaṇa, therefore, an intelligent man should devoutly give a gift to please Viṣṇu. The wise have declared giving gifts to be superior even to penance. Therefore, a wise man should, even with an effort, give gifts. O brāhmaṇa, there is none like him in this world who does both—giving gifts and practising penance.

CHAPTER TWENTYONE

Brāhmaṇas; *Gift of Food and Water*

Vyāsa said:

1. Having heard Brahmā's words, that best brāhmaṇa, Hariśarman, again saluted him devoutly, and spoke, O Jaimini:

Hariśarman said:

2. O lord, please tell me as to whom the many gifts that you narrated should be given.

Brahmā said:

3-4. Of all the castes brāhmaṇa is the most venerable person. Gifts should be given to him by men having devotion and faith. A brāhmaṇa is the resort of all deities. He is actually a god on the earth. He saves a giver in this ocean of the universe, which is difficult to cross.

The brāhmaṇa said:

5. O best god, you have declared brāhmaṇa to be the most

respectable of all castes. But out of them (i.e. brāhmaṇas) who is the greatest? To whom is a gift given?

Brahmā said:

6-8. O best brāhmaṇa, all the brāhmaṇas are superior, and all are always respectable. But those brāhmaṇas who are spoilt by such blemishes as theft, so also our haters, are not respectable. So (gifts should) not be given to others. Brāhmaṇas of bad conduct are not respectable. Śūdras with their senses curbed are respectable. So also those who eat what is prohibited (are not to be honoured). Cows are supposed to be the mothers of people. O best brāhmaṇa, I am now particularly telling the greatness of brāhmaṇas through affection for you. Listen to it attentively.

9-11. Brāhmaṇas are respectable to kṣatriyas, vaiśyas and śūdras. Brāhmaṇas are respectable to one another, and brāhmaṇas are to be honoured. O best man, the life, sons, fame, wealth of him who would worship a brāhmaṇa looking upon him as Viṣṇu, increase. O brāhmaṇa, Viṣṇu desires to cut off the head of that foolish man who hoards (wealth) on the earth.

12-15. O Jaimini(?), a wise man should not salute a brāhmaṇa who has flowers in his hand, who has water in his hand, who has (the idol of) a god in his hand, and whose body is smeared with oil. A wise man should not salute a brāhmaṇa who is in water, who is in a temple of a deity, whose mind is absorbed in meditation, and who is worshipping a deity. O best brāhmaṇa, a wise man should not salute a brāhmaṇa performing outside (i.e. morning) duties, who is taking his meal, so also a brāhmaṇa who is singing Sāmans. An intelligent man should not salute everyone of the brāhmaṇas (separately) where many brāhmaṇas are present, O best brāhmaṇa.

16. He who would not salute (in return) a brāhmaṇa who has devoutly saluted, should be known to be like a cāṇḍāla, and should never be saluted.

17. Parents saluted by their son, should not salute him (in return). All brāhmaṇas saluted by (other) brāhmaṇas, should salute them (in return).

18. The wise ones do not hate brāhmaṇas and cows who have committed faults. If through folly they hate, Viṣṇu is always angry with them.

19. Yama puts a needle into both the eyes of him who looks angrily at suppliants (and) brāhmaṇas.

20. O brāhmaṇa, Yama puts a heated iron rod into that mouth with which fools reproach (others).

21. In that house where a brāhmaṇa eats (food), Viṣṇu himself (lives). So also all deities, manes and divine sages.

22-28. Yama quickly destroys all the sin in the body of him, the wise one, who would carry just a drop of water from the foot of a brāhmaṇa. All the holy places that exist in crores of worlds, exist in the right foot of a brāhmaṇa. He whose head is sprinkled with water from the feet of a brāhmaṇa, has bathed at all holy places and is initiated for all sacrifices. By carrying (on his head) the water from the foot of a brāhmaṇa all his fierce sins like the murder of a brāhmaṇa perish at once. By carrying (on the head) the water from the foot of a brāhmaṇa, all diseases like consumption, highly afflicting, perish instantly. The dead ancestors gratified by the water offered at the feet of a brāhmaṇa for the dead ancestors, live in heaven as long as the moon and the stars (exist). By a wise man who would worship a brāhmaṇa's feet with dūrvās after washing them, Viṣṇu, the lord of the world and the best of all gods, is worshipped.

29-33. I am telling the truth (and) the truth (only). That mortal who would carry on his head the remains of the offering at the feet of brāhmaṇas, obtains eternal liberation. That best man who goes round a brāhmaṇa while keeping him to his right, has gone round the earth with the seven islands. He who would give a fruit or a tāmbūla after wetting the feet of brāhmaṇas is free from a disease if he is ill, and from a sin if he is a sinner. One that is bound gets free from his bond on washing the feet of brāhmaṇas. By washing the feet of brāhmaṇas those women who have no children or whose children are dead, have many children and their children live (long). O best brāhmaṇa, listen to the greatness (of the wetting of a brāhmaṇa's feet) which removes all sins.

34a. I (shall) tell you in brief about (the importance of) wetting the feet of a brāhmaṇa.

34b-46a. Formerly there was a brāhmaṇa named Bhadrakriya, born in a pure family and highly devoted to worshipping Viṣṇu. He knew the Vedas, he was tranquil, and was highly devoted to his parents. He honoured guests; so also he honoured his kinsmen. Once that best brāhmaṇa, with his body smeared with oil, went, taking with him clothes used for bathing, to a lake to bathe (then). That best brāhmaṇa who knew all holy texts and who was engaged in the well-being of all people, having bathed made offerings to his dead ancestors in the proper manner. Having finished the bath-rite, and repeating Viṣṇu's names, he came to his own house and was engrossed in worshipping Viṣṇu. With very cold water he washed both his feet. That brāhmaṇa who honoured (other) brāhmaṇas, who had washed his feet and hands, placed all utensils for the bath (of the deity). O best brāhmaṇa, to the region of the door came a dog that was tormented by the heat of the summer sun, resembling that of fire. He lay in the very cold water used by the brāhmaṇa for washing his feet. Due to the touch of the water used by the brāhmaṇa for washing his feet, the extremely sinful dog was freed from all sins committed during crores of existences. The dog lying at the door of the house and overcome by thirst, begged water. He was beaten by the brāhmaṇa's servants. O brāhmaṇa, the dog died there only. Due to the touch of the wetness of the brāhmaṇa's feet, the dog was free from sins. Seeing the noble one, as it were, the lord of the universe in an embodied form, the brāhmaṇa ascetic bowing with modesty, said to him:

The brāhmaṇa said:

46bc. O noble one, tell (me) who you are. Due to which act are you afflicted? (How) are you born in the stock of a dog, full of many afflictions?

Brahmā said:

47-57. Having heard the words of the brāhmaṇa sage, the very glorious one told all his account from the beginning. "I was a very powerful sovereign emperor named Śaṁkha. I protected the whole earth for four thousand years. All obeyed my orders. I conquered all enemies in battles. I gave all (kinds of) gifts, and protected my relatives. O glorious one, once I, struck by the arrows of Cupid, forcibly kidnapped a very beautiful bride of a man. As a result of that sin my glory was in danger. Then, I, very powerful one, was expelled by all people. Then, I, deprived of my kingdom, lived in a forest. Fatigued with hunger and thirst, I sometime died (there). Having gone to Yama's city I experienced distress for a long time. O best brāhmaṇa, listen to it, causing pain to the heart of the listeners. I experienced a very fearful mass of the flames of blazing fire on the land full of redness due to heated iron weapons. Then by Yama's order I remained clasping a very fearful iron pillar, heated by a blazing fire. Then Yama's servants sprinkled me with streams of cold water (sharp) like razors. There in Yama's abode I experienced another great misery. Then again and again being born in the remaining hells, I experienced great misery in a sinful stock for a long time.

58-59. Due to the contact of the water (flowing) from your feet I am rescued from the bond of sin. I am going to the highest position difficult to be obtained even by meditating saints. O best brāhmaṇa, you are my preceptor. My salutation to you, the noble one. Being freed from sins due to your grace I (shall) go to Viṣṇu's city."

Bhadrakriya said:

60-71. O king, a man should never (forget) the account of the previous existence. Therefore, abandoning one's son, one should always follow a wise course of action. A king who practises wisdom never faces misery. He enjoys the earth free from troublesome fellows for a long time. That wicked king who does not like wisdom is soon deprived of glory. There is no doubt about this. A king who desires a (long) life, strength, glory, friends, victory and happiness should always appoint wise ministers. Wise men, disregarding a king, abandon him with care. In an assembly without the wise, statesmanship is not strong. Then, when statesmanship of a king has suddenly vanished, the royal glory along with the treasure, the army and the elephants, vanishes. Kings desiring (their) well-being never hate brāhmaṇas, astrologers, physicians and kinsmen. A king who hates astrologers loses his glory. The one hating physicians loses his life. One who hates his kinsmen loses his family. One who hates brāhmaṇas suffers from all afflictions. Kings are said to be the fathers and subjects to be the sons. Therefore, kings protect the subjects as sons born of themselves. A king should love his citizens as his own sons. The wise ones should know that calamities hang over the heads of those very sinful kings who harass their subjects. Viṣṇu, the lord of gods, protects wise kings as they protect their own subjects. The two, viz. looking after and punishing the subjects, bring him good fortune.

72-75. Kings without (these) two should be known to be mean kings. Kings curbing the wicked and protecting the virtuous rejoice on the earth for a long time. A king should preserve with care the wealth that is obtained justly. A king of bad conduct would not prosper in a calamity. O best brāhmaṇa, kings desiring their own good, always speedily observe the auspicious and inauspicious (happenings) in their kingdom through spies as their eyes. A king should entertain fear till an invasion by an enemy takes place.

76-80. When that fear (of an invasion) has come, the king should act fearlessly. Towards his kinsman, or a friend, or a minister, he should be serious on his face (i.e. outwardly) but should mentally have love only (for him). His ministers, kinsmen, sons, subjects and brothers do not look upon a king without seriousness as a king. First they keep away, so also they do not stand before him. People do not desire the shelter of a king who has given up seriousness. O brāhmaṇa, a king desiring to be (i.e. continue) a king for a long time, should not have only one minister in the entire kingdom for its prosperity. He would take away the position of very intelligent servants.

81-91a. Therefore, the king should appoint another man in the assembly. A king won over by foolish women and always engaged in singing and playing upon musical instruments, so also without horses and elephants, would suddenly face a calamity. O best brāhmaṇa, following (good) practices, truthfulness, keeping one's promise, seriousness are the characteristics of kings. How can he be (called) king who is without valour? How can he be (called) king who has not conquered the land of others? After the land of another (king) is conquered, the king obtains the inexhaustible fruit of a horse-sacrifice for every step that he would go over. When a king, desiring to conquer another king's land, is killed by other kings in a battle, then he, being freed from all sins, would go to the highest place. A king who gets victory in a battle, obtains the highest position. Or if he is killed in a battle he would obtain Indra's affluence in heaven. That king who kills a warrior who has abandoned his weapon, who has lost his energy, or who is bent upon fleeing, has a downfall. O best brāhmaṇa, both he who is bent upon fleeing and he who kills him, would stay in a hell extremely unbearable. O best brāhmaṇa, a courageous warrior and he who kills him would both live in heaven as long as the moon and the sun exist. What is the use of talking too much in this regard? I shall tell (you) in brief. A king who protects his subjects, never sinks.

Brahmā said:

91b-96a. O brāhmaṇa, when the king was speaking like this, a great shower of flowers fell on him whose sin had dropped, from the sky. Then messengers of the noble Viṣṇu came there taking (with them) a beautiful chariot to which royal swans were yoked. That king whose sins had gone away, got into the divine chariot made of gold and went to Viṣṇu's abode. I have told (you) this greatness of the water (flowing) from a brāhmaṇa's feet. Having listened to it devoutly, a man would obtain liberation. Thus I have told you everything that you desired to hear. O brāhmaṇa, go to the abode of Viṣṇu. Well-being to you.

Hariśarman said:

96b-98a. Due to the great fire of hunger my body is being burnt. O lord of gods, tell me by which means my hunger would be satiated. You are a devotee, loving your devotees. Everyday due to the very blazing fire of hunger I am having very great pain.

Brahmā said:

98b-99. O best brāhmaṇa, eat the flesh of your body which you have always fed with food; for, those who satisfy themselves with the food (meant) for another (person), eat the flesh of their own bodies in the other world.

Vyāsa said:

100. Hearing the cruel words of Brahmā, that best brāhmaṇa again praised the god with words having pleasing letters (i.e. with pleasing words).

The brāhmaṇa said:

101-105. O god of gods, O you who protect him who seeks your refuge, pardon all my faults. Salutation to you, O greatest god. O lord, there are all faults (i.e. committed by) and no virtues of men who carry bodies full of feces and urine. Please pardon the fault committed by me who was deluded. The good do not take into account the fault of those who have sought their shelter. O Brahman, it is not possible for living beings to eat the flesh of their own bodies. Tell what is proper for them, and by what they will be gratified.

Thus the brāhmaṇa devoutly spoke these words. The omniscient Brahmā, dear to brāhmaṇas, and kind, spoke (thus):

Brahmā said:

106-109a. O best brāhmaṇa, do not grieve. Listen to my good words as to the means by which you will now obtain food. The son is born from oneself. (Therefore) the son is like one's own self. Therefore, the manes obtain (the fruit of) the deed of their sons. For a long time you will stay in the very beautiful abode of the god.

Then that brāhmaṇa, thus addressed by him, and oppressed by hunger, appeared before his son in a dream and said to him:

The brāhmaṇa said:

109b-116. O best son, you are initiated. May you have the highest good! O dear one, I am your father. Listen to my grief. O son, due to the efficacy of penance I have obtained the highest abode. Tormented by the fire of hunger I have always been sinking there. O son, O brāhmaṇa, if you have affection for me as your father, then now give food and water to me. Whatever is offered by sons to their fathers on the earth, is obtained by the fathers, since sons are born from (their) fathers' bodies. Formerly I very devoutly worshipped the lord with songs, musical instruments, dances and auspicious recitals of hymns, sandals, incenses, offerings of eatables and lamps full of ghee, so also with water for washing the feet, respectful offerings and water for sipping, so also meditations and invocations. O son, I, a miser, never gave the lord of the world food, or (other) offerings of eatables. I never honoured a guest with water or other (articles).

117-122a. I never satisfied my kinsmen or suppliants. O son, due to that act only, I, being tormented by the fire of hunger, am everyday sinking (while I live) in Viṣṇu's abode. Therefore, O best of the learned men, by giving the gifts of food and water to brāhmaṇas, protect my life. If, through cruelty you do not do so, then I shall eat my flesh only in Viṣṇu's abode.

Then that hungry brāhmaṇa, with his throat, lips and palate dried up, speaking like this to his son, suddenly disappeared. Then when in the bright morning the sun appeared, the (son who was) initiated thought over what his father had said to him in his dream.

122b-124a. 'Due to the fault in his acts my father, with his body burnt by hunger, everyday is sinking. Fie upon me who am a dull, miserly person. I too am giving nothing through my father's religious merit.'

124b-125. Thinking like this in many ways the brāhmaṇa, though initiated, with faith and devotion gave gifts to brāhmaṇas, O best brāhmaṇa.

126-131a. Listen for how much period he remained in Viṣṇu's abode free from hunger and thirst due to the efficacy of that religious merit. The day of Brahmā is said to be (i.e. to consist) of four thousand yugas. During that day only fourteen periods of Manu pass. During that day only fourteen Indras are said (to rule). O best brāhmaṇa, they enjoy their separate domains. Having enjoyed their auspicious domains during one day of Brahmā, the fourteen Indras and Manus perish. When that Hariśarman lived in the very bright world of Viṣṇu, which gave pleasure and which was charming, one day of Brahmā passed. There, he, having enjoyed charming pleasures for this much period, obtained the highest knowledge and entered Viṣṇu's body.

Vyāsa said:

131b-132. O Jaimini, in the world there is no other gift like that of food and water. Fruits of all gifts are had from the gifts of food and water. (For them) there is no test of a worthy recipient, or any restriction about time.

133-134. The wise have expressed (their view) regarding the gifts of food and water. (They say:) Gifts of food and water should always be made. Those men who, with great respect, recite this (description of the) greatness (of the gifts) of food and water and of brāhmaṇas, obtain the fruit of the gift of food and water and go to Viṣṇu's abode, giving happiness.

CHAPTER TWENTYTWO

The Greatness of Ekādaśī

Jaimini said:

1-2. O preceptor, by your grace I have heard the sin-destroying greatness along with its history, of the water flowing from a brāhmaṇa's feet, the auspicious greatness of Gaṅgā, so also the fruit of the worship of Viṣṇu, the excellent (account of the) greatness of the gift of food and of water.

3-5. O best sage, now I desire to hear carefully the entire fruit of (the vow of) Ekādaśī, which destroys all sins. Why is the Ekādaśī(-vow) the greatest? What is declared to be the mode of (its observance)? When is it observed? What is its fruit? Tell me. O you ocean of virtues, who is the most adorable deity there? Please tell me what fault (accrues) to him who does not observe it.

Vyāsa said:

6-12. O brāhmaṇa sage, none else but Viṣṇu is able to narrate the entire fruit of the Ekādaśī(vow). Therefore, I shall tell it in brief. The highest Puruṣa (Brahman) having first created the world with the mobile and the immobile, created the 'Man of Sin' (sin personified) for curbing all. His head was the murder of brāhmaṇas. His eyes were the drink of liquor. His face was the theft of gold. His ears were the violation of the preceptor's bed (i.e. his wife). His nose was the murder of women. His arms were the sin of killing cows. His neck was the snatching of deposits. His throat was causing abortions. The tip of his heart was adultery. His belly was the murder of friends. His waist ending with the hollow of his navel was the murder of those who sought his shelter. His thigh was the preceptor's censure. His penis was the sale of (one's) daughter. His anus was the divulging of confidential words. His feet were the murder of love. The small hair on his body was misfortunes. His body was huge. He was fierce. His complexion was dark. His eyes were tawny. He gave great pain to those who sought his shelter.

13-14. Seeing that Man of Sin, the best among men (but) very fierce, the kind lord who removes the affliction of his creation (i.e. mankind), thought: 'For curbing my creation, I have created this wicked man, cruel and giving affliction to those that resort to him. (Now) I shall create the means (to control him)'.

15-16. Then lord Viṣṇu himself became Yama. He created hells like Raurava that gave affliction to the sinners. A fool who commits a sin does not go to the highest position. By Yama's order he would go to a hell like Raurava.

17. Once lord Viṣṇu, who removes the affliction of the created beings, mounted upon Garuḍa and went to Yama's abode.

18. The Sun's son, on seeing Anāmaya Viṣṇu, the lord of the worlds, was pleased in mind, and worshipped him with incense etc.

19. Viṣṇu, the only chief of all the worlds, honoured by Yama, sat on a seat made of gold, O best brāhmaṇa.

20. The lord, the killer of demons, seated there, heard crying, meditation (dhyānaṁ?), in the southern direction, O lord.

21. Then that lord of Lakṣmī, with his mind full of amazement, said to Yama: "Wherefrom is this sound of their crying (coming)?"

Yama said:

22-23. O god, sinful mortals sink in the hell giving great affliction, in my abode due to sins committed by their own hands. O Viṣṇu, it is extremely painful to eat the fruit of the tree of sins. Therefore, the sinners are crying. This big noise is theirs.

24-25. Thus told by the Sun's son, Kṛṣṇa, having lotus-like eyes, suddenly went where they were crying. Then the lord, the master, seeing those sinful mortals living in Raurava etc. had pity produced in his heart and thought:

26. 'I have created all these living beings in accordance with the fault in their acts. In spite of my presence they sink in hell, giving great distress.'

27. O best brāhmaṇa, thinking this and something else, he, full of pity, himself suddenly became the day of Ekādaśī.

28-30. Then he made it well-known to all the sinners. All of them, with their sins dropped went to the highest abode. Therefore, know Ekādaśī to be the embodiment of Viṣṇu, the highest soul. He made the Ekādaśī day, as the best of all vows, the best one (removing) all misdeeds, and as one purifying the three worlds. The Man of Sin, being afraid, went to Viṣṇu to praise him.

31. Then, O brāhmaṇa, that Man of Sin, devoutly joining the palms of his hands, praised lord Viṣṇu, the lord of Lakṣmī.

32. Hearing his hymn of praise the lord was pleased. He said: "I am pleased. Tell me what you desire."

The Man of Sin said:

33-34. O Viṣṇu, you, the lord, have created me, giving distress (to beings) by obliging them. Due to the power of Ekādaśī, I am perishing now. When I die, all the sentient beings will be free from the bonds of the worldly existence.

35-42. O lord, when all the best sentient beings will be freed, with whom will you sport in this play-house in the form of the worldly existence? O Viṣṇu, if you have a desire to sport in the play-house in the form of the world, then protect me from the fear of the Ekādaśī day. I cannot be killed by thousands of other (kinds of) religious merit. The meritorious Ekādaśī (alone) can kill me. Grant me a boon. For me who ran away through the fear of Ekādaśī, I do not find any place free from fear among men, insects, other living beings, on mountains, trees, dry grounds, in water, rivers, seas, forests, on desolate roads, in heaven, on the earth, in the nether world, (or) among gods, gandharvas, birds. O god of gods, O eternal one, due to this Ekādaśī day I am not getting a place to stay in the crores of universes. O lord, O lord of gods, tell me where I shall live without fear on the Ekādaśī (day). You have created me without a purpose.

Vyāsa said:

43-44. The Man of Sin spoke like this to Viṣṇu who removes affliction. He, with tears in his eyes, fell down on the ground and wept. Then the lord, the destroyer of Madhu and Kaiṭabha, laughed and said to the Man of Sin who was alarmed through the fear of Ekādaśī:

The lord said:

45-47. O Man of Sin, give up your grief. Be joyful. I shall tell you where you will have your place on the Ekādaśī day. O Man of Sin, when Ekādaśī, the purifier of the three worlds, arrives, you should resort to food. This Ekādaśī day, my embodiment, will not kill you, the Man of Sin, who have taken shetler inside food.

48-49. Then, O brāhmaṇa sage, the god also disappeared there only. The Man of Sin, being satisfied, went as he had come. Therefore, those best ones who desire their welfare should never eat food when the day of (i.e. sacred to) Viṣṇu, has come.

50-52. By the order of glorious Viṣṇu all the sins that are there in the world, save themselves by resorting to food on the Ekādaśī day. (Even) those committing all (kinds of) sins would be discharged from hell. But those who eat food even on this day should be known to be the greatest sinners (and have no requittal). Repeatedly I am telling firmly. O people, listen, listen. Never, never eat food (on the Ekādaśī day).

53-56. O best brāhmaṇa, all brāhmaṇas, kṣatriyas, vaiśyas, śūdras and others should observe the Ekādaśī (vow), which gives (the fruit of) the four goals of human life. The wise say that a *kāṣṭhā* is formed by eighteen *nimeṣas*. Those who know everything say that a *kalā* is formed by thirty *kāṣṭhās*. A *kṣaṇa* is formed by thirty *kalās*, and a *muhūrta* by twelve *kṣaṇas*. The day and night of people is declared to be of thirty *muhūrtas*. O best brāhmaṇa, a fortnight should be known (to be formed) by those fifteen (days). A month is formed by the two fortnights—the bright and the dark.

57-58a. O best brāhmaṇa, he who, even having committed great sins, observes the Ekādaśī (vow) in both the bright and dark halves in the month, would, after being freed from all sins, obtain Viṣṇu's world.

58b-62. A mother is not said to be mother. The mother is the Ekādaśī day. A mother would look after (one) in this world only. But the Ekādaśī day (looks after one) everywhere. That dull person who, abandoning the Ekādaśī vow observes another vow, takes up a clod after giving up a gem in his hand. Those who, full of devotion, have observed the Ekādaśī vow, have performed all sacrifices, and have observed all vows. Viṣṇu is always angry with those sinful men who, through folly, eat (food) on the Ekādaśī of the bright half or of the dark half (of a month). He, who has fasted on the Ekādaśī day has performed all religious rites.

63-71. As Viṣṇu is declared to be the greatest of all gods, so is the Ekādaśī vow the greatest of all vows. As the Sun is (said to be the greatest) among Ādityas, as the Moon is (said to be the greatest) among the constellations, so the vow of Ekādaśī is said to be the greatest of all vows. As the holy fig tree is declared (to be the greatest) of all trees, as the Sāma (Veda) is (declared to be the greatest) of all Vedas, so is the Ekādaśī vow said to be the greatest of all vows. As Uśanas (i.e. Śukrācārya) is (said to be the greatest) of (all) thinkers, as brāhmaṇa is (said to be the best) among castes, so is the Ekādaśī vow said to be the greatest of all vows. Among the sages Vyāsa is the greatest. Nārada is the greatest among the divine sages. Similarly the Ekādaśī vow is the greatest of all vows. As the gift of food is said to be the best of all gifts, similarly the Ekādaśī vow is said to be the greatest of all vows. As there is no friend like religious merit, as there is no teacher like the holy texts, similarly there is no vow comparable to the Ekādaśī vow in the three worlds. As the wise have declared mind to be the greatest of the senses, the month of Kārtika to be the greatest among the months, Arjuna to be the greatest of the Pāṇḍavas, as the Vedas are declared to be the greatest of all holy texts, so is the Ekādaśī vow said to be the best among vows.

72-74. O brāhmaṇa, the wise have not declared any other vow equal to the Ekādaśī vow in the Vedas, scriptures, Purāṇas and other holy texts. Having observed the Ekādaśī vow all men remain without fear on the earth. What will (Yama), the Sun's son, do (to them)? Yama is the servant of those who properly observe (even) one Ekādaśī. Therefore, one should observe the Ekādaśī vow, giving happiness.

75. I am telling you in brief the manner of (observing) the Ekādaśī vow. O best one, O Jaimini, being of (i.e. with) an attentive mind listen (to it).

76-81. Having got up in the morning on the tenth (day) a man should brush his teeth. Then he should bathe without (smearing his body with) oil and (remain) without food. Then having worshipped Viṣṇu by offering water for washing his feet etc., he should, being highly devoted to the meditation of Viṣṇu, take one meal (only). On the tenth he should avoid (eating) flesh, salt, meat, pulses, big beans, so also vegetables. On the tenth he should avoid eating twice, the food of another (man), spirituous liquors, sexual union, so also taking food from vessels of bell-metal. On the tenth he should avoid nimba-leaf, egg-plant-fruit, and dry citron, so also milk without ghee. On the tenth he should avoid eating too much, very much enjoying and eating food and tāmbūla.

82. O best brāhmaṇa, just those articles which are prohibited on the tenth are also undoubtedly prohibited on the twelfth.

83. O best brāhmaṇa, a devotee of Viṣṇu desiring the proper fruit of his vow should not eat at night on the tenth, so also on the twelfth.

84. Therefore, he who observes a vow, having quickly eaten food proper for a fast should, in the proper manner, brush his teeth in the afternoon on the tenth.

85-87. In the evening, having gone to (Viṣṇu's) temple with a handful of flowers, he, meditating mentally upon Viṣṇu, should utter this prayer: 'O Govinda, I have taken up this vow before you. By the grace of your feet, may it reach its completion without any obstacle. Can I, a man of a very fickle mind, full of greed and delusion, observe it without your favour?'

88-93. Having recited these two hymns, and having offered just that handful of flowers to Viṣṇu, he should salute (Viṣṇu) prostrating himself like a staff on the ground. In that very abode of Viṣṇu, he, engaged in remembering Viṣṇu, should sleep on the ground after covering his bed with kuśa (grass). Then when it is the bright morning, he should not brush his teeth. The wise one should clean his mouth with twelve mouthfuls of water. He should (then) perform his daily rites like Viṣṇu's worship etc. Then, O best brāhmaṇa, at night, he should, together with all other men observing the vow, keep awake in front of the lord of worlds. O best brāhmaṇa, he who observes the vow for a long time along with his mother, wife, brother or also his father, his son, friend, and who would keep awake before Viṣṇu, would dwell in Viṣṇu's abode.

94. Viṣṇu would take away the sin of (i.e. committed by) him during many existences, who would draw the picture of a conch, or a disc etc. in Viṣṇu's temple.

95-100. Listen to the fruit of (i.e. obtained by) him who would draw in Viṣṇu's temple a picture with the paste of rice-powder or with other sylvan materials. He enjoys all auspicious (things) along with his sons, grandsons, and great-grandsons. And afterwards, he, going to Viṣṇu's abode, would get liberation there. A man hoisting a flag on the day of (i.e. sacred to) Lakṣmī's lord, would go to Viṣṇu's city after emancipating crores of men. That man who would decorate Viṣṇu's temple with lines of banners would be a king in every birth. As soon as the banner moves due to breezes all the sin of the maker of it perishes just then. Wise men desiring the highest position, should put up the lines of banners of various colours in Viṣṇu's temple on the day of (i.e. sacred to) Viṣṇu.

101-105. O brāhmaṇa sage, that man who holds a very beautiful umbrella over Viṣṇu's head, becomes (i.e. is born as) a kṣatriya in every existence on the earth. He who, on the day of (i.e. sacred to) Viṣṇu, prepares a pavilion of flowers, would obtain for every flower the religious merit due to more than a hundred horse-sacrifices. A wise man should even with effort prepare a pavilion with flowers on the day of (i.e. sacred to) Viṣṇu in order to obtain (the fruit of) the four goals of human life. He who makes an abode of cloth (i.e. a tent) on the day of (i.e. sacred to) Viṣṇu, lives in a mansion in heaven, O brāhmaṇa sage. Having fashioned an abode of cloth, a man, dear to Viṣṇu, (or to whom Viṣṇu is dear), ties there a white, or red or black (piece of) cloth.

106. The observer of the vow should devoutly install there

a śālagrāma stone or idol of the lord of Lakṣmī after bathing it with pañcāmṛta.

107. A wise man should first perform, even with effort the *svastyayana* (recitation of mantras for averting evil) and then declare the purpose in order to obtain (the fruit of) the four goals of human life.

108. Having performed one's *bhūtaśuddhi* (the removal of ghosts from oneself) in accordance with the formality prescribed by scriptures he should take with a concentrated mind an excellent flower.

109-110. He should meditate upon Viṣṇu residing in the lotus of his heart, seated on a golden seat and on a jewelled one. "Constantly looking from the corners of my eyes at him, seated on a golden seat, adorned with fire-like (bright) gems, having donned a sporting attire, having a beautiful body like the sky, having the digit (of the moon), always shining with the four arms holding weapons, looking with his lotus-like eyes at Lakṣmī's face that removes his fatigue, I worship him.

111-123. O lord, O lord of Lakṣmī, O dear one, come along with the gods. In this vow I have to worship you with devotion. O you endowed with all good characteristics, O lord of the world, remain with Lakṣmī on this excellent seat till I worship you. O you whose fame is well-known in all the worlds, O Nārāyaṇa, O lord, I hope you are quite all right. Tell me all that, O you who are worshipped by the gods. O lord of gods, O Nārāyaṇa, accept the fragrant water for washing your feet. It will remove the dust-particles from both your feet; it is pure and very cold. O Viṣṇu, I offer you materials of worship along with dūrvā grass. It is along with unbroken rice grains, O you whose eyes resemble lotuses. I am offering you this very pure water for sipping. O you highest joy, accept it which enhances great joy. O you destroyer of Jarāsandha, O you lord of Lakṣmī, may your body be decorated with the fragrant sandal offered by me. O god, O lord of gods, to you the first cause of the worlds I am offering this water for sipping, for purifying. (Please) accept it. For increasing the joy of the god, this incense was formerly created by Brahmā. Therefore, I offer it to you, O greatest among gods. O Janārdana, O god, may this lamp, full of ghee, and destroyer of the mass of darkness, please you. This garment along with the upper one will very well decorate your abdomen and hips. O lord of gods, O master of the world, I am giving it to you along with the sacred thread. O highest god, I have devoutly offered to you four kinds of food having six agreeable tastes. (Please) accept it. O Viṣṇu, O you very intelligent one, accept this tāmbūla removing the bad odour of the mouth, with (i.e. containing) camphor and khadira, and giving beatitude".

124-126. Full of devotion he should in this way worship Viṣṇu with excellent offerings in (all) the four watches (of the day). He who would offer various offerings on the day of (i.e. sacred to) Viṣṇu should not show guile about wealth if he desires the fruit of his acts. Then all the observers of the vow, highly devoted to Viṣṇu, should keep awake at night while dancing, singing and eulogizing etc.

127. O best brāhmaṇa, those who are engaged in the vow, should remember Viṣṇu's names destroying all sins, while going round (the image of Viṣṇu) keeping it to their right.

128. Those who hear the sound of Viṣṇu's name coming from every mouth would be free from great heaps of sins.

129. On the day of (i.e. sacred to) Viṣṇu one should not talk to heretics. Due to a mere talk with heretics (one's) entire religious merit perishes.

130. Fools are not pleased on hearing the song of Viṣṇu's glory which comes out from every mouth, as dogs are not pleased on hearing the sound of a lute.

131. The good ones are pleased on hearing the song about the lord of the world, which destroys all sins, as the deer are pleased on hearing the sound of a lute.

132-134. They sing songs about Viṣṇu. They dance an excellent dance. They are pleased on seeing the observers of Viṣṇu's vow. They are pleased with what the observers of Viṣṇu's vow are pleased with in the temple of Viṣṇu, O brāhmaṇa. Those observers of (Viṣṇu's) vow who do not sing on the day of (i.e. sacred to) Viṣṇu, attain beasthood eternally in every existence. They, without (the power of uttering) words (i.e. being dumb) roam in every existence.

135. Musical instruments like tabor should be beaten in front of (the image of) Viṣṇu, since lord Viṣṇu would be pleased with (the sound of) musical instruments.

136. The devotees of Viṣṇu keeping awake (in front) of Viṣṇu study Vedas (in his temple) or recite a Purāṇa (in the temple).

137. On the day of (i.e. sacred to) Viṣṇu, Rāmāyaṇa, Bhāgavata, or Bhārata narrated by Vyāsa or other Purāṇas should be read.

138. Those who read (these) before (the image of) Viṣṇu and those who listen to them on the day of (i.e. sacred to) Viṣṇu, obtain for every letter the fruit due to the gift of a tawny cow.

139. A devotee of Viṣṇu should joyfully keep awake at night. He should curb his sleep. He properly meditates upon Viṣṇu with his heart.

140-142. On the day of (i.e. sacred to) Viṣṇu, he should salute Viṣṇu by falling (i.e. prostrating himself) on the ground like a staff while going round (the image keeping it to his) right. Then the devout observer of the vow, after having performed the five great sacrifices in the bright morning, should bathe (the image of) Viṣṇu with milk and worship him. The observer of the vow should give a present according to his capacity to a brāhmaṇa. Then on the twelfth day he should break the fast.

143-147. The religious merit earned during crores of existences by him who breaks his fast after having observed a fast on the twelfth day, perishes. The wise ones, desiring the fruit of the vow, should break the fast on the twelfth day, and never on the thirteenth day. O brāhmaṇa, the devotee of Viṣṇu, desiring the fruit of the fast, should, with effort, avoid sleep even at night on the day of the fast. Without keeping awake the fast is useless. Therefore, (on the Ekādaśī days) in both the fortnights he should keep awake. O greatest brāhmaṇa, all those who observe the Ekādaśī vow in this manner truly go to (i.e. attain) liberation.

148. O Jaimini, even hosts of gods like Indra and others should observe this essence of the vow of the day of (i.e. sacred to) Viṣṇu, which is the only cause of avoiding birth and death. You also observe it carefully.

CHAPTER TWENTYTHREE

Queen Suprajñā on the Efficacy of Ekādaśī Vow

Vyāsa said:

1-2. Formerly on the earth there was a king named Kocaraśa. He was calm. He knew the excellent ways of life. He was the best among those who know statesmanship. He, the great one, spoke the truth. He had conquered his anger. He had vanquished the multitude of his enemies. He was very much devoted to Nārāyaṇa's worship. He was engrossed in the service of Hari.

3-4. His queen was Suprajñā by name, who spoke pleasing words, was endowed with all (good) characteristics, and was absorbed in serving her husband. She was engaged in (observing) the Ekādaśī vow, and desired the good of all living beings. She remembered her (past) births. She was noble and of an excellent complexion.

5-6. That king who knew the highest truth, having observed the Daśamī (vow), was along with his wife engrossed in keeping awake at night on the Ekādaśī day. In the meantime a certain brāhmaṇa named Śauri, who was very lustrous, came to the king's pavilion where people kept awake.

7-8. The king, highly devoted to Viṣṇu, seeing him coming, was highly delighted and honoured him by offering him water for washing his feet etc. The brāhmaṇa, knowing the entire truth, and comfortably seated among them, saw there many observers (of the Ekādaśī vow) engaged in Viṣṇu's worship.

9-14. Some worshipped Viṣṇu with many lovely flowers, sandal, incense, lamps and excellent presents. Some observers of the vow decorated with the clay from Gaṅgā, and adorned with garlands of tulasī leaves, gladly danced in front of (the image of) Viṣṇu. (Some) observers of the vow, dear to the lord, sang, keeping rhythm with clapping their hands, charming songs about Viṣṇu. Some (others) praised Anāmaya, Viṣṇu, the lord of the worlds, with excellent hymns having divine meanings and containing pleasing letters. Some fanned (the image of) Viṣṇu, the lord of the world, with white chowries to his great delight. Some played upon the charming, pure, auspicious musical instruments like the lute. Some noble ones sang (songs) to (i.e. in honour of) Viṣṇu.

15-16. The two—the king and the queen—being very much delighted, sang a charming song, and danced an excellent dance. That best brāhmaṇa, Śauri, spoke with gentle words to the noble couple, dancing and singing:

Śauri said:

17-20. O king, you are fortunate, so also is your queen fortunate. This auspicious behaviour of you two is difficult to be found on the earth. I shall speak something to you, since I have not seen an excellent devotee of Viṣṇu (like you). There is no doubt that the earth, with you as the king, is blessed. O king, along with your wife you are observing this pure Ekādaśī vow, dear to the lord. Therefore, you are the chief among Viṣṇu's devotees, since, O best king, you, the only lord of (the earth with) the seven islands, are, along with your wife, joyfully dancing and singing before (the image of) Viṣṇu.

21. This behaviour of you, the couple, is seen to be wonderful. For what reason such an extremely pure thought has arisen in (the mind of) you?

Vyāsa said:

22. Having heard these words of that brāhmaṇa, Śauri, Suprajñā, with a face having a slight smile on it, spoke to the brāhmaṇa:

Suprajñā said:

23-24. O best brāhmaṇa, we two, very great sinners, were formerly freed by the noble (Yama), the son of the Sun, due to the efficacy of the Ekādaśī (vow). O best brāhmaṇa, due to (my) power of recollecting (the past) existences, we two are now observing this divine Ekādaśī vow with a desire for (reaching) the highest place.

Śauri said:

25-26. O beautiful lady, if you know your former birth, then tell me (about it). In my heart a great curiosity is produced to listen to it. Who were you formerly? Who was your husband? How was it that you, though sinners, were released by Yama?

Suprajñā said:

27-28. Though these words are not to be divulged (I shall tell you), O best brāhmaṇa. I, proficient in the science of love, was the chief prostitute. O best brāhmaṇa, in that existence, I committed very many fearful sins, giving torment in hell.

29-30. This (king) was a śūdra named Nityodaya, who had given up the practices of his own (caste), who, the cruel one, kidnapped other's wives and snatched other's wealth. He drank liquor, killed his friends, caused abortions, harmed others, was very proud, and always censured the prescribed course of conduct.

31-33. Once he, abandoned by all his kinsmen of good vows, and longing for the amorous movements of prostitutes, came to my house. O best brāhmaṇa, seeing this handsome youth, I too, having love for him, pleased him with sexual unions (with him). Then, O you rich in penance, he, having had sexual union with me, being humble with modesty, spoke to me (these) words with love:

34. "I am proficient in the science of sexual union. I am abandoned by my relatives. If you agree about it (i.e. the sexual union), then I shall stay here with you."

35-40. Hearing these polite words, O brāhmaṇa, I forming the relation of a couple, stayed with him. O best brāhmaṇa, once on a day of (i.e. sacred to) Viṣṇu, I was tormented by major (diseases) harming the body. On that (day) only, O best brāhmaṇa, I, with my body dull by fever, did not drink water, nor did I eat food due to great fear. This one, in whom love for me was begotten, abandoned food and water on the same day, and was as it were unhappy with existence. Then, O best brāhmaṇa, I, with my mind smitten with fever, burnt a lamp with ghee, and kept awake. He too, repeatedly saying, 'Nārāyaṇa, Hari, Kṛṣṇa,' kept awake during the night.

41. O brāhmaṇa, due to the efficacy of the fast, and the utterance of (the name) Keśava, all our sin perished.

42-43. Then, O best brāhmaṇa, when the morning dawned,

and the sun rose, I, oppressed by fever, expired. Then he, seeing me dead, and censured by all people, resorted to death with me.

44-45. Then we two, after being bound with a strong noose by the servants of Yama, whose eyes were like blazing fire, were taken (to him) along a difficult path. That wise Citragupta considered, from the beginning, all our good and evil acts by Yama's order.

Citragupta said:

46-49. O you large-armed one, even though these two are the greatest sinners, yet they are freed from sins due to their fasting on the Ekādaśī day. Even he who would observe the meritorious Ekādaśī vow unintentionally would, being free from all sins, go to the highest place.

The very glorious Dharmarāja, thus addressed by Citragupta, suddenly rose from his seat, and saluted her and him. The two, free from sins, were adorned with fragrant sandal, divine incense, and flowers, so also with golden ornaments by Yama.

50-51. Then the Sun's son affectionately fed us with various kinds of fruits, sweet and resembling nectar. Then lord Yama himself praised us with divine eulogies and having put us in a divine chariot said to us with the palms of his hands joined:

Yama said:

52. You are the greatest among the meritorious. You are free from sins. Now go there where Viṣṇu dwells.

53-54. When we two were thus addressed by Yama, humble with modesty, we, bowing at his lotus-like feet, said to him: "O god, we would not go anywhere (else). (We would go to) the highest position of Viṣṇu. But we have a desire to see the hell situated in your dwelling."

55. Then, O brāhmaṇa, by Yama's order we two got into a beautiful chariot and we two saw there extensive hells, difficult to be seen.

The brāhmaṇa said:

56-58. O you chaste lady, please tell (me) in detail all the conditions of the sinners which you saw there. O you beautiful lady, tell me in detail by which path the meritorious ones go to Yama's house, and by which way the sinners go. How would a pious soul see there lord Yama and the paths of the pious and of the sinners, giving pleasure and pain (respectively)?

Suprajñā said:

59-64. I shall first describe the path of the pious men, which increases the pleasure of the meritorious. O best brāhmaṇa, listen. The path of the pious, built with big stones and covered with divine pieces of cloth, appears to be free from all troubles. At places wonderful songs are sung by gandharva-maidens. At places celestial nymphs of beautiful bodies dance. At places they produce the sound of the lute and the charming (sound) of various musical instruments. At places there is a shower of flowers; at places cold breezes blow. At places there are stalls where water is distributed to travellers, at places there are houses for eating. At places god and gandharvas recite excellent eulogies. At places there are very beautiful lakes with fully bloomed lotuses. At places there are very shady trees like blossomed aśoka trees.

65-73. From there, O best brāhmaṇa, the pious men endowed with happiness, and meeting with a happy death, go along the path. Some are mounted on horses; some are decorated with various ornaments. They go covering their heads with white umbrellas with their handles raised. Some mounted on elephants, some mounted on chariots, some having got into vehicles, happily go to Yama's abode. Some men, fanned with breezes from the chowries placed in the hands of divine ladies, and praised by great sages, go (to Yama's abode). Certain pious men, holding divine weapons, adorned with garlands and sandal and eating tāmbūla go to Yama's abode. Some living in houses built near water, blazing the ten quarters with the lustre of their bodies go to Yama's abode. O best one, certain (men), enjoying rice boiled in milk, and eating well go happily to Yama's abode. Some drinking milk, some drinking sugarcane juice, also some drinking butter-milk go to Yama's abode. Some meritorious ones eating curd, some eating various fruits, some drinking spirituous liquor go (to Yama's abode).

74-76. Seeing many (such) pious men, securing Yama's

love and coming there, Viṣṇu would himself appear there. He has four arms; his complexion is dark; his eyes are like full-blown lotuses. He holds a conch, a disc, a mace and a lotus. His vehicle is Garuḍa. His sacred thread is golden. His great face is lovely like that of Cupid. He puts on a crown and ear-rings. He is adorned with a garland of wood flowers.

77-79. All like the very wise Citragupta, Yama's servants like Caṇḍa, speaking sweetly have the forms of Viṣṇu. O brāhmaṇa, then Yama himself, having great affection, would worship all those excellent men. Having (honoured) the pious men with divine gems (and) fed them fruits the Sun's son (i.e. Yama) said:

Yama said:

80-81. O you noble ones afraid of the torment in the hell, you (will) go to the highest position due to the efficacy of your acts. The man who, being born in the world, does (acts of) merit, is my father, my brother, and is my friend and like my kinsmen.

82. O best brāhmaṇa, all those, thus addressed by Yama, got into a divine chariot and went to Viṣṇu's city.

83-98. O best brāhmaṇa, I have told you in brief (about) the fate of the meritorious. Listen to the fate of sinners. I shall tell it in detail. The expanse of the path, full of all afflictions, of the wicked ones, is said to be eighty-six thousand yojanas. At places there is a shower of fire. At places there is a shower of stones, and O best brāhmaṇa, at places there is hot sand. At places there are sharp stones. At places there are hot stones. At places there is a shower of weapons. At places there is a shower of burning charcoals. At places breezes, very hot like fire, blow. At places are deep places of darkness with their openings covered with grass, O brāhmaṇa. At places there is a shower of thorns, along with thorny arrows. At places there are rows of rocks, difficult to climb, along with serpents. The sinners, with their throats and palates parched up, go there. O best brāhmaṇa, the unhappy sinners go along that path full of various kinds of sufferings and without shade or water. The sinners named Vimuktakeśa, some of the form of goblins, fierce, wet with steams of blood, some adorned (i.e. smeared) with mud, some with dark bodies, go along the path. Some sinners waiting with agony, some with their eyes full of tears that are trickling, some repenting for their deeds, go along the path. Round the neck of some sinner a hide-noose is tied. (Chains) are bound round someone's skeleton and someone's both feet. Yama's servants, angrily putting a noose round the sinners' necks pierced with needles, drag them. The sinners carrying in the cavities of their ears heavy stones lying on the path, and (carrying) iron-loads on the tops of their heads, go along the path. Yama's servants take some sinners after putting nooses round their arms and (after keeping) strong weapons on their necks. By tossing the sinners Yama's servants take them. Some walk with their heads down, and some with their feet up. Some walk on their hands; some walk on one foot. Thus they are deformed, and cry piteously.

99-102. The sinners, being beaten by Yama's messengers go along that path. When they had come, evil-minded Yama, angrily gave up his divine form and became very fierce. His body was thirty yojanas long, and his eyes resembled wells. His complexion was smoky. He was very lustrous. He was prominent. His sound was gurgling. He had rows of very long teeth. His rows of nails resembled winnowing baskets. He was mounted on a strong he-buffalo. He bit his lips. He had a staff in his hand. He had a noose of hide. His face had curved eyebrows.

103. With him shone Citragupta who had great illusory power, whose eyes were red due to anger, and who was laughing loudly.

104-105. All (Yama's) servants, with nooses and mallets in their hands, who were fierce and angry, thundered like clouds. Yama's servants, running from every side said boastfully: "Quickly kill the most sinful ones. Break them, cut them, pierce them."

106. Lord Yama threatened all the sinners that were running, giving out a 'hum' sound with these words:

Yama said:

107-113a. O sinners, O wicked ones, you thoughtless ones have committed sins which trouble yourselves. You do not see me remaining over your heads. Even knowing me, the lord of life, (to be observing your deeds), you committed sins. Nowhere have you heard with your own ears that I am the brother of the meritorious and the enemy of sinners. Hells are unbearable; they are full of various afflictions. The sinners experience them (i.e. undergo tortures there). Have you not heard this? O you wicked-hearted ones, you regarded my inquiry to be just untrue. O you who have committed sins, today see it with your own eyes. In the blindness due to wealth, all of you being insolent, never followed my words. You always committed heaps of sins. In accordance with that (heap of sins), O wicked ones, experience the fruit of your sins. What is the use of crying?

Suprajñā said:

113b-116a. Speaking (to them) like this, Yama said to Citragupta: "O you noble one, take into account the sinful deeds of these."

Hearing those great words of Yama, Citragupta being (thus) directed (by Yama) told as many sins of them (as they had committed). Then, O best brāhmaṇa, all the sinners waited. They, who were frightened, and who were controlled with a noose of hide (said):

The sinners said:

116b-119a. O Sun's son, who were the witness presented by you to the sins which we had committed. Tell us who witnessed the good or evil deeds that we did formerly.

Then, O brāhmaṇa, Yama having laughed spoke these words very angrily after summoning all the witnesses:

Yama said:

119b-120. You were all nearby and witnesses to whatever took place. The sky, the earth, so also the water, the dates, the day, the night, both the twilights and Dharma—these are the witnesses.

121-122. They narrated all the good and evil deeds of the sinners, and the deed of each one of them and the time when it was done. Each witness told (the deeds) in Yama's presence.

Hearing them, the minds of all sinners were overpowered by fright.

123-125a. They stood with their hearts trembling as deer (remain) on seeing a cloud. Then making a 'Kaḍa Kaḍa' sound with the rows of his teeth (i.e. gnawing his teeth), Yama separately struck them with his fatal staff. All those sinners, struck separately by Dharmarāja (i.e. Yama) wailed over their deeds and being alarmed lamented.

125b-132. Then, Caṇḍa and others, the messengers of Yama, threw, by Yama's order, all those sinners into hells. They dropped some sinners into (the hell called) Tapana, and some into (the hell called) Avīci. (They threw others) into Saṁghāta, Kālasūtra, Mahāraurava, into a hot basin containing sand, and into Kumbhīpāka. They threw the sinners into (hells like) Pramardana which was breathless (i.e. where breathing was not possible) and which was very fierce; so also in the fearful (hell called) Asipatravana, and into (hells) containing various kinds of foods. Certain servants of Yama similarly threw (some) sinners into Vaitaraṇā. Yama's servants threw some sinners into a fierce pool of feces; some (sinners) into (a hell) full of thorns along with bones and chaff-fire, and extremely hot; so also Yama's servants threw them into hells where smearing was done with feces, where the foods was feces, so also in the hell where one's own flesh was eaten. Some (sinners) ate phlegm; some drank semen. Some sinners drank urine; some drank blood. In the mouths of some were leeches, resembling serpents.

133-151. Some (hells) were filled with serpents by the fierce messengers of Yama. O best brāhmaṇa, the very angry (servants of Yama) extracted the tongues of some (sinners). The cruel servants of Yama filled (i.e. put) heated oil into the cavities of the ears and into the mouths of some. They cut off with the edges of swords (i.e. with sharp swords) a hand and a foot also, so also ears and noses of some wicked ones. Some slept on the heap of burning charcoals; some on thorns resembling arrows. O best brāhmaṇa, Yama's servants pulled out the hair of sinners and threw them into hot mud. They repeatedly inserted thousands of heated needles into the mouths and joints of nails of certain sinners. They put certain (sinners) on the tip of a heated pike. With sharp thorns they hurt the heads of some (sinners). (Yama's servants) seized some sinners crying piteously by their hands and feet, and cut them asunder with the thorns of śālmali trees. Yama's servants, after tying a stone round the necks (of the sinners) repeatedly threw some into ditches full of blood and into ditches full of pus. The messengers of Yama devoured the heads of the sinners. They angrily again and again crushed them with stones. They put into the chests of the wicked ones who were crying, masses of iron nails. The eyes of certain sinners were extracted with hooks. O brāhmaṇa, the noses of some were filled with scorpions. Yama's servants tied the feet of some with ropes to the branch of a tree and burnt fire with smoke at the root (of the tree). There the sinners inhaled smoke. They remained there with their faces down and feet up as long as the moon and stars (shine in the sky). Some (sinners), being repeatedly beaten with pestles and mallets by Yama's messengers, and overcome by agony, vomitted blood, Certain sinners sank into an abode full of darkness and having the odour of pus, along with gad-flies and gnats. Some ate ash; some ate insects. Some ate ill-smelling flesh, and some earth with pus. Some, being eaten by dogs, tigers, jackals and hogs, so also by bears, and wet with blood, wail(ed). Some others were being eaten by serpents with extremely strong poison. O brāhmaṇa, the chests of others were being torn asunder by the horns of he-buffaloes.

152-161. Sprinkling the ground with their blood, they fell in a swoon on the earth. With their entire bodies shattered with arrows, resembling snakes, which (arrows) were discharged from the bows of Yama's servants, others rolled on the ground. They (crush) a mass of heated iron balls and a heated stone with a cutting weapon into their mouths. Yama's messengers sewed the nostrils and mouths of some in order to suppress breath. The arrogant, very strong servants of Yama, pulled out, with Yama's sharp-edged (weapons called) Śakti, the skin of the bodies of some. They seized some by their hair, and dropped them on the ground. They always struck (the sinners) with weapons and (their) feet etc. Some sinners were tormented with streams of saline water. O brāhmaṇa, they wailing in various ways, drank saline water. Certain sinners drank bile, O noble one. Some great sinners drank the mucus resembling thick milk flowing from the nose. Yama's servants placed on the chests of some lying on the ground, big, heated stones, resembling mountains. They tied with strong cords the faces of some turned upwards, after putting a pair of logs at their necks and into their throats. They dropped some on the ground after placing them on the branch of a tree.

162-167. They raised them and again and again threw them on the ground. In this way all the sinners, hungry and thirsty, and murmuring 'save me, save me' cried in the abode of torment (i.e. in hell). Having, till the end of the yuga experienced torment in hell, and having not experienced (the fruit of) the remaining sins, they are born in sinful stocks. They, born in sin ful stocks, are troubled by diseases. They are defective in a limb, or have an excess limb. They are unhappy and resort to sins. They are sonless. They are great fools. They are absorbed in harming others. They have a short (span of) life. They are dull. They are the husbands of bad wives. Everyday they do sinful acts through (physical) deeds, mind and words. Again as a result of their sins they go to hell as before. Therefore, the best ones should never commit a sin.

168-175a. Men who have committed sins, cannot escape from hell. O best brāhmaṇa, I have explained to you in brief the affliction of sinners. Who is able to describe it properly even with hundreds of myriads of years? Then, having observed the sinners with a bad plight, we, getting into an aeroplane, went to Viṣṇu's city. Having enjoyed pleasures in Viṣṇu's house for thousands of crores of kalpas, we were born in this very pure royal family, O best brāhmaṇa. Having enjoyed here (i.e. in this existence) all pleasures with all affluence, O best brāhmaṇa, we had a happy (i.e. peaceful) death, and we would go to the highest place. In the three worlds, there is no (other) vow like the Ekādaśī vow. Such is our mode of existence even after our having observed the vow unintentionally. I do not know what would happen to them, through Viṣṇu's grace, who observe the Ekādaśī vow with devotion. O best brāhmaṇa, I have thus told you all that (you) had asked (me) about the importance of the day of (i.e. sacred to) Viṣṇu. What else do you want to listen to?

Vyāsa said:

175b-178. Hearing these words of him, the brāhmaṇa, knowing the highest truth, put his mind very firmly into (observing) the Ekādaśī vow. The king and the queen having, for a long time, enjoyed the earth, in the end went to Viṣṇu's city and obtained the highest position. Those who listen to or recite the importance of this king of vows are freed from the heaps of sins and obtain (a place) near Viṣṇu.

CHAPTER TWENTYFOUR

The Greatness of Tulasī and Dhātrī

Sūta said:

1-2. Jaimini, being very much pleased on hearing the fruit of the Ekādaśī (vow), spoke, with the palms of his hands joined, these (words) to lord Kṛṣṇa Dvaipāyana (i.e. Vyāsa): "Through your grace I have heard the greatness of god Viṣṇu. (Now) tell me about the greatness of tulasī which destroys the sins of the listeners."

Vyāsa said:

3-6. O brāhmaṇa, this revered tulasī should always be worshipped by all deities like Indra. It gives the fruit of the four goals of human life. To the good tulasī is difficult to be obtained in heaven, in the mortal world and in the nether world. Devotion to it secures the four goals of human life. O best one, at that place only where one tulasī-plant stands, all gods like Brahmā, Viṣṇu and Śiva dwell. Always Keśava dwells in the middle of the leaf, Prajāpati at the tip of the leaf, and Śiva at the foot-stalk of the leaf of tulasī.

7-10. Lakṣmī, Sarasvatī, so also Gāyatrī and Caṇḍikā, likewise all other wives of (other) gods dwell in the leaves of that (tulasī-plant). These, viz. Indra, Agni, Śamana, Nairṛti, so also Varuṇa, Vāyu and Kubera dwell in the branch of the tulasī-plant. All planets like the Sun, the Viśvedevas,[1]

1. Viśvedevāḥ—Name of a particular group of deities ten in number and supposed to be sons of Viśvā; their names are: Vasu, Satya, Kratu, Dakṣa, Kāla, Kāma, Dhṛti, Kuru, Purūravas, and Mādravas.

Vasus,[1] all sages and all divine sages, so also all the holy places that are there in the crores of universes and on the earth, live by resorting to (i.e. in) the tulasī plant.

11-17. He who devoutly worships tulasī, has worshipped the holy places, so also all gods like Brahmā. Viṣṇu just at that moment destroys (the sin of) the murder of a brāhmaṇa remaining in the body of those who remove the masses of grass at the root of tulasī. O best brāhmaṇa, by sprinkling the tulasī plant with fragrant and cold water in summer a man would obtain eternal bliss. He who gives it moonlight or an umbrella, especially in summer, is freed from all sins. A man who would everyday sprinkle the tulasī plant with continuous streams in Vaiśākha obtains the fruit of a horse-sacrifice. He who would sprinkle the tulasī plant with water from the hand stretched out and hollowed also obtains heaven after being freed from all sins. O brāhmaṇa sage, in the house of that man who would sometime sprinkle the tulasī plant with milk, Lakṣmī is steady.

18-22. O brāhmaṇa sage, listen to the fruit of the merit of him who would smear the root of the tulasī plant with cowdung. For as many thousands of kalpas as the dust particles removed from there, he rejoices with Viṣṇu, O Jaimini. He who would place a lamp at the root of the tulasī plant at twilight, goes along with a crore (members) of his family to Viṣṇu's abode. Viṣṇu would always protect him who protects the tulasī plant from cows, dogs, asses, men and children. There is no doubt that he who devoutly plants a tulasī plant, obtains the highest liberation after death.

23. That best devout man who would see the tulasī plant in the morning uninterruptedly obtains the fruit of seeing Viṣṇu.

24. The life, strength, fame, wealth, progeny of one who would devoutly salute the tulasī plant, grow.

25. By remembering tulasī, all sin perishes. The diseases of men perish on just touching the tulasī (plant).

26-27. The sin in the body of him who eats the auspicious tulasī leaf, removing all sins, perishes at that moment (only).

---

1. Vasavaḥ—Vasus are a class of deities. They are eight in number: Āpa, Dhruva, Soma, Dhara or Dhava, Anila, Anala, Pratyūṣa, and Prabhāsa.

In the body of the man who wears a rosary made of tulasī wood there is no sin. This is the truth that I tell.

28. There is no doubt that he who bears on his head the water dropped from the leaves of tulasī, obtains the religious merit due to a bath in Gaṅgā.

29. A man having devoutly worshipped the auspicious tulasī with dūrvās, sacred rice grains, flowers, offerings of eatables, would obtain the fruit of the worship (offered) to Viṣṇu.

30. O brāhmaṇas(?), what is the use of worshipping Viṣṇu's feet to him who has sometime worshipped revered tulasī, giving the highest nectar of piety, material welfare and sensual enjoyment, with offerings of eatables, flowers, excellent incense and ghee-lamps?

31. O brāhmaṇa, Viṣṇu is pleased with them who plant tulasī pleasing Viṣṇu and fit to be worshipped by gods, at places free from blemishes; and Mura's enemy, the lord of the three worlds, quickly gives them the highest position.

32. Whatever auspicious act—a sacrifice, a vow, honouring the dead ancestors, worship of Viṣṇu, giving gifts—and other auspicious act(s) that men perform at the blemishless root of tulasī—all those indeed become inexhaustible.

33. O best brāhmaṇa, all that pious act which a man does on the earth without tulasī, dear to Viṣṇu, becomes fruitless. The god of gods, the lotus-eyed one (i.e. Viṣṇu) is also not pleased.

34. A man who, with devotion, sees the auspicious, pure tulasī during pilgrimages, quickly gets the fruit of the pilgrimages through Viṣṇu's grace. This statement is very firm.

35-36. Ananta (i.e. Viṣṇu), the only lord of the world, abandoning fragrant flowers like mandāra, kunda, lotus, gladly accepts even dry tulasī full of virtues and the security for the destruction of sins. Hari (i.e. Viṣṇu) to whom tulasī is dear always snatches the wealth of those wicked men who, through ignorance, uproot a tulasī (plant) purifying like the nectar-giving creeping plant, and place it on the ground. This is the truth.

37. Viṣṇu quickly snatches the wealth of those men who always urinate or excrete or put dirt at the root of tulasī, the abode of gods, and thus collect sins.

38-42. "I am collecting (the leaves of) you for worshipping Viṣṇu. I am collecting (the leaves of) you since even with flowers like (those of) pārijāta, so also with sandal etc., put without you Viṣṇu is not satisfied. O holy one, without you every act is fruitless. Therefore, O goddess Tulasī, I am collecting (the leaves of) you. Grant me a boon. O leader of the world, pardon me that pain which is produced in your heart due to (your leaves) being plucked. O Tulasī I salute you." A devotee of Viṣṇu, joining the palms of his hands recites these two hymns and then clapping twice collects tulasī leaves in such a way that the tulasī branch does not shake, O best brāhmaṇa.

43. When at the time of plucking a leaf, a branch of goddess (Tulasī) would be broken, then anguish is produced in the heart of Viṣṇu, Tulasī's lord.

44. Viṣṇu, the destroyer of (the demons) Madhu and Kaiṭabha should be worshipped even with every old leaf fallen from the tip of a branch.

45. He who would worship lord Viṣṇu with tender tulasī leaves, quickly gets whatever he desires with (i.e. in) his heart.

Jaimini said:

46. O best brāhmaṇa, what (other) tree is like that of tulasī? I desire to know it. O son of Satyavatī, (please) tell it.

Vyāsa said:

47-51. O brāhmaṇa, as tulasī is always most dear to Viṣṇu, so is dhātrī, destroying all sins. O best brāhmaṇa, all those deities who dwell in the plant after having reached it, stay at the root of āmalakī. O best brāhmaṇa, holy places like Gaṅgā dwell just there where pure dhātrī, most dear to Viṣṇu, remains. That act, auspicious or inauspicious, which is done by men at the root of āmalakī, would certainly become inexhaustible, O brāhmaṇa. He who would worship Viṣṇu with pure, fresh leaves of dhātrī, is freed from mass of sins and secures absorption into Viṣṇu.

52-56. O Jaimini, that place where there would be neither dhātrī nor tulasī is impure. (A man) does not obtain the fruit of his act (performed there). All the (pious) acts done by him in his hermitage where the auspicious dhātrī or tulasī does not exist indeed become fruitless. O brāhmaṇa, (in the house) of him, which is without dhātrī and tulasī, poverty and sin (remain) and by that Kali is pleased. The wise should look upon that place where there is neither tulasī nor dhātrī as a cremation ground, O best brāhmaṇa. All gods dwell there where dhātrī and tulasī exist. All sin exists there where there is neither a leaf of dhātrī nor of tulasī.

57-60. Viṣṇu, along with Lakṣmī, would remain by resorting to the body of the wise man who would wear a rosary of dhātrī-fruits. All deities live by resorting to the body of the intelligent man who would wear a garland of dhātrī wood. All the act, auspicious or inauspicious, which a man wearing a garland (i.e. rosary) of dhātrī fruits does, is said to be inexhaustible. The entire sin remaining in the body of that man knowing the entire nature of Brahman, who eats the dhātrī fruit, perishes.

61-63. O best brāhmaṇa, I (shall) tell (you) the greatness destroying all sins (of the man) who would wear a rosary of the dhātrī fruits. Listen (to it). Even if he by chance dies in a cremation ground, he obtains the religious merit due to a bath in Gaṅgā. There is no doubt about it. Seeing him, all sinners are instantly freed from very fierce heaps of sins, (committed) even during hundreds of crores of existences.

64-66. There is no doubt, O best brāhmaṇa, that he who everyday takes a lump of the dhātrī fruit would obtain religious merit everyday and store it. There is no doubt that he who harms the dhātrī tree, the resort of all gods, gives blows on the body of Viṣṇu. Dhātrī is full of all gods. It is especially dear to Viṣṇu. Even Brahmā cannot correctly describe its virtues.

67. That man who, having known the entire truth, has devotion for dhātrī and tulasī, enjoys all pleasures, and then in the end obtains liberation due to Viṣṇu's grace.

CHAPTER TWENTYFIVE

The Importance of Honouring a Guest

Jaimini said:

1. O glorious one, tell me in detail again about tulasī's greatness destroying sins, so also about the importance of honouring a guest.

Sūta said:

2. Then, O best brāhmaṇa, that very lustrous Vyāsa, started telling the greatness of tulasī, destroying the sins of the listeners.

Vyāsa said:

3-4. This tulasī, dear to the lord, is actually great Lakṣmī. Therefore, O Jaimini they do not recognise it as a tree. As a mortal always worships tulasī on the earth, so gods along with Indra worship it in heaven.

5-6. I am telling firmly that everything is prosperous there only where this tulasī, of the nature of the highest Brahman, stands. Even a sinner who gets, at the time of his death, water dropped from a leaf of tulasī, goes near Viṣṇu.

7. He who would have, at the time of his death, a vertical sectarian mark (*ūrdhvapuṇḍra*) is freed from all sins and goes to Viṣṇu.

8. O best brāhmaṇa, Yama is not the master of him who would have a tulasī leaf in his mouth, on his head or in his ears at the time of his death.

9-12a. There was a pious brāhmaṇa by name Pavitra, who knew the highest truth. His wife had the name Bahulā. The chaste lady belonged to a good family and was highly devoted to serving her husband. There (also) lived an excellent brāhmaṇa named Anapatyapati. That Pavitra, serving brāhmaṇas, formed friendship with him. Then, O best one, Pavitra, through love (for his friend) and with a desire to have talk, sat with Anapatyapati on an excellent seat.

12b-13a. In the meanwhile a good brāhmaṇa, of a great lustre, named Lomaśa, came there and saw the two telling (each other) wonderful stories.

13b-14a. Then the two brāhmaṇas, getting up from the seat, honoured that brāhmaṇa Lomaśa with water for washing his feet, with respectful offerings and water for rinsing his mouth.

14b-16a. That Lomaśa, highly devoted to Viṣṇu, was very much pleased with them, and narrating (tales of) Viṣṇu, sat on the seat, O best brāhmaṇa. The two sages, Pavitra and Anapatya, said devoutly to the magnanimous Lomaśa who had joined the palms of his hands:

16b-20a. "O revered one, O you who know all the worldly practices, indeed our hermitage is purified by the couple of your feet which are fit to be seized (i.e. touched) by the good. By seeing the couple of your feet, all the sins that we had formerly committed through delusion, have perished. You are actually lord Viṣṇu fit to be worshipped even by gods. How are we, men, able to worship you properly? With the worship that we have, according to our capacity, offered to you, our guest, be pleased. Pardon the faults of us two."

20bc. O best brāhmaṇa, speaking like this, the two high-souled friends, the two householders, fell at the couple of the feet of the guest.

Vyāsa said:

21-23. Then Lomaśa, best among the learned, was very much pleased. (He said to them:) "You are best among the polite, You are the best brāhmaṇas, and are highly devoted to piety. By your polite words I am very much pleased. The wise say that a guest is actually Brahmā, Śiva, or Viṣṇu. You have shown so much devotion to me. May auspiciousness come to you. I, a guest, have been properly entertained by you with abundant eatables."

Vyāsa said:

24. Then the two brāhmaṇas got up, and saluting him by touching the couple of his feet, said to that sage Lomaśa:

The two brāhmaṇas said:

25-26. O brāhmaṇa, please tell us the importance of the worship of a guest, having done which, liberation, to be obtained by men but with difficulty, is obtained. Who is said to be a guest in the world? How is his worship (done)? What position do the one attentive to a guest and the guest obtain?

Lomaśa said:

27-28. Of the four stages of life that of the householder is said to be the best due to its honouring the anchorite, celibate and a religious mendicant. Among (the members of) the four stages of life the householders are said to be the chief. They should devoutly honour guests.

29-30. The greatest duty of householders is said to be honouring guests. They are said to be householders since they have not fallen from the duty of their stage of life. If householders take care in honouring guests, then what purpose do they have with other pious acts?

31-32. The wise call him to be a guest whose name, family and position are not heard of (before), and who would accidentally come to their house. The wise ones should honour like Viṣṇu brāhmaṇas, kṣatriyas, vaiśyas and śūdras who have come to their house.

33-34. Those others born in low castes, among whom cāṇḍālas are the chief ones, should be honoured like Viṣṇu with water for washing their feet, with respectful offerings and abundant eatables. When guests come, a householder goes forth (to greet them). A brāhmaṇa should quickly give them water for washing their feet and materials of worship.

35. With soft words he would make a friendly enquiry after the (guests') health. And the householder should gladly feed them with divine foods.

36. The wise one should prepare his bed in a comfortable chamber. Seeing him desirous to go in the morning he should give him leave.

37-38. O best ones, I shall tell you how a guest should be honoured with hospitality if the householder is unfortunately not wealthy. When guests have come he should devoutly offer them (a) grass (seat) etc. If there is no grass seat he should not devoutly say to him: "Sit on the ground."

39-41. For washing his feet he should give him excellent water. Then with sweet words he should ask in a friendly way about his health etc. Then he should devoutly give him fruit etc.

for eating. Without that an intelligent person should not gladly present himself (to the guest). And he should say: "O guest, I am a great sinner, very poor. I desire to offer you (worship with) devotion. But the destiny is opposing."

42-44. The poor one who has avoided honouring a guest in this manner and not anyone else fallen from his duty, would obtain the fruit as stated (in holy texts). The religious merit earned during crores of existences, of the householder from whose house a guest goes unhonoured, perishes. Viṣṇu would instantly remove the sin committed during crores of existences, of him who honours with devotion just one guest.

45-46. I am telling the truth. I am saying what is beneficial. I am making a firm statement. A householder does not go to heaven without carefully honouring a guest. It is truth, (nothing but) the truth. It is the repeated truth. For householders going to heaven is not (possible), is not (at all) possible, except by honouring a guest.

47-51. In the Dvāpara age there was a cowherd known as Jñātidharma. He knew all the ways of life. His wife was called Śrīvallabhā. He who served his kinsmen did all (good) acts. With his wife he lived in Saurāṣṭra. O brāhmaṇas, due to the movement of bad planets Indra did not shower water for twelve years. Therefore, there was a very great famine. During that great famine, the inhabitants of that country were distressed, and all of them gave up even the limit (of decorum). The great meditating saint Jñānabhadra, with his wealth lost due to the great famine, became very much distressed in the age called Dvāpara.

52-53. Seeing his wife and sons distressed with hunger, he with the brāhmaṇa's consent(?), went to the land at the foot of a mountain to eat fruits and roots. O you two best brāhmaṇas, the long-lived one, who was hungry, found one pumpkin gourd at the border of the land at the foot of the hill.

54-56. That very glorious best brāhmaṇa Jñānabhadra, being delighted on getting the fruit, speedily went (back) to his house. O brāhmaṇas, in the meanwhile, when the clouds had covered the sky, as it were, with dark blue feet, it rained with powerful showers. The sage's entire body was bathed with that shower. A forester, afflicted with cold, went to (his) house from the forest.

57-63. Seeing the guest afflicted with cold, he saluted him by (bowing) his head. He then devoutly gave him a grass-seat and water for washing his feet etc. Then with that guest only making an intelligent talk with sweet words the cowherd along with his wife diligent in serving her lord, remained with a composed mind. The chaste lady was delighted on having, with effort, secured a pumpkin gourd and gave a part to him after cutting it (into parts). Then that hospitable cowherd who had become weak due to fasting for twentyone days gladly gave a large part (of the fruit) to the guest. Then that chaste housewife highly devoted to her husband also gladly gave that (other) part (of the fruit) to the guest. O best brāhmaṇa, the guest having eaten both the parts (of the fruit) of (i.e. meant for) that noble couple, was very much delighted. The two with firm devotion worshipped the guest like Viṣṇu.

64. Having rested there only at night, he went in the morning after a long time after having bathed. (The two) passed twentyone days in fasting.

65-66a. Then that noble couple died. Due to the efficacy of that religious merit the noble-hearted couple obtained absorption into Viṣṇu, difficult to be obtained even by meditating saints.

66b-67. Due to the efficacy of their religious merit and the worship of the guest that they had done, the famine in the kingdom came to an end. The people were extremely happy and were free from grief and diseases.

68. They were rich in wealth and grains and were highly devoted to religion. The bandits there disappeared, and the king protected the people.

69-70. People were engaged in their own practices (i.e. practices laid down for their respective castes), and the clouds rained as desired. Crores of the ancestors and successors of the two, being freed from sins due to that act only obtained salvation. They were blemishless, endowed with wealth and were alone honoured by all the people.

71a. The progeny of the two grew without grief and diseases.

Lomaśa said:

71b-72a. I have told you the importance of the worship of

a guest along with its history. O brāhmaṇas, what else do you desire to hear for your pleasure?

Vyāsa said:

72b-76a. When that Lomaśa, rich in austerities was speaking like this, a black mouse, seized by death came up from its hole. Seeing that black mouse to have come from the hole, Pavitra, beside himself with anger got up, repeatedly speaking like this: "This wicked mouse of a sinful heart digs (the ground of) the hermitage with its sharp teeth at night, and destroys domestic things. For all the castes pity is said to be the best. It should be shown to all living beings, but not to wicked ones."

76b-80a. Speaking like this, O best brāhmaṇa, with a very sharp iron arrow he killed the mouse that had committed sins and the death of whom had approached. That rat, with its body bathed (i.e. wet) with the streams of flowing blood, fell on the ground with its consciousness affected due to agony, O brāhmaṇa sage. Seeing the mouse fallen, the kind, best brāhmaṇa, wailed loudly and speedily got up. Taking an excellent tulasī leaf from his own ear, he put it into the mouse's mouth, on its head and ears.

80b-82a. "O mother, O goddess Tulasī, O you causing delight to Govinda, give the best position to this mouse who has committed sins." O best brāhmaṇa, he who obliged all the world, loudly uttered the sound (i.e. the words): 'Hari, Nārāyaṇa Ananta'.

82b-83a. The mouse, due to the touch of the tulasī leaf, and due to hearing Viṣṇu's name, was free from sins and became free from the bond of the worldly existence.

83b-86a. Then the messengers of the great Viṣṇu, who were endowed with all (good) characteristics, quickly came there in good chariots to take (the mouse) whose sins had gone (to Viṣṇu's abode). The mouse surrounded by the hosts of Viṣṇu's messengers got into a divine chariot and went to the highest place. The mouse, having stayed in Viṣṇu's abode for thousands of crores of yugas, and having secured knowledge there only, went to (i.e. obtained) final emancipation.

Vyāsa said:

86b-87. O best brāhmaṇa, I have told you the importance of goddess Tulasī. O glorious one, tell me what you desire to hear now.

CHAPTER TWENTYSIX

Conduct in the Four Yugas

Jaimini said:

1. O glorious one, tell me how will all people be (i.e. behave) when the very fierce Kali age has come.

Vyāsa said:

2-5. The first (age) is called Satya-yuga. In it the people—brāhmaṇas and others—were devoted to worshipping Viṣṇu, and were free from grief and diseases. All of them spoke the truth, all were kind, and all lived long. They were rich in wealth and grains. They were free from (doing) harm (to others) and from religious hypocrisy. All obliged others. All knew sacred treatises. O best brāhmaṇa, in Satya-yuga all people were like this. And the kings followed royal duties and protected people. Oh! Who can relate the merit and the glory of Satya-yuga?

6-8. In it no man practised unrighteousness. When Tretā-yuga came, Dharma became deficient in one foot. Some people had little unhappiness. Some resorted to kindness. People were engaged in meditating upon Viṣṇu. They were highly devoted to (performing) sacrifices and (giving) gifts. They were engaged in (following) the practices of castes and stages of human life. They were happy and of a composed mind. All the śūdras tilled the soil and served brāhmaṇas.

9-11. Brāhmaṇas were noble and had mastered the Vedas and the Vedāṅgas. They were averse to accepting presents. They were true to their words. They had curbed their senses. They were always engaged in penance and vows. They always worshipped Viṣṇu. When at the end of Tretā-yuga, Dvāpara-yuga arrived.

Dharma would be deficient in two feet and some men would have happiness and unhappiness. Some would be engrossed in sins, and some were pious.

12. Some lacked some virtues. Some men of high virtues were extremely unhappy. Some were happy.

13. Sometime a brāhmaṇa longed for receiving (a present). At some time or other kings harassed their subjects through greed for wealth.

14-17. Brāhmaṇas were very much given to Viṣṇu's worship, and śūdras served brāhmaṇas. When, O brāhmaṇa, in yuga after yuga Dharma became deficient (foot) by foot, then Vyāsa of the form of Viṣṇu divided the Veda. O best brāhmaṇa, in Kali-yuga which is the only abode of all sins, Dharma would be having one foot (only), and all people would be engaged in (committing) sins. Brāhmaṇas, kṣatriyas, vaiśyas and śūdras will be very much addicted to sins, will be very voluptuous and cruel. They will censure the Vedas and indulge in gambling and stealing.

18-20. They will be engaged in cohabiting with widows in Kali-yuga. Certain brāhmaṇas, looking to their livelihood (only), will be acting very fraudulently. All will be exceedingly fond of women, all will drink intoxicating liquors. All will be engaged in sexual acts and snatch other's wealth. They will always ardently long for other's food. They will be averse to penance and vows. They will be bound by the company of heretics in Kali-yuga.

21-22. Brāhmaṇas following śūdras' practices, will be (vagrant devotees) wearing red garments. In Kali-yuga the accomplished one will reach a very low position. And the mean, being endowed with wealth, will go to a very high position. All men will give gifts to those who have obliged them.

23-24. Even with effort (being made) cāṇḍālas will not abide by brāhmaṇas. In Kali-yuga people will give false testimony through affection for their friends. They will talk impious ideas. They will lament over righteous thoughts. They will censure (people) in (their) absence. They will be cruel, and will speak sweetly in the presence of other (people).

25-26. Unchaste women will speak like chaste women to their husbands. Brāhmaṇas will harm other's wives and will sell their possessions. In Kali-yuga, people will sell their daughters.

All men will be subjugated by women. Women too will be very fickle.

27-29. In Kali-yuga men will be wicked-hearted. The earth will have few crops and clouds will have little water. They will also shower (water) at a wrong time. O Jaimini, in Kali-yuga cows will eat feces and will yield little milk. And undoubtedly that milk will be ghee-less. People will be given to self-praise. They will be intent on censuring others.

30. Boys will have short bodies, and will eat too much food. In Kali-yuga, brāhmaṇas will offer libations to the dead ancestors for religious hypocrisy.

31. All will be affectionate in words (only) till their mission does not succeed. All will laugh at (certain) people, seeing them to be devoted to piety.

32-33. People will prosper through wicked deeds. Therefore, people will be addicted to sins. And they will completely perish within ten or twelve years. (They will prosper) as water will increase in the rainy season. People will lose their youth in Kali-yuga.

34. A girl will conceive in her fifth or eighth year. Men will have many children and (therefore) they will be very unhappy.

35. All will long for taking (gifts), none will long for giving. In Kali (yuga) Mlecchas will be kings, addicted to sins.

36. In Kali-yuga people will be of one caste (only) in order to satisfy carnal desires. In the first division of Kali (yuga) men (will) censure Viṣṇu.

37-38. In the middle (part) of Kali (yuga) men will only recognise Viṣṇu's names. Brāhmaṇas, kṣatriyas, vaiśyas, śūdras will have (but) one caste in Kali-yuga, and there will be only four castes.

39-40a. O best brāhmaṇa, whenever there will be a decrease in (the number of) the pious ones, it should be known that the sinners will be on the increase in Kali (yuga). O best brāhmaṇa, though I have described this Kali (yuga) to be fierce, yet O best among the virtuous, it has (one) great merit.

40b-41. In Satya (yuga) religious merit would be accomplished after twelve years. In Tretā (yuga) (it would be accomplished during half the period of that. In Dvāpara (it would be accomplished) within a month. But it would be produced in a day and night in Kali-yuga.

42-44a. Therefore, in the mortal world men do not at all reach a good position. A man obtains that fruit in Kali-yuga merely by uttering (the name of) Viṣṇu, which he would obtain by worshipping Viṣṇu for twelve years in another yuga. Kali does not trouble that man who utters only one name of Viṣṇu in Kali-yuga in this world. This is the truth, the (only) truth. There is no doubt in it.

Jaimini said:

44b-46a. Every act becomes fruitless due to the lack of the purity of mind. You have told this before. Therefore, my mind gives wonder (i.e. is amazed). In Kali-yuga all lack the purity of mind. O preceptor, tell me how their acts would be (done).

Vyāsa said:

46b-47. A man should devoutly offer whatever act he does in Kali-yuga to the great Viṣṇu. Every act that is dedicated to Viṣṇu would be inexhaustible.

Vyāsa said:

48. O best brāhmaṇa, I have thus told you the entire account, having devoutly heard which a man would obtain liberation.

Sūta said:

49. Jaimini thus informed by that highest soul, became engaged in the employment of rituals, and went to the highest position.

50-52. Those men desiring liberation, who devoutly recite or listen to this Essence of the Employment of Rituals are freed from all fierce sins committed during many existences, and obtain liberation. There is no doubt about this. Those men who, desiring liberation, recite and listen to this, get whatever is desired by them through the auspicious favour of Lakṣmī's lord.

53. A man, reciting or listening to half a verse, or a verse, or a quarter of a verse, gets the desired fruit.

54. That man who, after writing or getting written this holy text, would worship it, obtains the fruit of Viṣṇu's worship only.

55. May this Purāṇa which is very secret, has come out from Vyāsa's mouth, is very charming, gives delight to Viṣṇu's devotees, pleases the Disc-holder (Viṣṇu), Murāri whose feet are for a long time saluted by gods and others and who is the lord of the entire world.

May auspiciousness prevail.

May it be dedicated to Viṣṇu.

End of the Treatise.

INDEX